LABORATORY MA
& WORKBOOk

RILEY WHITE
ANDREW C. STAUGAARD, JR.

STRUCTURED &
OBJECT-ORIENTED
PROBLEM SOLVING
USING C++

THIRD EDITION

ANDREW C. STAUGAARD, JR.

LABORATORY MANUAL & WORKBOOK

RILEY WHITE
ANDREW C. STAUGAARD, JR.

STRUCTURED & OBJECT-ORIENTED PROBLEM SOLVING USING C++

THIRD EDITION

ANDREW C. STAUGAARD, JR.

Prentice Hall

Upper Saddle River, NJ 07458

Senior Editor: Petra Recter
Assistant Editor: Sarah Burrows
Executive Managing Editor: Vince O'Brien
Managing Editor: David A. George
Production Editor: Barbara A. Till
Supplement Cover Manager: Paul Gourhan
Supplement Cover Designer: PM Workshop Inc.
Manufacturing Buyer: Ilene Kahn

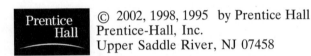

© 2002, 1998, 1995 by Prentice Hall
Prentice-Hall, Inc.
Upper Saddle River, NJ 07458

The author and publisher of this book have used their best efforts in preparing this book.
These efforts include the development, research, and testing of the theories and programs
to determine their effectiveness. The author and publisher make no warranty of any kind,
expressed or implied, with regard to these programs or the documentation contained in this
book. The author and publisher shall not be liable in any event for incidental or consequential
damages in connection with, or arising out of, the furnishing, performance, or use of these programs.

Printed in the United States of America

10 9 8 7 6 5 4 3 2 1

ISBN 0-13-067017-0

Pearson Education Ltd., *London*
Pearson Education Australia Pty. Ltd., *Sydney*
Pearson Education Singapore, Pte. Ltd.
Pearson Education North Asia Ltd., *Hong Kong*
Pearson Education Canada, Inc., *Toronto*
Pearson Educacíon de Mexico, S.A. de C.V.
Pearson Education—Japan, *Tokyo*
Pearson Education Malaysia, Pte. Ltd.

CONTENTS

Getting Acquainted With Your C++ Environment

LAB OBJECTIVES

In this lab, you will . . .
- Learn about various types of programming environments.
- Use your editor to enter a simple program.
- Use your compiler to compile and link a simple program.
- Test the ANSI/ISO standard compliance of your compiler.
- Use your compiler's error output to find a syntax error.

REQUIRED READING

Chapter 1: Structured & Object-Oriented Problem Solving Using C++, 3rd edition, by Andrew C. Staugaard, Jr.

INTRODUCTION

The goal of this project is to get you acquainted with your programming environment. You will learn a little about what types of environments are available and some of the advantages and disadvantages of each type. Armed with this knowledge, you will use your environment to create a simple executable program.

The next task you will complete has a difficulty level that depends on your programming environment. You will type a program that contains a syntax error (basically a typo) and use your compiler's error output to find and correct the problem with your program.

Your last task will be to test the ANSI/ISO compliance of your compiler with respect to strings (i.e. variables that hold text). Whether your compiler supports the relatively new C++ style string will drastically affect your programs. Major C++ compilers such as Microsoft Visual C++ and Borland C++ have been updated to support C++ strings, but there are many compilers, both free and commercial, that have yet to implement them.

COMPONENTS OF A TYPICAL PROGRAMMING ENVIRONMENT

There are three major components of most programming environments: the compiler, the editor, and the debugger. Of these, only the compiler and the editor are required; the debugger, is extremely useful, however, and most environments provide a debugger of some sort. Some environments, known as *Integrated Development Environments* (IDE's), have the editor, compiler, and debugger tied together in one cohesive unit.

Compiler

The compiler, as we will talk about it here, actually includes what is known as a *linker*. The actual compiler creates machine code from your program, and the linker puts everything together into a form that is executable by the operating system.

As a beginning programmer, you only need to know how to feed source code to your compiler and how to retrieve the executable program from it. Over time, you will pick up a lot about how your compiler works just by using it. You will know its little quirks in the same way you know that, for example, your car makes a quiet knocking noise if you keep a steady 35 MPH for a couple of seconds then let off the gas. You'll learn to work around any problems in your compiler's C++ implementation without thinking, the same way you automatically push a little harder to close the door in your house that gets hung up on the carpet.

Unfortunately, no C++ implementation is perfect. Every compiler you use will have imperfections. However, don't give in to the temptation to call all unexpected behavior a "bug in the compiler." If you do, you will be wrong. Until you've checked everything over several times, consulted the C++ Standard to find the correct behavior, and had a few other people double-check your work, assume that your code is incorrect. Most of the time you will find an error somewhere in your code, or you will find that you are using code that, though it makes sense to you (and possibly even works like you expect it to in some compilers), is not supported by the C++ Standard.

Compilers that are not part of an IDE, such as the GNU C++ compiler and Borland's free C++ command line compiler, generally have a command line interface. You usually have to create a source code file using an editor, and then use a command prompt or a shell interface to run the compiler with the source code file as one of the arguments. These compilers often have a wide variety of options available that can be specified within the command line. If a project has specific needs, the command line can get long and cumbersome to type, so these compilers generally support what is known as a *makefile*, or a file that contains all of the details on how to compile a program. You should consult your specific compiler's documentation for instruction if you need to use makefiles.

IDE's handle compilation details automatically. Compilers in an IDE, such as Microsoft's Visual C++, usually use makefiles, and the makefile options are usually customizable using the program's menus, but the default options will work for most noncommercial programs.

Editor

Your editor is whatever you use to create or change C++ source code. Since the source code must be saved as a simple ASCII text file, any text document editor program from Notepad, Pico, or Simpletext to Microsoft Word, Sun StarOffice, or Appleworks can be used as an editor for your C++ environment.

Editors created specifically for C++ usually are more useful for programming than any of the previously mentioned programs, for several reasons. Most C++ specific editors implement *syntax highlighting*. In an editor with syntax highlighting, C++ keywords and often-used objects such as *cin* and *cout* will be color coded. This makes the code generally easier to read and helps to prevent typos. Some of the more advanced editors take this a step further and actually complete keywords and/or function names for you, often drastically reducing the amount of typing that you have to do.

Editors that are not part of an IDE often will be customizable. You can point them to your C++ compiler and they will add a "compile program" option to a program menu, making program compilation a one-step process.

One-step compilation is built-in to IDE's. The tight integration between the editor and the compiler can make a programmer forget that they are two separate programs.

Debugger

While not absolutely required in a programming environment, a debugger is the single most useful tool for finding logic errors in your program code. A debugger lets you execute your code one line at a time, and provides a means for you to *watch* variables (i.e. view the values of the variables in real time as the program executes).

As useful as debuggers are, they do have a drawback—they make programmers lazy. Some might argue that this is not a problem. After all, the purpose of the debugger is to reduce the amount of work that a programmer has to do, resulting in a decrease in the time that it takes to do the work. However, a programmer may not sufficiently desk check an algorithm because he or she may think that any problems

2

will be easily caught in the debugger, or the programmer may decide to compose a particularly complex portion of code at the keyboard using the debugger in a "trial and error" sequence to find an algorithm that works. Both of these scenarios invariably will result in code that is not as polished as it could be. Often, the programmer will not even know exactly what is happening, and as long as the code "works," the programmer doesn't care.

If you remember that the debugger is not a design tool and you therefore do not use it as such, then your code will be cleaner, more readable, and infinitely more elegant.

Your debugger needs to be in sync with your compiler. The debugger needs to show the execution of your program such that when you tell the debugger to execute a line of C++ code, it always executes the exact portion of machine code that the compiler created from that line of C++ code. If you are working in an IDE, you will have no problem working with your debugger. In fact, most IDE's use the editor's interface to access the debugger so that when you find an error in your code, you can immediately fix the problem. Some IDE's, such as Microsoft Visual C++, don't even make you recompile your code in most cases when you edit the code while debugging—you can keep stepping through the code and it will implement the changes you made "on the fly."

If you are not working in an IDE, debugging will not be as easy. The debugger, if you have one, will probably be a separate program that you must launch with a command line, and it's interface will probably not double as an editor. When you find a problem, you will have to note where it is, quit the debugger, launch your editor, change the code, recompile the program, and run the debugger again.

IDE vs. Separate Components

You may be wondering now why anybody would want to program in a nonintegrated environment. After all, the IDE makes things easier. The programmer can concentrate on the code without thinking about any extra details.

There actually are several reasons that some programmers prefer using a nonintegrated environment. The three major reasons, however, are choice, control, and compatibility. In an environment where the components are separate, it is easy to change your compiler or your editor for a different one that you like better. You can even have multiple compilers set up on your machine and a menu command set up in your editor for each one of them. An IDE is a package deal. If you are not happy with one part of the environment, you have to live with it or replace the entire environment. Setting up compile options with a makefile, or finding the perfect editor and customizing it to meet particular needs of a project, give a programmer a sense of control that is rarely felt when working in an environment that is set up to make everyone happy. Some programmers feel that IDE's, in trying to please everyone, cater to the lowest common denominator. While it's true that IDE's don't show most of the complexity dealing with project compilation and that many who learn to program in an IDE never bother learning about these details, the options are usually just a menu click away. However, the customization options of a single editor available in IDE's cannot compete with the wide array of different editors available for a nonintegrated environment and the multitude of customization options available in those editors. Also, the tight integration of the editor, compiler, and debugger in an IDE means that the programmer has very little control over the exact details of how the compiler and debugger are executed. This is a sharp contrast to a non-integrated setup, where the compiler and debugger are called either explicitly by the programmer, or they are called with editor commands that have been set up explicitly by the programmer.

Compatibility is not generally a goal of an IDE, and, in fact, the selling points of IDE's rely heavily on incompatibility. To set their products apart from the competition, vendors will usually ship IDE's with a library of code that is not available in other environments (e.g., widgets, controls, etc.). A knowledgeable programmer could actually use that library with another compiler, but that would require the programmer to have access to the library, which is only available as part of the IDE package. Not that you can't write code using an IDE that will compile with other compilers, but if you use any of the proprietary widgets in your program, particularly if you use a "drag and drop" Rapid Application Development environment such as is available in Microsoft Visual C++ and Borland C++ Builder, don't expect to be able to easily port your code to another development environment.

While there are many advantages to a nonintegrated environment, the ease of use of an IDE such as Microsoft Visual C++ is hard to argue with, and even programmers who prefer another compiler for some reason often will compromise, developing and debugging code in an IDE using only standard syntax and libraries, then compiling a final release with the preferred compiler.

Whether you are a new programmer or an experienced programmer testing a new environment or learning a new programming language, a simple "Hello World" program is the traditional way to test that everything in your programming environment is working correctly. In this lab, you will explore your environment, and use it to create a "Hello World" program. This is your first step to becoming a C++ programmer.

If you are working with Microsoft Visual C++, you may want to read Sections 1 and 2 in Appendix B in addition to working through this lab.

 # Pre-Lab

PROBLEM

Learn to use your programming environment by writing a simple "Hello World" message to the display.

Learning About Your Programming Environment

As you go through this project, try to answer the following questions about your programming environment. If you need help, ask your professor or a lab assistant (if you are in a class), or consult your environment or component on-line help and documentation.

1. Are you working in an IDE or in a nonintegrated environment?

---

2. If you are working in an IDE, who is the vendor and what is the name and version of the environment? (e.g. Microsoft Visual C++ 6.0, Borland C++ Builder 5.0)

---

3. If you are working in a nonintegrated environment, who is the vendor and what is the name and version of the compiler?

---

4. If you are working in a nonintegrated environment, who is the vendor and what is the name and version of the editor?

---

5. If you are working in a nonintegrated environment, do you have a debugger, and, if so, who is the vendor, and what is the name and version of the debugger?

---

6. How do you begin a new C++ program using your environment? (e.g., "create a new file" or "create a new project, and then add a new file to the project")

_____

_____

7. How do you launch your editor?

_____

_____

8. Does your editor do syntax highlighting? _____

9. Does your editor auto-complete function names? _____

10. How do you save the C++ source file?

_____

_____

11. How do you compile a program? Can you compile from within your editor?

_____

_____

_____

_____

12. How does your compiler communicate syntax errors (i.e., typos)?

_____

_____

_____

13. How do you launch your debugger (if one is available)? Can you launch your debugger from within your editor?

_____

_____

_____

14. Does your debugger use the same interface as your editor? _____

15. Can you edit from within your debugger? If so, can you make changes "on the fly" (i.e., without stopping the debugger, recompiling the program, and restarting the debugger)?

_____

16. Where does your compiler save the executable generated by your program?

_____

17. How does your compiler name the executable?

_____

18. Can you run the executable that is generated from within your editor? How? (i.e. not within the "debugger")

_____

19. How can you get a printout of your source code?

_____

20. How can you get a program output screen? (Note: See *Printing Console Output From Microsoft Windows* in *Appendix A* if you are working with Microsoft Windows.)

_____

21. How do you close a project?

_____

22. How do you close your programming environment?

_____

 # In-the-Lab

Coding Your First Program

✓ Start Your Editor

Start your C++ editor / IDE.

✓ Create a New Project

Make sure that a new file (and project if required) is open.

✓ Enter the Source Code

Type in the following C++ program.

```
#include <iostream.h>

int main()
{
    cout << "Hello World!" << endl;

    return 0;
}
```

✓ Save the Program

After you have entered the source code, you need to save the program. Name this program *L1_1.cpp*.

Testing and Debugging the Program

✓ Compile the Program

Now that you have entered and saved the program, compile it. (See Question 11 in the Pre-Lab exercise.)

✓ Errors?

If there were any errors in the program you will have to edit the program code to fix the errors and then compile the program again before you can link and run the program. (See Question 11 in the Pre-Lab exercise.) Be sure to save the program again after you correct any errors.

✓ Link the Program

If you used a "compile" option rather than a "build" or "make" option, you may have to explicitly tell your compiler to link your program after compiling it. (See Question 11 in the Pre-Lab exercise.)

✓ Run the Program

When the program is successfully compiled and linked, run it to make sure that it does what it is supposed to do. (See Questions 16, 17, and 18 in the Pre-Lab exercise.)

✓ Check the Program Output

A sample output of the "Hello World!" program is shown in Figure 1-1. If your output does not look similar to the one shown in Figure 1-1, double-check that you typed the program code in exactly as shown, then rebuild the executable.

Depending on your particular environment, there may be other things on the screen. If you are working in a command line environment, the "Hello World!" message may simply be written on the line following the command to run the program, and your command prompt will be flashing on the line following the program output. If you are in a graphical environment, a new console window probably appeared to show you the program output, and there may be an additional message instructing you on how to close the window.

Figure 1-1 Sample "Hello World" output

Documenting the Program

✓ Test and Print a Sample Run of the Program

Get a printout of the program run. (See Question 20 in the Pre-Lab exercise.) See *Printing Console Output From Microsoft Windows* in *Appendix A* if you are running Microsoft Windows and need help with this.

✓ Print the Source Code

Get a printout of the program source code. (See Question 19 in the Pre-Lab exercise.)

✓ Close the File

When you are finished with the program file, make sure that you have saved any final changes and then close the file (and project or workspace if required). (See Questions 21 and 22 in the Pre-Lab exercise.)

Syntax errors occur when your compiler does not understand your code. They usually are just typos. Most compilers are "smart" enough to point you to the specific line that contains the error. In an IDE, you are usually given a visual cue within your editor as to where the syntax error is. In a non-integrated environment, you may be given only a line number and an error message, and you must use your editor to manually search for the line with the error, and then fix it.

 # In-the-Lab

PROBLEM

Use your compilers error reporting to find and correct a syntax error

Coding the Program

✓ Start Your Editor

Start your C++ editor / IDE.

✓ Create a New Project

Make sure that a new file (and project if required) is open.

✓ Enter the Source Code

Type in the following C++ program exactly as it is shown. Note that there is a syntax error in this program.

```cpp
#include <iostream.h>

int main()
{
    cout << "Hello Syntax Error!" << endl

    return 0;
}
```

✓ Save the Program

After you have entered the source code, you need to save the program. Name this program *L1_2.cpp*.

Testing and Debugging the Program

✓ Compile the Program

Now that you have entered and saved the program, compile it.

✓Errors?

When you try to compile the program, your compiler will generate a syntax error. See Question 12 in the Pre-Lab exercise for information on how your compiler generates the error. Using the information given find the line where the syntax error exists.

The actual error is on the line containing the *cout* statement. The line is missing a semi-colon (;). This is one of the most common syntax errors, and many compilers will actually generate an error indicating the line following the line that is missing the semi-colon.

Fix the error by putting a semi-colon at the end of the *cout* line, and try to compile again. If your compiler generates any more errors, try to use the error messages to locate the line containing the error, then check that line against the code listing above, and fix the error.

✓Link the Program

If you used a "compile" option rather than a "build" or "make" option, you may have to explicitly tell your compiler to link your program after compiling it.

✓Run the Program

When the program is successfully compiled and linked, run it to make sure that it does what it is supposed to do.

✓Check the Program Output

A sample output of the "Hello Syntax Error!" program is shown in Figure 1-2. If your output does not look similar to that shown in Figure 1-2, double-check that you typed the program code in exactly as shown, then rebuild the executable.

Depending on your particular environment, there may be other things on the screen. If you are working in a command line environment, the "Hello Syntax Error!" message may simply be written on the line following the command to run the program, and your command prompt will be flashing on the line following the program output. If you are in a graphical environment, a new console window probably appeared to show you the program output, and there may be an additional message instructing you on how to close the window.

Figure 1-2 Sample "Hello Syntax Error" output

Documenting the Program

✓ Test and Print a Sample Run of the Program

Get a printout of the program run. See *Printing Console Output From Microsoft Windows* in *Appendix A* if you are running Microsoft Windows and need help with this.

✓ Print the Source Code

Get a printout of the program source code.

✓ Close the File

When you are finished with the program file, make sure that you have saved any final changes and then close the file (and project or workspace if required).

A string is a type of variable that holds text. You need to know about two basic types of strings: C++ strings and C-strings. It is generally preferable to use C++ strings if you are programming in C++. However, your compiler may not support C++ strings, in which case you must use C-strings. Working with C-strings is more difficult than working with C++ strings, but programmers who work with C-strings will have a head start on programmers who work with C++ strings when it is time to learn arrays. The purpose of this project is simply to test which style of strings you must work with.

You may wonder why no other aspects of the ANSI/ISO C++ standard are discussed in a lab titled "ANSI/ISO" Standard. Two relatively new additions to the C++ standard will affect the way you program: Namespaces and C++ strings. As a beginning programmer, you will not worry about namespaces except to put a particular line (*using namespace std*) into your programs.

C++ string support, however, can drastically change the way you program. With C-strings, the programmer has to either explicitly state the maximum length of a string variable, or explicitly provide a means of dynamically (during the run of the program) changing the maximum size of a string object. Programming texts generally use the former method, while professionals usually use the latter.

C++ strings require less thought. The programmer can simply define and use a string variable. All details are taken care of within the compiler.

Even if your compiler supports C++ strings, it will be worth your while to learn how to use C-strings, even if you put it off until later. A lot of C++ code has been written using C-strings—code that you may have to maintain someday. Also, at some point in your programming career you may find yourself working with a compiler that does not support C++ strings, or you may find yourself working on a project in which you cannot use C++ strings because of compatibility issues. While it's okay to take the academic approach while you are in training and ignore C-strings, it is much better to take the realistic approach and learn to use them since you will probably have to deal with them in the real world. Staugaard's new text covers both C++ strings and C-strings.

It's time to test the ANSI/ISO compliance of your compiler with respect to strings. Major C++ compilers such as Microsoft Visual C++ and Borland C++ have been updated to support C++ strings, but there are many compilers, both free and commercial, that have yet to implement them.

In-the-Lab

PROBLEM

Find out if your compiler supports C++ strings.

Testing Your Compiler for C++ String Support

✓ Start Your Editor

Start your C++ editor / IDE.

✓ Create a New Project

Make sure that a new file (and project if required) is open.

There are two code listings here. Listing 1 contains a C++ string, and Listing 2 is modified to work with a C string instead. The changed lines are shaded in Listing 2. Type in Listing 1 first.

Listing 1:

```
#include <iostream>
#include <string>
using namespace std;

int main()
{
    string helloString = "";
    helloString = "Hello Standard!";
    cout << helloString << endl;

    return 0;
}
```

Listing 2:

```
#include <iostream.h>
#include <string.h>
//THE namespace LINE IS DELETED. THIS LINE IS A COMMENT, AND NEED NOT BE INCLUDED.

int main()
{
    char helloString[16] = "\0";
    strcpy ( helloString, "Hello Standard!" ) ;
    cout << helloString << endl;

    return 0;
}
```

✓ **Save the Program**

After you have entered the source code, you need to save the program. Name this program *L1_3.cpp*.

Testing and Debugging the Program

✓ **Compile the Program**

Now that you have entered and saved the program, compile it.

✓ **Errors?**

If your program does not compile, then your compiler will generate syntax errors. If the errors generated indicate that your compiler does not know where to find the files "iostream" and "string," then modify your code to match Listing 2, save the file, and try to compile again. You should make sure that your code matches Listing 1 exactly and still does not compile before you make the modifications.

If you have other errors, check your code and try again. It should be noted that the second listing will work in all compilers, whether or not they support C++ strings.

✓ Link the Program

If you used a "compile" option rather than a "build" or "make" option, you may have to explicitly tell your compiler to link your program after compiling it.

✓ Run the Program

When the program is successfully compiled and linked, run it to make sure that it does what it is supposed to do.

✓ Check the Program Output

A sample output of the "Hello Standard!" program is shown in Figure 1-3. If your output does not look similar to the one shown in Figure 1-3, double-check that you typed the program code in exactly as shown, then rebuild the executable.

Depending on your particular environment, there may be other things on the screen. If you are working in a command line environment, the "Hello Standard!" message may simply be written on the line following the command to run the program, and your command prompt will be flashing on the line following the program output. If you are in a graphical environment, a new console window probably appeared to show you the program output, and there may be an additional message instructing you on how to close the window.

Figure 1-3 Sample "Hello Standard" output

Documenting the Program

✓ Test and Print a Sample Run of the Program

Get a printout of the program run. See *Printing Console Output From Microsoft Windows* in *Appendix A* if you are running Microsoft Windows and need help with this.

✓ Print the Source Code

Get a printout of the program source code.

✓ Close the File

When you are finished with the program file, make sure you have saved any final changes, and then close the file (and project or workspace if required).

You should now know whether your compiler supports C++ style strings. Chances are that your compiler does support them, and Listing 1 worked. However, if you had to resort to Listing 2, don't despair. You can do everything with C-strings that you can with C++ strings, you just have to go about it differently.

LAB PROJECT #2

The Programmer's Algorithm

■ LAB OBJECTIVES

In this lab, you will . . .

* Practice how to solve problems using the *programmer's algorithm.*
* Define a problem in terms of computer output, input, and processing.
* Plan a problem solution using problem abstraction and stepwise refinement.
* Construct problem solving diagrams of your problem solutions.
* Develop algorithms that are easily converted to C++ code.

■ REQUIRED READING

Chapter 2: Structured & Object-Oriented Problem Solving Using C++, 3rd edition,
by Andrew C. Staugaard, Jr.

■ INTRODUCTION

Programming reduces to the art and science of problem solving. To be a good programmer, you must be a good problem solver. To be a good problem solver, you must attack a problem in a methodical way, from initial problem inspection and definition to final solution, testing, and documentation. In the beginning, when confronted with a programming problem, you will be tempted to get to the computer and start coding as soon as you get an idea of how to solve it. However, you *must* resist this temptation. Such an approach might work for simple problems, but will *not* work when you are confronted with the complex problems found in today's real world. A good carpenter might attempt to build a dog house without a plan, but would never attempt to build your "dream house" without a good set of blueprints.

In this lab project, you will practice the steps required to solve just about any programming problem using a *top-down structured* approach. You will begin by defining the problem in terms of input, output, and processing. Then, use your problem definition to construct a main algorithm that ignores the implementation details required by a computer language. From this initial abstract algorithm, you will refine the solution step by step until it reaches a level that can be coded directly into a computer program. As you become more experienced in programming, you will find that the secret to successful programming is good planning through abstract analysis and stepwise refinement, which results in top-down structured software designs. Such designs are supported by languages like C++.

■ PROBLEM SOLVING REVIEW

Here is a problem from Staugaard's text that is similar to what you will be asked to do in this project. Read it over carefully and use it as a guide to complete the problems in this project.

PROBLEM

Develop a set of algorithms to calculate the amount of sales tax and the total cost of a sales item, including tax. Assume the sales tax rate is 7 percent and the user will enter the cost of the sales item.

Defining the Problem

Look for the nouns and verbs within the problem statement, as they often provide clues to the required output, input, and processing. The nouns suggest output and input, and the verbs suggest processing steps. The nouns relating to output and input are *sales tax*, *total cost*, and *cost*. The total cost is the required output, and the sales tax and item cost are needed as input to calculate the total cost of the item. However, the sales tax rate is given (7 percent), so the only data required for the algorithm is an entry of the item cost by the user.

The verb *calculate* requires us to process two things: the amount of sales tax and the total cost of the item, including sales tax. Therefore, the processing must calculate the amount of sales tax and add this value to the item cost to obtain the total cost of the item. In summary, the problem definition in terms of output, input, and processing is as follows:

Output: The total cost of the sales item, including sales tax to be displayed in a console screen on the system monitor.

Input: The cost of the sales item to be entered by the user on the system keyboard.

Processing: $tax = 0.07 \times cost$
$totalCost = cost + tax$

Planning the Solution

Using the foregoing problem definition, we are now ready to write the initial algorithm as follows:

Initial Algorithm

main()
BEGIN
   Obtain the cost of the sales item from the user.
   Calculate the sales tax and total cost of the sales item.
   Display the total cost of the sales item, including sales tax.
END.

Again, we have divided the problem into three major tasks relating to input, processing, and output. The next task is to write a pseudocode algorithm for each task. We will refer to these algorithms as *setdata()*, *calculateCost()*, and *displayResults()*. Due to the simplicity of this problem, we need only one level of refinement as follows:

First Level of Refinement

setData()
BEGIN
   Write a user prompt to enter the cost of the item (*cost*).
   Read *cost*.
END

calculateCost()
BEGIN
   Set *tax* to $(0.07 \times cost)$.
   Set *totalCost* to $(cost + tax)$.
END

displayResults()
BEGIN
   Write *totalCost..*
END

The problem solving diagram in Figure 2-1 shows the block structure required for the program.

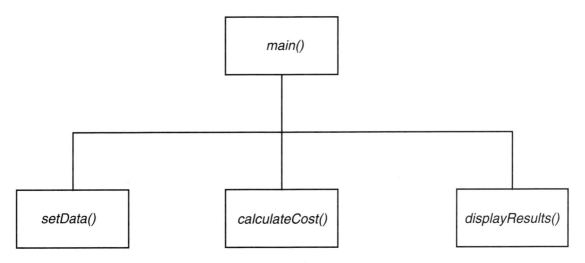

Figure 2-1   Problem solving diagram for the tax problem.

In this lab you will create a problem definition and a set of algorithms to calculate and report the gross pay for an employee who works 40 hours or less per week. Then you will enter the C++ code to solve the problem, and compile, link, run, and print the program.

 # Pre-Lab

PROBLEM

Calculate and report the weekly gross pay for a part-time employee.

Defining the Problem

Output: What output is needed according to the problem statement?

_____

Input: What input will be needed for processing to obtain the required output?

_____

Processing: What processing is required to calculate gross pay from the given input values?

_____

According to the problem statement, you will be calculating the gross pay for an employee that works 40 hours or less per week. This means that you will not have to worry about overtime pay. The output should be the employee's name, rate of pay, hours worked, and the total amount of gross pay. The employee's name, hours worked, and rate of pay are needed as input. To process the gross pay, you must multiply the employee's hours by the pay rate.

Planning the Solution

Develop the initial algorithm using the input, output, and processing described previously.

main()
BEGIN

END

Develop the pseudocode for each task in your initial algorithm. This is your first level of refinement.

setdata()
BEGIN

END

calculatePay()
BEGIN

END

displayResults()
BEGIN

END

Does your problem solution look similar to the one below?

main()
BEGIN
    Obtain the employee's name, rate of pay, and hours worked.
    Calculate the employee's gross pay.
    Display the employee's name, rate of pay, hours worked, and gross pay.
END

setdata()
BEGIN
    Write a user prompt to enter the employee's name (*name*).
    Read *name*.
    Write a user prompt to enter rate of pay (*rate*)..
    Read *rate*.
    Write a user prompt to enter weekly hours worked (*hours*).
    Read *hours*.
END

calculatePay()
BEGIN
    Set *grossPay* to *hours* × *rate*.
END

displayResults()
BEGIN
    Write *name, rate, hours, grossPay*.
END

Use the space below to construct a problem-solving diagram for the solution to the payroll problem.

22

In-the-Lab

Coding the Program

✓ Start Your Compiler

Start your C++ program development environment.

✓ Open a new File

Make sure that a new file (and project if required) is open.

✓ Enter the Source Code

Enter one of the three listings that follow using your editor. Listing 1 is a fully standards-compliant listing, which you should use if you determined in Project 1 that your compiler supports C++ style strings, unless you're using Microsoft Visual C++ 6.

You should use Listing 2 only if you are using Microsoft Visual C++ 6. It addresses a bug in this compiler's implementation of the *getline()* function. In Microsoft Visual C++ 6 (as of service pack 5), the *getline()* function reads an input string incorrectly. The user of the program will have to press enter twice at the name prompt. (See http://support.microsoft.com/ support/kb/articles/Q240/0/15.ASP for details and a fix.)

Listing 3 uses C-strings instead of the ANSI/ISO style strings. Enter Listing 3 if your compiler does not support C++ strings. Listing 2 and Listing 3 have changes with respect to Listing 1 shaded.

Listing 1: (ANSI/ISO Compliant Compilers)

```cpp
// LAB 2-1 (L2_1.CPP)
// AUTHOR : type your name here
// DATE WRITTEN : type the date here

// PREPROCESSOR DIRECTIVES
#include <iostream>      //FOR cin AND cout
#include <iomanip>       //FOR setw()
#include <string>        //FOR string
using namespace std;

int main()
{
    // DEFINE VARIABLES
    string name = "";          // EMPLOYEE NAME
    float hours = 0.0;         // WEEKLY HOURS WORKED
    float rate  = 0.0;         // HOURLY RATE OF PAY
    float grossPay = 0.0;      // WEEKLY GROSS PAY

    // DISPLAY PROGRAM DESCRIPTION MESSAGE
    cout << "This program will calculate the gross pay for a\n"
         << "part time employee, given his/her rate of pay\n"
         << "and number of weekly hours worked. It is assumed\n"
         << "that the employee has worked less than 40 hours." << endl << endl << endl;
```

```cpp
    // OBTAIN USER DATA
    cout << "Enter employee name:" << endl;
    cin >> ws;
    getline(cin,name);
    cout << "\nEnter the rate of pay:" << endl;
    cin >> rate;
    cout << "\nEnter the hours worked this week:" << endl;
    cin >> hours;

    // CALCULATE GROSS PAY
    grossPay = rate * hours;

    // DISPLAY REPORT
    cout.setf(ios::fixed);
    cout.setf(ios::showpoint);
    cout.precision(2);
    cout << "\n\nPAYROLL REPORT FOR: " << name << endl << endl;
    cout << setw(20) << "RATE" << setw(20) << "HOURS"
         << setw(20) << "GROSS PAY" << endl << endl;
    cout << setw(15) << "$" << rate << setw(20) << hours
         << setw(13) << "$" << grossPay << endl;

    return 0;
}// END main()
```

Listing 2: (Visual C++ 6.0)

```cpp
// LAB 2-1 (L2_1.CPP)
// AUTHOR : type your name here
// DATE WRITTEN : type the date here

// PREPROCESSOR DIRECTIVES
#include <iostream>        //FOR cin AND cout
#include <iomanip>         //FOR setw()
#include <string>          //FOR string
using namespace std;

int main()
{
    // DEFINE VARIABLES
    string name = "";            // EMPLOYEE NAME
    float hours = 0.0;           // WEEKLY HOURS WORKED
    float rate  = 0.0;           // HOURLY RATE OF PAY
    float grossPay = 0.0;        // WEEKLY GROSS PAY

    // DISPLAY PROGRAM DESCRIPTION MESSAGE
    cout << "This program will calculate the gross pay for a\n"
         << "part time employee, given his/her rate of pay\n"
         << "and number of weekly hours worked. It is assumed\n"
         << "that the employee has worked less than 40 hours." << endl << endl << endl;

    // OBTAIN USER DATA
    cout << "Enter employee name, then press Enter twice:" << endl;
    cin >> ws;
    getline(cin,name);
    cout << "\nEnter the rate of pay:" << endl;
```

```cpp
            cin >> rate;
            cout << "\nEnter the hours worked this week:" << endl;
            cin >> hours;

            // CALCULATE GROSS PAY
            grossPay = rate * hours;

            // DISPLAY REPORT
            cout.setf(ios::fixed);
            cout.setf(ios::showpoint);
            cout.precision(2);
            cout << "\n\nPAYROLL REPORT FOR: " << name << endl << endl;
            cout << setw(20) << "RATE" << setw(20) << "HOURS"
                 << setw(20) << "GROSS PAY" << endl << endl;
            cout << setw(15) << "$" << rate << setw(20) << hours
                 << setw(13) << "$" << grossPay << endl;

            return 0;
}// END main()
```

Listing 3: (ANSI/ISO Noncompliant Compilers)

```cpp
// LAB 2-1 (L2_1.CPP)
// AUTHOR : type your name here
// DATE WRITTEN : type the date here

// PREPROCESSOR DIRECTIVES
#include <iostream.h>      //FOR cin AND cout
#include <iomanip.h>       //FOR setw()
//THE string HEADER IS NOT INCLUDED, AND THE namespace LINE HAS BEEN DELETED

int main()
{
            // DEFINE VARIABLES
            char name[22] = "\0";       // EMPLOYEE NAME
            float hours = 0.0;          // WEEKLY HOURS WORKED
            float rate  = 0.0;          // HOURLY RATE OF PAY
            float grossPay = 0.0;       // WEEKLY GROSS PAY

            // DISPLAY PROGRAM DESCRIPTION MESSAGE
            cout << "This program will calculate the gross pay for a\n"
                 << "part time employee, given his/her rate of pay\n"
                 << "and number of weekly hours worked. It is assumed\n"
                 << "that the employee has worked less than 40 hours." << endl << endl << endl;

            // OBTAIN USER DATA
            cout << "Enter employee name:" << endl;
            cin.getline(name,22);
            cout << "\nEnter the rate of pay:" << endl;
            cin >> rate;
            cout << "\nEnter the hours worked this week:" << endl;
            cin >> hours;

            // CALCULATE GROSS PAY
            grossPay = rate * hours;
```

```
    // DISPLAY REPORT
    cout.setf(ios::fixed);
    cout.setf(ios::showpoint);
    cout.precision(2);
    cout << "\n\nPAYROLL REPORT FOR: " << name << endl << endl;
    cout << setw(20) << "RATE" << setw(20) << "HOURS"
         << setw(20) << "GROSS PAY" << endl << endl;
    cout << setw(15) << "$" << rate << setw(20) << hours
         << setw(13) << "$" << grossPay << endl;

    return 0;
}// END main()
```

✓Save the Program

After you have entered the source code, you need to save the program. Name this program *L2_1.cpp*.

Testing and Debugging the Program

✓Compile the Program

Now that you have entered and saved the program, compile it.

✓Errors?

If there were any errors in the program you will have to edit the program code to fix the errors, and then compile the program again before you can link and run the program. Be sure to save the program again after you correct any errors.

✓Link the Program

If you used a "compile" option rather than a "build" or "make" option, you may have to explicitly tell your compiler to link your program after compiling it.

✓Run the Program

When the program is successfully compiled and linked, run it to make sure that it does what it is supposed to do, and then answer the following questions about the program:

What C++ statements are causing the program's messages to be displayed on the screen?

_____

What C++ statements are causing the computer to wait for information to be entered?

_____

What do you think the \n and *endl* parts of the program code are doing?

_____

What C++ function within the *cout* statement is positioning the *RATE, HOURS,* and *GROSS PAY* headers on the screen?

What do you think the *setf( )* and *precision( )* functions in the program code are doing?

As you run the program, the user messages are displayed on your screen with the *cout* statements in the program and when input is needed the *cin* and *getline( )* (or *cin.getline( )* if you used Listing 3) statements wait for you to enter information from the keyboard and then place the information into a specified variable.

As you may have guessed, \n and *endl* cause the cursor to move to a new line. Output can be placed where you want it to be displayed by using the *setw( )* function. The *setw( )* function is used to position the *RATE, HOURS,* and *GROSS PAY* headers where you see them on the screen. The *setf( )* function sets the *ios::fixed* and *ios::showpoint* flags to force fixed decimal output and the display of trailing zeros for currency format, respectively. The *precision( )* function forces a decimal output to the number of places specified.

✓ Check the Program Output

Check the program output to make sure that it is correct. Figure 2-2 shows a sample output from the payroll program. If your program results look similar, congratulations, it worked!

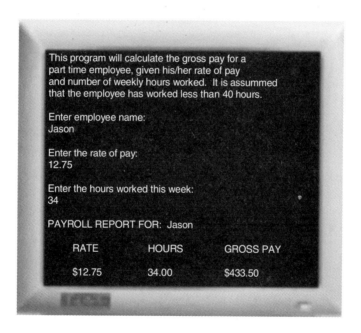

Figure 2-2 Input sample and tabular output required for the circle problem

Documenting the Program

✓ Test and Print a Sample Run of the Program

Running the program several times with different input information is an important part of program testing. Run the program several times with different values for the *name, rate,* and *hours.* Be sure to check the program output each time.

Printed copies of sample program runs are part of the documentation process in programming. To obtain these, you will need to have access to a printer. Make sure that the printer is on and on-line. Get a printout of your program runs. See *Printing Console Output From Microsoft Windows* in *Appendix A* if you are running Microsoft Windows and need help with this.

✓ Print the Source Code

A printed copy of the program source code is also an important part of program documentation. Make sure that the printer is ready and then print the source code.

✓ Close the File

When you are finished with the program file, make sure that you have saved any final changes and then close the file (and project or workspace if required).

In this problem you will create a problem definition and use a set of algorithms to calculate the interest on a credit card account balance. Then you will enter the code for the problem, compile, run, test, and print the code sample runs.

 **Pre-Lab**

Read the following problem statement, complete the problem definition, and revise the algorithms that follow to use a single *If/Then/Else* operation in place of the two *If/Then* operations:

PROBLEM

The interest charged on a credit card account depends on the remaining balance, according to the following criteria:

> Interest charged is 18 percent of the balance up to $500 and 15 percent of the balance for any amount over $500.

Define the problem and develop a set of algorithms to find the total amount of interest due on any given account balance.

Defining the Problem

Output: What output is needed according to the problem statement?

_____

Input: What input will be needed for processing to obtain the required output?

_____

Processing: According to the criteria defined in the problem statement, the amount of interest is divided into two cases.

Case 1: What processing is required if the balance is less than or equal to $500?

_____

Case 2: What processing is required if the balance is greater than $500?

_____

According to the problem statement, the output will be the total amount of interest due. The account balance is needed as input for processing. If the balance is less than or equal to $500, the first $500 must be multiplied by 0.18. If the balance is greater than $500, the first $500 must be multiplied by 0.18 and the portion of the balance that is over $500 must be multiplied by 0.15. See the following set of algorithms to help you understand the structured design required to calculate the interest:

Planning the Solution

main( )
BEGIN
    Obtain the account balance.
    Calculate the interest.
    Display the interest.
END

setdata( )
BEGIN
    Write a user prompt to enter the account balance (*balance*).
    Read *balance*.
END

calculateInterest( )
BEGIN
    If *balance* <= 500 Then
        Set *interest* to $(0.18 \times balance)$.
    If *balance* > 500 Then
        Set *interest* to $(0.18 \times 500) + (0.15 \times (balance - 500))$.
END

displayResults( )
BEGIN
    Write *interest*.
END

Use the space below to construct a problem-solving diagram for the solution to the credit card interest problem.

30

Revise the *calculateInterest()* algorithm for this problem to replace the two *If/Then* control structures with a single *If/Then/Else* control structure.

calculateInterest()
BEGIN

END

An *If/Then/Else* control structure performs the statements that follow the *If* only when the test condition is true. The statements that follow the *Else* are performed only when the test condition is false. The *If/Then/Else* structure creates exactly two possibilities for the flow of the program. Regardless of which code branch runs, the program execution picks up directly after the close of the *If/Then/Else* structure after the *If* or *Else* statements are executed.

The condition to test in this problem is whether the *balance* is $500 or less. If this is false, then the *balance* is greater than $500–this is exactly what the second *If/Then* statement in the original *calculateInterest()* algorithm was testing. Thus, the second *If/Then* statement is true only when the first is false and vice versa. Therefore, the second *If/Then* statement can be combined with the first to create a single *If/Then/Else* statement as shown:

If *balance* <= 500 Then
  Set *interest* to (0.18 × *balance*).
Else
  Set *interest* to (0.18 × 500) + (0.15 × (*balance* – 500)).

This algorithm says that *interest* will be set to (0.18 × *balance*) if the *balance* is less than or equal to $500; otherwise *interest* will be set to (0.18 × 500) + (0.15 (*balance* – 500)).

 # In-the-Lab

Coding the Program

✓ Start Your Compiler

Start your C++ program development environment.

✓ Open a new File

Make sure that a new file (and project if required) is open.

✓ Enter the Source Code

Enter one of the following two listings using your editor: Listing 1 is a fully ANSI/ISO standard compliant listing, which you should use if your compiler's standards compliant header files do not end with ".*h*". The only differences between the Listing 1 and Listing 2 are the *namespace* line in Listing 1 and the ".*h*" on the header files in Listing 2. Because of the lack of string objects, this is one of the few programs in which the standards compliance of your compiler makes no difference in the way the program is written. Thus, Listing 2 will work with all compilers, compliant or not, whereas Listing 1 will only work with compilers that are ANSI/ISO compliant.

Listing 1: (ANSI/ISO Compliant Compilers)

```cpp
// LAB 2-2 (L2_2.CPP)
// AUTHOR : type your name here
// DATE WRITTEN : type the date here

// PREPROCESSOR DIRECTIVES
#include <iostream>      //FOR cin AND cout
#include <iomanip>       //FOR setw()
using namespace std;

int main()
{
    // DEFINE VARIABLES
    float interest = 0.0;       // AMOUNT OF INTEREST
    float balance  = 0.0;       // AMOUNT OF ACCOUNT BALANCE

    // DISPLAY PROGRAM DESCRIPTION MESSAGE
    cout << "This program will calculate total interest due for a credit\n"
        << "card account." << endl << endl;

    // OBTAIN USER DATA
    cout << "Enter the credit card balance:" << endl;
    cin >> balance;

    // CALCULATE INTEREST
    if (balance <= 500)
    {
        interest = 0.18 * balance;
    }
    else
    {
        interest = (0.18 * 500) + (0.15 * (balance-500));
    }

    // DISPLAY REPORT
    cout.setf(ios::fixed);
    cout.setf(ios::showpoint);
    cout.precision(2);
    cout << "\n\nThe total interest for the account balance of $" << balance
        << " is $" << interest << endl;
    return 0;
}// END main()
```

Listing 2: (ANSI/ISO Noncompliant Compilers)

```cpp
// LAB 2-2 (L2_2.CPP)
// AUTHOR : type your name here
// DATE WRITTEN : type the date here

// PREPROCESSOR DIRECTIVES
#include <iostream.h>      //FOR cin AND cout
#include <iomanip.h>       //FOR setw()

int main()
{
    // DEFINE VARIABLES
    float interest = 0.0;        // AMOUNT OF INTEREST
    float balance  = 0.0;        // AMOUNT OF ACCOUNT BALANCE

    // DISPLAY PROGRAM DESCRIPTION MESSAGE
    cout << "This program will calculate total interest due for a credit\n"
         << "card account." << endl << endl;

    // OBTAIN USER DATA
    cout << "Enter the credit card balance:" << endl;
    cin >> balance;

    // CALCULATE INTEREST
    if (balance <= 500)
    {
        interest = 0.18 * balance;
    }
    else
    {
        interest = (0.18 * 500) + (0.15 * (balance-500));
    }

    // DISPLAY REPORT
    cout.setf(ios::fixed);
    cout.setf(ios::showpoint);
    cout.precision(2);
    cout << "\n\nThe total interest for the account balance of $" << balance
         << " is $" << interest << endl;
    return 0;
}// END main()
```

✓**Save the Program**

After you have entered the source code, you need to save the program. Name this program *L2_2.cpp*.

Testing and Debugging the Program

✓**Compile the Program**

Now that you have entered and saved the program, compile it.

✓Errors?

If there were any errors in the program you will have to edit the program code to fix the errors, and then compile the program again before you can link and run the program. Be sure to save the program again after you correct any errors.

✓Link the Program

If you used a "compile" option rather than a "build" or "make" option, you may have to explicitly tell your compiler to link your program after compiling it.

✓Run the Program

When the program is successfully compiled and linked, you can run and test it. Try entering several different values for *balance*.

As you run the program, the user messages are displayed on your screen with the *cout* statements in the program, and when input is needed the *cin* statements wait for you to enter information from the keyboard. The *cin* statement assigns the information you entered to the specified variable.

✓Check the Program Output

Check the program output to make sure it is correct. Figure 2-3 shows a sample output with a *balance* of $725.

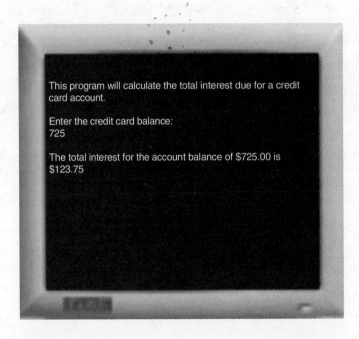

Figure 2-3 Sample output for the credit card program.

Documenting the Program

✓ Test and Print a Sample Run of the Program

Get a printout of three sample runs as follows:
 One with the *balance* less than $500.
 One with the *balance* equal to $500.
 One with the *balance* greater than $500.

See *Printing Console Output From Microsoft Windows* in *Appendix A* if you are running Microsoft Windows and need help with this.

✓ Print the Source Code

Make sure that your printer is ready, and then print the source code.

✓ Close the File

When you are finished with the program file, make sure you have saved any final changes, and then close the file (and project or workspace if required).

Using Data Types & Classes

OBJECTIVES

In this lab, you will . . .
* Learn about data types
* Decide when to use integers and when to use floating point numbers.
* Decide when to use characters and when to use strings.

REQUIRED READING

*Chapter 3: Structured & Object-Oriented Problem Solving Using C++, 3rd edition,
by Andrew C. Staugaard, Jr.*

INTRODUCTION

The goal of this project is to acquaint you with some standard data types that are a part of the C++ language. Problem 1 deals with when it makes sense to use integer types and when to use floating point data types—a desicion that is not always obvious. Problem 2 deals with a decision that is usually more straightforward, when to use character and string data.

PROBLEM SOLVING REVIEW

Here is a problem from Staugaard's text that illustrates basic problem-solving concepts and the programmer's algorithm.

Problem

Your local bank has contracted you to design a C++ application program that will process savings account data for a given month. Assume that the savings account accrues interest at a rate of 12 percent per year and that the user must enter the current account balance, amount of deposits, and amount of withdrawals. Develop a problem definition, a set of algorithms, and a C++ program to solve this problem.

Defining the Problem

Output: The program must display a report showing the account transactions and balance for a given savings account in a given month.

Input: To process a savings account, you need to know the initial balance, amount of deposits, amount of withdrawals, and interest rate. We will assume that these values will be entered by the program user, with the exception of the interest rate, which will be coded as a constant.

Processing: The program must process deposits and withdrawals and calculate interest to determine the monthly balance.

We will divide the problem into individual subproblems to solve the overall banking problem. Now, try to identify the separate tasks that must be performed to solve the problem. First, the user must enter the required transaction data, which will include the previous month's balance, current month's deposits, and current month's withdrawals. Once the transaction data are entered, the program must add the deposits to the account balance, subtract the withdrawals from the account balance, calculate the interest, and generate the required report. As a result, we can identify the following five program tasks:

- Obtain the transaction data entered by the program user.
- Add the deposits to the account balance.
- Subtract the withdrawals from the account balance.
- Calculate the account interest.
- Generate the monthly account report.

The problem-solving diagram in Figure 3-1 shows the structure required for the program.

Planning the Solution

Now we will employ stepwise refinement to develop the required set of algorithms. The initial algorithm level, *main()*, will reflect the problem definition and call the individual subprogram, or function, or modules, as follows:

Initial Algorithm

main()
BEGIN
    Call a function to obtain the transaction data from user.
    Call a function to add the account deposits.
    Call a function to subtract the account withdrawals.
    Call a function to calculate the account interest.
    Call a function to generate the account report.
END.

The first level of refinement requires that we show a detailed algorithm for each subprogram module, or function. They are as follows:

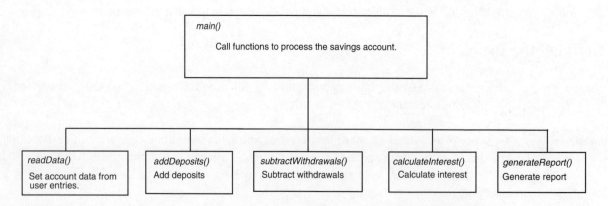

Figure 3-1 A problem-solving diagram for the banking problem.

readData()
BEGIN
    Write a prompt to enter the current account balance.
    Read *balance*.
    Write a prompt to enter the monthly deposits.
    Read *deposits*.
    Write a prompt to enter the monthly withdrawals.
    Read *withdrawals*.
END.

addDeposits()
BEGIN
    Calculate *balance = balance + deposits*.
END.

subtractWithdrawals()
BEGIN
    Calculate *balance = balance − withdrawals*.
END.

addInterest()
BEGIN
    Calculate *balance = balance + (balance * interest)*.
END.

generateReport()
BEGIN
    Write *balance*.
    Write *deposits*.
    Write *withdrawals*.
END.

Coding the Program

Here is how the foregoing algorithms are translated into C++ code:

```
/**********************************************************************************

ACTION 3-2 (ACT03_02.CPP)
THIS PROGRAM REPRESENTS THE FLAT SOLUTION TO THE BANKING PROBLEM

**********************************************************************************/

//PREPROCESSOR DIRECTIVE
#include <iostream.h> //FOR cin AND cout

//DEFINE GLOBAL INTEREST CONSTANT
const double INTEREST = 0.01;    //CURRENT MONTHLY INTEREST RATE
                                 //IN DECIMAL FORM
```

```
//MAIN FUNCTION
int main()
{
    double balance = 0.0;              //ACCOUNT BALANCE
     double deposits = 0.0;            //MONTHLY DEPOSITS
     double withdrawals = 0.0;         //MONTHLY WITHDRAWALS

    cout << "This program will generate a banking account report based"
         << "on information entered by the user" << endl << endl;

    //readData(): GET THE MONTHLY ACCOUNT INFORMATION
    //FROM THE USER
    cout << "Enter the account balance:  $";
    cin  >> balance;
    cout << "Enter the deposits this month:  $";
    cin >> deposits;
    cout << "Enter the withdrawals this month:  $";
    cin >> withdrawals;

    //addDeposits(): ADD THE MONTHLY DEPOSITS
    //TO THE ACCOUNT BALANCE
    balance = balance + deposits;

    //subtractWithdrawals(): SUBTRACT THE MONTHLY WITHDRAWALS
    balance = balance - withdrawals;

    //addInterest(): ADD MONTHLY INTEREST
    balance = balance + (balance * INTEREST);

    //FORMAT OUTPUT IN DOLLARS AND CENTS
    cout.setf(ios::fixed);
    cout.setf(ios::showpoint);
    cout.precision(2);

    //generateReport(): DISPLAY THE MONTHLY ACCOUNT REPORT
    cout << "The account balance is currently:  $" << balance << endl;
    cout << "Deposits were  $" << deposits << endl;
    cout << "Withdrawals were  $" << withdrawals << endl;

    //RETURN
     return 0;
} //END main()
```

At this point, the code might look a little overwhelming. However, don't agonize over the coding details; just observe the things that relate to what was discussed in Chapter 3 of Staugaard's text. You will learn all the coding details in time. First, notice the overall structure of the program. A general program comment is at the top of the program, followed by the preprocessor directives, followed by function *main()*, which is followed by the individual function code. Second, notice the constant and variable definitions. The constant *INTEREST* is defined prior to *main()* to make it a global constant and accessible to the entire program. The variables *balance*, *deposits*, and *withdrawals* are defined at the beginning of *main()*. You should define constants just before *main()*, after your preprocessor directives, and you should define variables before anything else within *main()*. You will understand the reason for this when you start coding highly structured programs in Project 8. Finally, notice the extensive use of comments. The purpose of the program is commented, as well as the purpose of each function. Furthermore, a comment is placed with each constant and variable definition to specify its purpose in the program. The comments are easily identified from the executable code, because they are coded in uppercase characters.

Here we have used a *flat* or *inline* implementation of the program. The term *flat* comes from the idea that we will flatten the hierarchical structure of the algorithms by coding all the program steps as one long *inline* sequence of statements as part of function *main()*. As you can see, each of the former algorithms have been coded inline as part of *main()*. This type of implementation is adequate for simple problems like this. The program code is clear and easy to understand, given the appropriate program comments. For the next few projects, we will employ flat implementations. Then, as the problems get more complex, we will be forced to implement the program modules as C++ functions and replace the inline program statements with calls to those functions. However, before you can do this, you need to learn the basic implementation details of the C++ language. The next four projects are devoted to this purpose. We will get back to highly structured C++ programs in Project 8, where functions are discussed in detail.

This code is available on Staugaard's text CD as *ACT03_02.cpp*. It can be downloaded from the text Web site at www.prenhall.com/staugaard. You may wish to compile and execute the code to observe its operation.

There are two basic types of numeric data in C++: integers and floating point values. Both types of data are limited in range by the compiler because of practical issues. Different compilers impose different limitations on these ranges. In order to implement the ranges and still give the programmer the ability to work with very large numbers, C++ has several different primitive integer and floating point types, some of which have a relatively small range and take a very small amount of resources, and some of which have larger ranges and use more resources.

 # Pre-Lab

PROBLEM

Your professor wants you to develop a program to divide the students in the class into four groups. This means that, if possible, each of the four groups must have the same number of students. If the students cannot be evenly divided into four groups, then the first three groups should contain the same number of students, and the fourth group should contain that number plus any left over students. (For example if your class has 20 students, each group will have 5 students, but if your class has 23 students, the first three groups will each have 5 students and the fourth group will have 8 students.) Additionally, your professor would like to know the average number of students per group.

Defining the Problem

Output: What output is needed according to the problem statement?

_____

Input: What input will be needed for processing to obtain the required output?

_____

Processing: What processing is required to calculate the number of students in Group 1?

_____

What processing is required to calculate the number of students in Group 2?

_____

What processing is required to calculate the number of students in Group 3?

_____

What processing is required to calculate the number of students in Group 4?

_____

What processing is required to calculate the average number of students per group?

Your program should first output the number of students in Groups 1, 2, 3 and 4, and then it should output the average number of students in each group. Your program must accept the number of students in the class as input from the user. Since you cannot have only part of a student in a group, you must use integer division to divide the number of students by 4 to calculate the size of the groups. *Integer division* divides two numbers and produces an integer result (i.e. it *does not* compute the decimal portion of the answer). To calculate the number of students in Group 4, you must again use integer division to divide the number of students by 4, but you must also add the result of the *modulus*, or remainder, of the number of students divided by 4.

For some insight into how this works, assume that there are 11 students in the class. The long division below shows how the integer division and modulus operations are calculated:

$$
\begin{array}{r}
2 \quad \text{r3} \\
4\overline{\smash{)}11} \\
-8 \\
\hline
3
\end{array}
$$

The integer division result of 11 ÷ 4 is 2 and the modulus, or remainder of 11 ÷ 4, is 3. In C++, integer division is denoted by the / operator used with two integer operands, and modulus is denoted by the % operator used with to integer operands. Therefore, in C++, 11 / 4 = 2 and 11 % 4 = 3. Thus, in the case of 11 students, Groups 1, 2, and 3 will contain 2 students each (calculated by 11 / 4), and Group 4 will contain 5 students (calculated by (11 / 4) + (11 % 4)).

When reporting an average, you should report a floating point result. You must use *floating point division* to calculate the average number of students in each group. Again, assume there are 11 students in the class. Here is the long division that shows how floating point division is calculated:

$$
\begin{array}{r}
2.75 \\
4\overline{\smash{)}11.00} \\
-8 \\
\hline
30 \\
-28 \\
\hline
20 \\
-20 \\
\hline
0
\end{array}
$$

The floating point result of 11 ÷ 4 is 2.75. In C++, floating point division is denoted by the / operator, but, in order to produce a floating point result, *at least one of the two operands must be a floating point type*. All you have to do to make a C++ division operation calculate a floating point answer is add a ".0" to the one of the operands to make it a floating point number rather than an integer. In C++, 11 / 4 = 2, but 11 / 4.0 = 2.75.

43

Planning the Solution

Here is the algorithm for function *main()* developed from the problem definition.

main()
BEGIN

    Write a program description message.
    Set the number of students from information entered by the user.
    Set number of students in Group 1 = number of students / 4.
    Set number of students in Group 2 = number of students / 4.
    Set number of students in Group 3 = number of students / 4.
    Set number of students in Group 4 = (number of students / 4) + (number of students % 4).
    Set average students per group = number of students / 4.0.
    Write the number of students in each group and the average number of students per group.
END.

In-the-Lab

Coding Your The Program

✓ Start Your Editor

Start your C++ editor/IDE.

✓ Create a New Project

Make sure that a new file (and project if required) is open.

✓ Enter the Source Code

Type in the C++ program that follows, filling in the blanks as you go. If your compiler does not support the latest ANSI/ISO standard, you may need to include *iostream.h* rather than *iostream*, and you will want to drop the *using namespace std* line.

```
// LAB 3-1 (L3_1.CPP)
// AUTHOR: type your name here
// DATE WRITTEN: type the date here

//PREPROCESSOR DIRECTIVES
#include <iostream>

using namespace std;

int main()
{
    //DEFINE LOCAL VARIABLES
    [          ] numberOfStudents;
```

```
[        ]   group1Students;

[        ]   group2Students;

[        ]   group3Students;

[        ]   group4Students;

[        ]   averageStudentsPerGroup;

    //DISPLAY PROGRAM DESCRIPTION MESSAGE
    cout << "Given the number of students in a class, this program will"
         << "\ndivide the students into 4 groups, display the number of"
         << "\nstudents in each group, and display the average number"
         << "\nstudents per group.\n\n" << endl;

    //SET THE NUMBER OF STUDENTS FROM USER INPUT
    cout << "Enter the number of students in the class:  ";
    cin >> numberOfStudents;

    //CALCULATE THE NUMBER OF STUDENTS IN GROUP 1
    group1Students = numberOfStudents / [    ] ;

    //CALCULATE THE NUMBER OF STUDENTS IN GROUP 2
    group2Students = numberOfStudents / [    ] ;

    //CALCULATE THE NUMBER OF STUDENTS IN GROUP 3
    group3Students = numberOfStudents / [    ] ;

    //CALCULATE THE NUMBER OF STUDENTS IN GROUP 4
    group4Students = (numberOfStudents / [    ] ) + (numberOfStudents % [    ] );

    //CALCULATE THE AVERAGE STUDENTS PER GROUP
    averageStudentsPerGroup = numberOfStudents / [    ] ;

    //DIPLAY NUMBER OF STUDENTS IN EACH GROUP
    //AND AVERAGE STUDENTS PER GROUP
    cout << numberOfStudents << " are in the class." << endl;
    cout << group1Students << " students are in Group 1." << endl;
    cout << group2Students << " students are in Group 2." << endl;
    cout << group3Students << " students are in Group 3." << endl;
    cout << group4Students << " students are in Group 4." << endl;
    cout << "There are an average of " << averageStudentsPerGroup
         << " students per group." << endl;

    //EXIT PROGRAM
    return 0;
} //END main()
```

✓Save the Program

After you have entered the source code, you need to save the program. Name this program *L3_1.cpp*.

Testing and Debugging the Program

✓ Compile the Program

Now that you have entered and saved the program, compile it.

✓ Errors?

If there were any errors in the program, you will have to edit the program code to fix the errors and then compile the program again before you can link and run the program. Be sure to save the program again after you correct any errors.

✓ Link the Program

If you used a "compile" option rather than a "build" or "make" option, you may have to explicitly tell your compiler to link your program after compiling it.

✓ Run the Program

When the program is successfully compiled and linked, run it to make sure that it does what it is supposed to do.

✓ Check the Program Output

Sample output for the student group program is shown in Figure 3-2. If your output does not report the information correctly, double-check your choice of data types and division operand types.

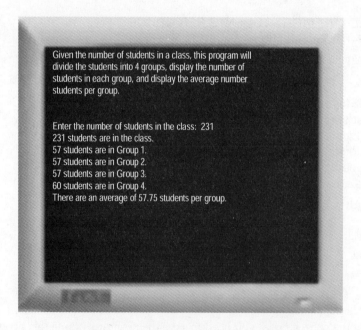

Figure 3-2 Sample student group output

46

Documenting the Program

✓ Test and Print a Sample Run of the Program

Get a printout of the program run. See *Printing Console Output From Microsoft Windows* in *Appendix A* if you are running Microsoft Windows and need help with this.

✓ Print the Source Code

Get a printout of the program source code.

✓ Close the File

When you are finished with the program file make, sure that you have saved any final changes and then close the file (and project or workspace if required).

In C++ there are two kinds of data made to store text: *characters* and *strings*. Character variables can contain exactly one character and are always denoted by the **char** type. The **char** type is a primitive type that actually stores an integer value in memory. When it comes time to display its value, it takes the integer value that it contains and displays the ASCII equivalent of the integer value. A list of ASCII values can be found in Appendix D of this lab manual.

Strings contain 0 to several chararacters. The number of characters contained in a string is known as the string *length*. A string with length 0 (i.e. it contains no characters) is known as an *empty string*. Older compilers use C-strings (*arrays*, or lists, of characters) to store string data. In these compilers, you will define a string variable using the following syntax (where *MAX* is a constant or a literal integer value that is equivalent to one more than the maximum length of the string):

> **char** *stringVariableName*[*MAX*];

Compilers that conform to the latest ANSI/ISO standard use the C++ *string* class to store string data. In these compilers, you must include the *string* header file and use the following syntax to define a string variable (*Note:* C++ *string* class objects do not have a maximum length specified as part of the variable definition):

> string *stringVariableName*;

Pre-Lab

PROBLEM

Your professor wants you to develop another program. This program should accept the first names of four students and the letter grade that each student has earned in the class. It should then output a report of the names and grades.

Defining the Problem

Output:　　　What output is needed according to the problem statement?

_____

Input:　　　What input will be needed for processing to obtain the required output?

_____

Processing:　What processing, if any, is required to obtain the output?

_____

This program should output a report of the student's first names and letter grades. As input, the program should read in the names and letter grades. The names should be stored as strings and the letter grades should be stored as characters. No processing is required to obtain the output.

Planning the Solution

Here is the algorithm for function *main()* developed from the problem definition:

main()
BEGIN
    Write program description message.
    Set the first name of student 1 from information entered by the user.
    Set the letter grade of student 1 from information entered by the user.
    Set the first name of student 2 from information entered by the user.
    Set the letter grade of student 2 from information entered by the user.
    Set the first name of student 3 from information entered by the user.
    Set the letter grade of student 3 from information entered by the user.
    Set the first name of student 4 from information entered by the user.
    Set the letter grade of student 4 from information entered by the user.
    Write the name of student1, letter grade of student1, name of student2, letter grade of student2, name of
        student3, letter grade of student3, name of student4, letter grade of student4.
END.

In-the-Lab

Coding the Program

✓ Start Your Editor

Start your C++ editor/IDE.

✓ Create a New Project

Make sure that a new file (and project if required) is open.

✓ Enter the Source Code

Type in one of the C++ program listings that follow, filling in the blanks as you go. Listing 1 is fully compliant with the ANSI/ISO standard, and Listing 2 should be used with compilers that do not yet fully support the standard. The differences between Listing 2 and Listing 1 are marked in Listing 2.

Listing 1:

```
// LAB 3-2 (L3_2.CPP)
// AUTHOR: type your name here
// DATE WRITTEN: type the date here
```

```cpp
// PREPROCESSOR DIRECTIVES
#include <iostream>
#include <string>
using namespace std;

int main()
{
    //DEFINE LOCAL VARIABLES
    [_____] student1FirstName = " ";

    [_____] student1LetterGrade = ' ';

    [_____] student2FirstName = " ";

    [_____] student2LetterGrade = ' ';

    [_____] student3FirstName = " ";

    [_____] student3LetterGrade = ' ';

    [_____] student4FirstName = " ";

    [_____] student4LetterGrade = ' ';

    //DISPLAY PROGRAM DESCRIPTION MESSAGE
    cout << "Given four students first names and letter grades,"
        << "\nthis program will display a report of the student's"
        << "\nnames and grades.\n\n" << endl;

    //SET STUDENT 1 INFORMATION FROM USER INPUT
    cout << "Please enter the first name of student 1:  ";
    cin >> student1FirstName;
    cout << "Please enter the letter grade of student 1:  ";
    cin >> student1LetterGrade;

    //SET STUDENT 2 INFORMATION FROM USER INPUT
    cout << "Please enter the first name of student 2:  ";
    cin >> student2FirstName;
    cout << "Please enter the letter grade of student 2:  ";
    cin >> student2LetterGrade;

    //SET STUDENT 3 INFORMATION FROM USER INPUT
    cout << "Please enter the first name of student 3:  ";
    cin >> student3FirstName;
    cout << "Please enter the letter grade of student 3:  ";
    cin >> student3LetterGrade;

    //SET STUDENT 4 INFORMATION FROM USER INPUT
    cout << "Please enter the first name of student 4:  ";
    cin >> student4FirstName;
    cout << "Please enter the letter grade of student 4:  ";
    cin >> student4LetterGrade;

    //DISPLAY STUDENT GRADE REPORT
    cout << "\n\n\nSTUDENT GRADE REPORT\n" << endl;
    cout << student1FirstName << "'s letter grade is " << student1LetterGrade << endl;
    cout << student2FirstName << "'s letter grade is " << student2LetterGrade << endl;
```

```cpp
    cout << student3FirstName << "'s letter grade is " << student3LetterGrade << endl;
    cout << student4FirstName << "'s letter grade is " << student4LetterGrade << endl;

    //EXIT PROGRAM
    return 0;

} //END main()
```

Listing 2: (*Hint:* You will need to supply a number for the maximum string length within square brackets [ ] in string variable definitions *only*. Make the number sufficiently large to hold a first name, but do not make it too large, because that will waste resources by causing excess memory to be allocated.)

```cpp
// LAB 3-2 (L3_2.CPP)
// AUTHOR: type your name here
// DATE WRITTEN: type the date here

// PREPROCESSOR DIRECTIVES
#include <iostream.h>

//THE using namespace std LINE IS NOT NEEDED

int main()
{
    //DEFINE LOCAL VARIABLES
    [      ] student1FirstName[      ] = "\0";

    [      ] student1LetterGrade = ' ';

    [      ] student2FirstName[      ] = "\0";

    [      ] student2LetterGrade = ' ';

    [      ] student3FirstName[      ] = "\0";

    [      ] student3LetterGrade = ' ';

    [      ] student4FirstName[      ] = "\0";

    [      ] student4LetterGrade = ' ';

    //DISPLAY PROGRAM DESCRIPTION MESSAGE
    cout << "Given four students first names and letter grades,"
         << "\nthis program will display a report of the student's"
         << "\nnames and grades.\n\n" << endl;

    //SET STUDENT 1 INFORMATION FROM USER INPUT
    cout << "Please enter the first name of student 1:  ";
    cin >> student1FirstName;
    cout << "Please enter the letter grade of student 1:  ";
    cin >> student1LetterGrade;

    //SET STUDENT 2 INFORMATION FROM USER INPUT
    cout << "Please enter the first name of student 2:  ";
    cin >> student2FirstName;
```

```
        cout << "Please enter the letter grade of student 2:  ";
        cin >> student2LetterGrade;

        //SET STUDENT 3 INFORMATION FROM USER INPUT
        cout << "Please enter the first name of student 3:  ";
        cin >> student3FirstName;
        cout << "Please enter the letter grade of student 3:  ";
        cin >> student3LetterGrade;

        //SET STUDENT 4 INFORMATION FROM USER INPUT
        cout << "Please enter the first name of student 4:  ";
        cin >> student4FirstName;
        cout << "Please enter the letter grade of student 4:  ";
        cin >> student4LetterGrade;

        //DISPLAY STUDENT GRADE REPORT
        cout << "\n\n\nSTUDENT GRADE REPORT\n" << endl;
        cout << student1FirstName << "'s letter grade is " << student1LetterGrade << endl;
        cout << student2FirstName << "'s letter grade is " << student2LetterGrade << endl;
        cout << student3FirstName << "'s letter grade is " << student3LetterGrade << endl;
        cout << student4FirstName << "'s letter grade is " << student4LetterGrade << endl;

        //EXIT PROGRAM
        return 0;

} //END main()
```

✓ Save the Program

After you have entered the source code, you need to save the program. Name this program *L3_2.cpp*.

Testing and Debugging the Program

✓ Compile the Program

Now that you have entered and saved the program, compile it.

✓ Errors?

If there were any errors in the program, you will have to edit the program code to fix the errors and then compile the program again before you can link and run the program. Be sure to save the program again after you correct any errors.

✓ Link the Program

If you used a "compile" option rather than a "build" or "make" option, you may have to explicitly tell your compiler to link your program after compiling it.

✓ Run the Program

When the program is successfully compiled and linked, run it to make sure that it does what it is supposed to do.

✓ Check the Program Output

A sample output of the student grade report program is shown in Figure 3-3. If your output does not look right, double-check your data type choices and then rebuild the executable.

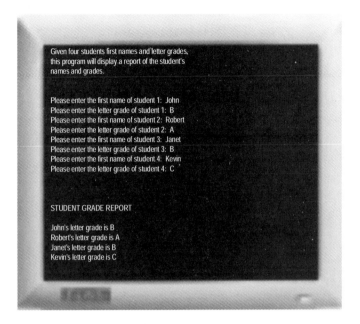

Given four students first names and letter grades, this program will display a report of the student's names and grades.

Please enter the first name of student 1: John
Please enter the letter grade of student 1: B
Please enter the first name of student 2: Robert
Please enter the letter grade of student 2: A
Please enter the first name of student 3: Janet
Please enter the letter grade of student 3: B
Please enter the first name of student 4: Kevin
Please enter the letter grade of student 4: C

STUDENT GRADE REPORT

John's letter grade is B
Robert's letter grade is A
Janet's letter grade is B
Kevin's letter grade is C

Figure 3-3 Sample student grade report program output

Documenting the Program

✓ Test and Print a Sample Run of the Program

Get a printout of the program run. See *Printing Console Output From Microsoft Windows* in *Appendix A* if you are running Microsoft Windows and need help with this.

✓ Print the Source Code

Get a printout of the program source code.

✓ Close the File

When you are finished with the program file, make sure that you have saved any final changes and then close the file (and project or workspace if required).

Getting Things In and Out

LAB OBJECTIVES

In this lab, you will . . .
* Generate output messages in a console screen on the display monitor.
* Obtain input from the keyboard.
* Use special functions and syntax to format and manipulate program output.
* Perform simple read/write disk file I/O operations.

REQUIRED READING

Chapter 4: Structured & Object-Oriented Problem Solving Using C++, 3rd edition, by Andrew C. Staugaard, Jr.

INTRODUCTION

In this project you will be displaying information in a console screen on the display monitor. Generating output from your program is called ***writing***. In C++ you will write information to a console screen in a display monitor using a *cout* (pronounced "see-out") statement. The word *cout* is not considered a keyword within C++; rather, *cout* is an object defined in the *iostream.h* header file (or the standardized *iostream* header file) for a class called *iostream*. We refer to *cout* as an ***output stream object*** that is attached to a console window on your system monitor.

You will also be accepting input from the keyboard. Accepting input into your program is called ***reading.*** The primary C++ statement that we will use for reading keyboard data is the *cin* (pronounced "see-in") statement. Like *cout, cin* is a predefined stream object in C++ and is part of the *iostream.h* header file (or the standardized *iostream* header file). The *cin* stream is an input stream attached, by default, to your system keyboard. Thus, as you enter information via the keyboard, it will flow into the *cin* stream.

Seveal ***I/O manipulators*** are listed in Table 4-1, several common I/O functions are listed in Table 4-2, and several I/O *escape sequences* are listed in Table 4-2. Manipulators and escape sequences are used with the *cout* object to format your output. To use some of the the I/O manipulators in Table 4-1, you must include the iomanip.*h* header file (or the standardized *iomanip* header file) in your program. To use the escape sequences in Table 4-2, you must include the *iostream.h* or the *iostream* header file, one of which, of course, must be included to use the *cout* object.

Any of the manipulators in Table 4-1 can be inserted in the *cout* << statement just like any other output item. To use an I/O stream function in Table 4-2, it must be called by the *cout* object using the dot, ., operator. To use any of the escape sequences in Table 4-3, simply include it as part of a string or enclose it within single quotes in the output stream in your program. Each escape sequence is treated as a separate character by the compiler.

TABLE 4-1 I/O STREAM MANIPULATORS FOR C++

Manipulator	Action
setw(n)	Sets field width to *n*
setprecision(n)	Sets floating point precision to *n*
setfill(n)	Sets fill character to *n*
ws	Extracts white space characters
endl	Inserts a new line in the output stream, then flushes the output stream
flush	Flushes the output stream

TABLE 4-2 FORMATTING FUNCTIONS AND FLAGS

Function/Flag	Description
setf()	Sets a formatting flag
unsetf()	Unsets a formatting flag
precision(n)	Sets decimal output to *n* decimal places
fixed	Forces fixed decimal point output
left	Forces left justification within field
right	Forces right justification within field
scientific	Forces exponential (*e*) output
showpoint	Forces a decimal point to be displayed along with trailing 0's.(Used for currency outputs)
showpos	Forces a + sign output for positive values

TABLE 4-3 ESCAPE SEQUENCES DEFINED FOR C++

Sequence	Action
\a	Beep
\b	Backspace
\n	CRLF
\r	CR
\t	Horizontal tab
\v	Vertical tab
\\	Backslash
\'	Single quote
\"	Double quote
\?	Question mark

Here is a problem from Staugaard's text that is similar to what you will be asked to do in this project. Read it over carefully, and use it as a guide to complete the problems in this project.

PROBLEM

Write a user-friendly program that will calculate the monthly payment for an installment loan from different values of principle, interest rate, and term entered by the user. We will format a four-column table for principle, interest rate, term, and payment and underscore each column heading. Thus, the final program output will be a table showing the loan principle, interest rate, term, and monthly payment. In addition, we will display the program user's name and the date the program was run.

To solve this problem, we will walk through the first three steps defined in the *programmer's algorithm* as described in Staugaard's text: define the problem, plan the problem solution, and code the program.

Defining the Problem

Output: The final program output must be a table showing the calculated monthly loan payment along with the loan principle, interest rate, and term used in the calculation. The user's name and date the program was run will be displayed above the table. In addition, user prompts should be provided on the monitor to direct the user to enter the required values.

Input: The input must be the user's name, date the program was run, and values for the loan principle, interest rate, and term.

Processing: $payment = principle * rate/(1- (1+rate)^{-term})$

where: *principle* is the amount of the loan.
rate is a monthly interest rate in decimal form.
term is the number of months of the loan.

Planning the Solution

The next step is to construct a set of algorithms from the problem definition. Try to identify the separate tasks that must be performed to solve the problem. First, the program must obtain the required data from the user. Once the data are entered, the program then must calculate the payment. Finally, the program must display the results. Thus, we can identify three program tasks, or functions, as follows:

- Obtain the user's name, date of program run, loan principle, interest rate, and term from the user.
- Calculate the monthly payment using the equation
  $payment = principle * rate/(1- (1+rate)^{-term})$
- Display the user's name, date the program was run, and table of results.

The problem solving diagram in Figure 4-1 shows the structure required for the program.

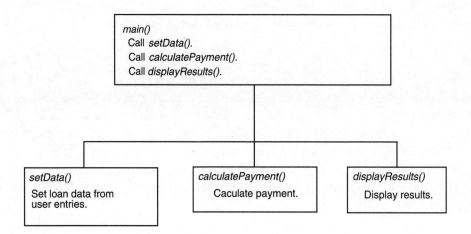

Figure 4-1   A problem-solving diagram for loan problem.

Because we are using the modular technique to design the program, we must employ stepwise refinement to develop the algorithms. The initial algorithm level, *main()*, will simply reflect the problem definition and call the individual subprogram functions, as follows:

Initial Algorithm

main()
BEGIN
    Call function to obtain the input data from the user.
    Call function to calculate the loan payment.
    Call function to display the results.
END.

The first level of refinement requires that we show a detailed algorithm for each subprogram module, or function. They are as follows:

First Level of Refinement

setData()
BEGIN
    Write a user prompt to enter the user's name.
    Read *name*.
    Write a user prompt to enter the date.
    Read *date*.
    Write a user prompt to enter the loan principle, or amount.
    Read *principle*.
    Write a user prompt to enter the annual interest rate of the loan.
    Read *rate*.
    Write a user prompt to enter the term of the loan, in months.
    Read *term*.
END.

calculatePayment()
BEGIN
    Calculate *decRate = rate/12/100.*
    Calculate *payment = principle * decRate/(1 - (1+decRate)* $^{-term}$ *).*
END.

displayResults()
BEGIN
    Display user's name and date of program run.
    Display table headings for principle, rate, term, and payment.
    Display the principle, rate, term, and payment values under the respective   headings.
END.

Notice that *rate* is converted to a monthly value in decimal form. Why? Because the user entry is an annual value in percentage form. However, the payment calculation formula requires a monthly value in decimal form.

Coding the Program

Here is the fully standards compliant code. Remember that if you are using Visual C++ 6.0, the *getline()* function will require you to press the *Enter* key twice for each string entry. (The bug is a known issue as of Service Pack 5; see http://support.microsoft.com/support/kb/articles/Q240/0/15.ASP for details and a fix.) Listing 1 is fully standards compliant. Listing 2 uses older C-strings for compilers that have not yet implemented the string class. The Listing 1 code (*ACT04_01.cpp*) is available on Staugaard's text CD or can be downloaded from the text Web site at <u>www.prenhall.com/staugaard</u>. You may wish to compile and execute the code to observe its operation.

Listing 1: (ANSI/ISO Compliant Compilers)

```
/*
ACTION 4-1 (ACT04_01.CPP)
OUTPUT:     A TABLE MENU SHOWS THE LOAN AMOUNT, INTEREST, TERM, AND MONTHLY
            PAYMENT.
            USER PROMPTS AS NECESSARY.

INPUT:      LOAN AMOUNT, INTEREST RATE, AND TERM.

PROCESSING: PAYMENT = PRINCIPLE * RATE/(1-(1+RATE) –TERM)

WHERE:      PRINCIPLE IS THE AMOUNT OF THE LOAN.
            RATE IS A MONTHLY INTEREST RATE IN DECIMAL FORM.
            TERM IS THE NUMBER OF MONTHS OF THE LOAN.
*/


//PREPROCESSOR DIRECTIVES
#include <iostream>   //FOR cin and cout
#include <string>     //FOR string CLASS
#include <math.h>     //FOR pow()

using namespace std; //REQUIRED WHEN INCLUDING iostream
```

```cpp
//MAIN FUNCTION
int main()
{
    //DEFINE AND INITIALIZE OBJECTS AND VARIABLES
    string name = " ";          //CUSTOMER NAME
    string date = " ";          //DATE OF REPORT
    double principle = 0.0;     //LOAN PRINCIPLE
    int term = 0;               //TERM OF LOAN IN MONTHS
    double rate = 0.0;          //ANNUAL INTEREST IN PERCENT FORM
    double payment = 0.0;       //MONTHLY PAYMENT
    double decRate = 0.0;       //MONTHLY INTEREST IN DECIMAL FORM

    //DISPLAY PROGRAM DESCRIPTION MESSAGE
    cout << "\nThis program will calculate a monthly loan interest"
         << "\npayment, total loan interest, and total loan amount." << endl;

    //setData() FUNCTION: SET VARIABLES TO DATA ENTERED BY USER
    cout << "\nPlease enter your name: ";
    cin >> ws;
    getline(cin,name);
    cout << "\nEnter the date in XX/XX/XX format: ";
    cin >> ws;
    getline(cin,date);
    cout << "\nEnter the amount of the loan: $";
    cin >> principle;
    cout << "\nEnter the duration of the loan in months: ";
    cin >> term;
    cout << "\nEnter the annual interest rate in percent: ";
    cin >> rate;

    //calculatePayment() FUNCTION
    decRate = rate/12/100;
    payment = principle * decRate/(1-pow((1+decRate),-term));

    //displayResults() FUNCTION
    cout.setf(ios::fixed);
    cout.setf(ios::showpoint);
    cout.precision(2);
    cout << endl << endl;
    cout << "Name: " << name << endl;
    cout << "Date: " << date << endl;
    cout << "\n\n"
         << "LOAN AMOUNT"
         << "\tINTEREST RATE"
         << "\t\tTERM"
         << "\t\tPAYMENT" << endl;
    cout << "-----------"
         << "\t-------------"
         << "\t\t----"
         << "\t\t-------" << endl;
    cout << "$" << principle
         << "\t" << rate << "%"
         << "\t\t\t" << term << " Months"
         << "\t$" << payment << endl;
    //RETURN
    return 0;
} //END main()
```

Listing 2: (ANSI/ISO Non-Compliant Compilers)

```
/*
OUTPUT:    A TABLE MENU SHOWS THE LOAN AMOUNT, INTEREST, TERM, AND MONTHLY
PAYMENT.
               USER PROMPTS AS NECESSARY.

INPUT:     LOAN AMOUNT, INTEREST RATE, AND TERM.

PROCESSING: PAYMENT = PRINCIPLE * RATE/(1-(1+RATE) -TERM)

WHERE:     PRINCIPLE IS THE AMOUNT OF THE LOAN.
           RATE IS A MONTHLY INTEREST RATE IN DECIMAL FORM.
           TERM IS THE NUMBER OF MONTHS OF THE LOAN.
*/

//PREPROCESSOR DIRECTIVES
#include <iostream.h> //FOR cin and cout
#include <math.h>     //FOR pow()

//DECLARE CONSTANTS
const int NAME_SIZE = 31;    //SIZE OF NAME ARRAY
const int DATE_SIZE = 10;    //SIZE OF DATE ARRAY

int main()
{
    char name[NAME_SIZE] = "\0";    //CUSTOMER NAME
    char date[DATE_SIZE] = "\0";    //DATE OF LOAN
    double principle = 0.0;       //LOAN PRINCIPLE
    int term = 0;                 //TERM OF LOAN IN MONTHS
    double rate = 0.0;            //ANNUAL INTEREST IN PERCENT FORM
    double payment = 0.0;         //MONTHLY PAYMENT
    double decRate = 0.0;         //MONTHLY INTEREST IN DECIMAL FORM

    //DISPLAY PROGRAM DESCRIPTION MESSAGE
    cout << "\nThis program will calculate a monthly loan interest"
        << "\npayment, total loan interest, and total loan amount." << endl;

    //setData() FUNCTION: SET VARIABLES TO DATA ENTERED BY USER
    cout << "\nPlease enter your name: ";
    cin.getline(name,NAME_SIZE);
    cout << "\nEnter the date in XX/XX/XX format: ";
    cin.getline(date,DATE_SIZE);
    cout << "\nEnter the amount of the loan: $";
    cin >> principle;
    cout << "\nEnter the duration of the loan in months: ";
    cin >> term;
    cout << "\nEnter the annual interest rate in percent: ";
    cin >> rate;

    //calculatePayment() FUNCTION
    decRate = rate/12/100;
    payment = principle * decRate/(1-pow((1+decRate),-term));

    //displayResults() FUNCTION
    cout.setf(ios::fixed);
```

61

```
cout.setf(ios::showpoint);
cout.precision(2);
cout << endl << endl;
cout << "Name: " << name << endl;
cout << "Date: " << date << endl;
cout << "\n\n"
     << "LOAN AMOUNT"
     << "\tINTEREST RATE"
     << "\t\tTERM"
     << "\t\tPAYMENT" << endl;
cout << "-----------"
     << "\t-------------"
     << "\t\t----"
     << "\t\t-------" << endl;
cout << "$" << principle
     << "\t" << rate << "%"
     << "\t\t\t" << term << " Months"
     << "\t$" << payment << endl;

//RETURN
return 0;
} //END main()
```

If you don't know which of the two listings to use, try the first listing initially. If it doesn't work correctly, modify the code to match the second listing, depending on your compiler. The lines that need to be modified are shown on a shaded background. These modifications employ tried and true code that is backwards compatible with some of the oldest implementations of the C++ language. The C-style strings that it uses are not as easy to work with as the new C++ strings, but they always work.

Here is a sample of what the user would see when executing either program.

```
This program will calculate a monthly loan interest
payment, total loan interest, and total loan amount.

Please enter your name: Andrew C. Staugaard, Jr. ↵
Enter the date in XX/XX/XX format: 05/25/99↵

Enter the amount of the loan: $1000.00↵
Enter the duration of the loan in months: 12↵
Enter the annual interest rate in percent: 12↵

Name: Andrew C. Staugaard, Jr.
Date: 05/25/99
```

LOAN AMOUNT	INTEREST RATE	TERM	PAYMENT
$1000	12.0%	12 Months	$88.85

Now it is time for you to exercise your problem-solving muscle. The following are some problems for you to tackle:

In this exercise, you will develop a problem definition and a set of algorithms to calculate the circumference and area of a circle, given its radius from the user. You will then write the source code program that produces a formatted output. You will compile, link, run, test, and print your program.

 # Pre-Lab

PROBLEM

Write a user-friendly program to calculate the circumference and area of a circle from a user's entry of its radius. Generate a tabular display showing the circle's radius, circumference, and area.

Defining the Problem

Output: What output is needed according to the problem statement?

_____

Input: What input will be needed for processing to obtain the required output?

_____

Will the program user be required to enter all the values, or can you hard-code some of the needed values as constant amounts?

_____

Processing: What processing is required to calculate the circumference and area?

_____

According to the problem statement, the output will be a tabular report showing the circle's radius, circumference, and area. The input value required from the user is the circle's radius. The constant *pi* (3.14159) can be coded as a constant in the program. To calculate the circumference of the circle, you must multiply the radius by *2pi*. To calculate the area of the circle, you must square the radius and multiply it by *pi*.

Planning the Solution

Here is the initial algorithm for function *main()*, developed from the problem definition. Notice that the problem can be refined according to the three major tasks relating to input, processing, and output. Your job is to write the algorithms required for the first level of refinement.

main()
BEGIN
    Call function to set the radius of the circle from the user.
    Call function to calculate the circle's circumference and area.
    Call function to display the circle's radius, circumference, and area in tabular format.
END

SET THE RADIUS FROM USER ENTRY
BEGIN

END.

CALCULATE THE CIRCUMFERENCE AND AREA
BEGIN

END

DISPLAY THE RESULTS IN TABLUAR FORMAT
BEGIN

END

64

 **In-the-Lab**

Coding the Program

✓ Start Your Compiler

Start your C++ program development environment.

✓ Open a new File

Make sure that a new file (and project if required) is open.

✓ Enter the Source Code

Using the algorithm that you developed, complete the following program shell for the loan interest program:

```
// LAB 4-1 (L4_1.CPP)
// AUTHOR : type your name here
// DATE WRITTEN : type the date here

// PREPROCESSOR DIRECTIVES




// DECLARE CONSTANTS (IF NEEDED)



int main()
{
// DEFINE AND INITIALIZE VARIABLES AND OBJECTS





// DISPLAY PROGRAM DESCRIPTION MESSAGE


```

// SET RADIUS FROM USER ENTRY

// CALCULATE CIRCUMFERENCE AND AREA

// DISPLAY RESULT TABLE

```
//RETURN
    return 0;
} //END MAIN
```

✓ Save the Program

After you have entered the source code, you need to save the program. Name this program *L4_1.cpp*.

Testing and Debugging the Program

✓ Compile the Program

Now that you have entered and saved the program, compile it.

✓ Errors?

If there were any errors in the program you will have to edit the program code to fix the errors, and then compile the program again before you can link and run the program. Be sure to save the program again after you correct any errors.

✓ Link the Program

Once the program is successfully compiled, you need to link it with the C++ library files needed by the program.

✓ Run the Program

When the program is successfully compiled and linked, run it to make sure that it does what it is supposed to do.

✓ Check the Program Output

A sample output of the user input screen and corresponding output table for the circle is shown in Figure 4-2. If your output does not look similar to the one shown in Figure 4-3, edit your program code so that you obtain the correct output. You may need to adjust the *setw()* statements or *setprecision()* statements to obtain the formatting shown.

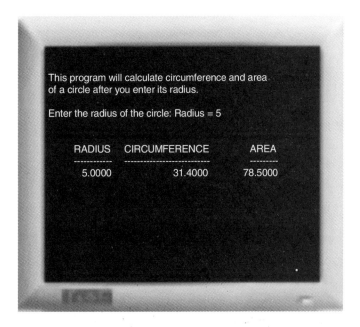

This program will calculate circumference and area of a circle after you enter its radius.

Enter the radius of the circle: Radius = 5

RADIUS	CIRCUMFERENCE	AREA
5.0000	31.4000	78.5000

Figure 4-2 Input sample and tabular output required for the circle problem

Documenting the Program

✓ Test and Print a Sample Run of the Program

Get a printout of the program run. See *Printing Console Output From Microsoft Windows* in *Appendix A* if you need help with this.

✓ Print the Source Code

Get a printout of the program source code. Obtain a printed copy of three sample program runs, entering different values for the radius in each sample run.

✓ Close the File

When you are finished with the program file, make sure that you have saved any final changes and then close the file (and project or workspace if required).

In this exercise you will develop a problem definition and set of algorithms to accept a student name, course name, and test scores from the program user. You will calculate the test average, and generate a report of the student name, course, test scores, and test average. You will then write the source code program that produces a formatted output. You will compile, link, run, test, and print your program.

 # Pre-Lab

PROBLEM

Write a user-friendly program that will allow a student to enter his/her name, course, and four test scores. Generate a display of the student's name, course name, individual test scores, and test average.

Defining the Problem

Output: What output is needed according to the problem statement?

_____

Input: What input will be needed for processing to obtain the required output?

_____

Processing: What processing is required to calculate the test average?

_____

According to the problem statement, the output will be a formatted report showing the student's name, course name, individual test scores, and test average. The student's name, course name, and test scores are needed as input. These items *cannot* be hard-coded into the program as constants and must be accepted as variable input from the keyboard. To calculate the test average, you need to add the test scores and divide by four.

Planning the Solution

Write a set of algorithms using the input, output, and processing that you developed in the problem definition.

Here is the initial algorithm for function *main()* developed from the problem definition. Notice that the problem can be refined according to the three major tasks relating to input, processing, and output. Your job is to write the algorithms required for the first level of refinement.

main()
BEGIN
    Call function to set the student's name, course name, and test scores from user entries.
    Call function to calculate the test average.
    Call function to display a report of the test results in tabular format.
END

SET STUDENT INFORMATION FROM USER ENTRIES
BEGIN

END.

CALCULATE THE TEST AVERAGE
BEGIN

END

DISPLAY THE RESULTS IN TABLUAR FORMAT
BEGIN

END

In-the-Lab

Coding the Program

✓ Start Your Compiler

Start your C++ program development environment.

✓ Open a new File

Make sure that a new file (and project if required) is open.

✓ Enter the Source Code

Using the algorithm that you developed, complete the following program shell for the test average program.

```
// LAB 4-2 (L4_2.CPP)
// AUTHOR : type your name here
// DATE WRITTEN : type the date here

// PREPROCESSOR DIRECTIVES




int main()
{

// DEFINE AND INITIALIZE VARIABLES AND OBJECTS




// DISPLAY PROGRAM DESCRIPTION MESSAGE


```

// SET STUDENT NAME, COURSE, AND TEST SCORES FROM USER ENTRIES

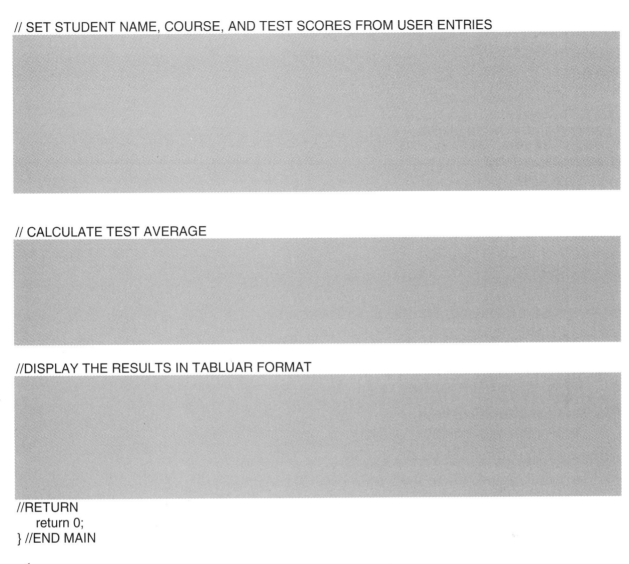

// CALCULATE TEST AVERAGE

//DISPLAY THE RESULTS IN TABLUAR FORMAT

//RETURN
   return 0;
} //END MAIN

✓ Save the Program

After you have entered the source code, you need to save the program. Name this program *L4_2.cpp*.

Testing and Debugging the Program

✓ Compile the Program

Now that you have entered and saved the program, compile it.

✓ Errors?

If there were any errors in the program you will have to edit the program code to fix the errors, and then compile the program again before you can link and run the program. Be sure to save the program again after you correct any errors.

✓ Link the Program

Once the program is successfully compiled, you need to link it with the C++ library files needed by the program.

✓ Run the Program

When the program is successfully compiled and linked, run it to make sure that it does what it is supposed to do.

✓ Check the Program Output

A sample output of the test scores and average program is shown in Figures 4-3 and 4-4. Your output screens do not have to look exactly like the ones shown here, but they should look similar. If your output does not look similar to the screens shown in the figures, edit your program code so that you obtain the correct output. You may need to adjust the *setw()* statements or *setprecision()* statements.

✓ Observe the Program Execution with the Debugger

User a debugger to step through the program, executing the code one line at a time, and observe the operation of the input and output statements in your program. Set a watch on your student name, course name, scores, and average objects using a watch window.

Documenting the Program

✓ Test and Print a Sample Run of the Program

Get a printout of the program run. See *Printing Console Output From Microsoft Windows* in *Appendix A* if you need help with this.

✓ Print the Source Code

Get a printout of the program source code. Obtain a printed copy of three sample program runs, entering different values for the radius in each sample run.

✓ Close the File

When you are finished with the program file, make sure you have saved any final changes, and then close the file (and project or workspace if required).

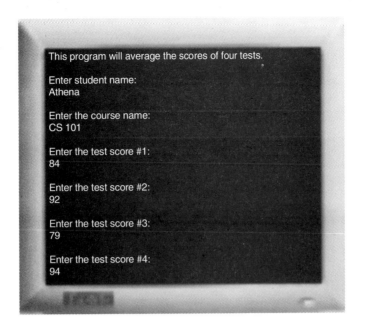

Figure 4-3 Sample input screen for the test average program.

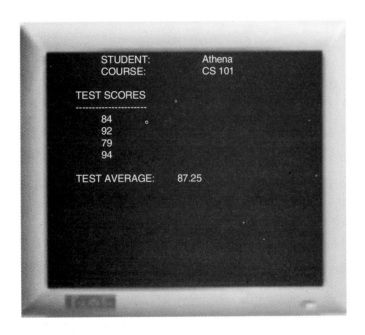

Figure 4-4 Sample output screen for the test average program.

In this exercise you will develop a problem definition and a set of algorithms to perform simple disk-file read-and-write operations.

 **Pre-Lab**

PROBLEM

Write a program that employs a loop to read a character file called *lowcase*, consisting of all lowercase characters. Convert the lowercase characters to uppercase by subtracting 32 from each character, and write the uppercase characters to a file called *upcase*.

Defining the Problem

Output: What output is needed according to the problem statement?

_____

Input: What input will be needed for processing to obtain the required output?

_____

Processing: What processing is required to generate an uppercase character file from the lowercase character file?

_____

According to the problem statement, the output will be a disk file of uppercase characters called *upcase*. The input will be a disk file of lowercase characters called *lowcase*. The input file must be created using a simple ASCII text editor, while the output file will be written by your program. To generate the uppercase equivalent of a lowercase character, you must subtract 32 from the lowercase ASCII code. The program will employ a loop that reads one character at a time from the lowercase character file, subtracts 32 from the character, then writes the resulting uppercase character to the uppercase character file.

Planning the Solution

Write a set of algorithms using the input, output, and processing that you developed in the problem definition.

Here is an algorithm for function *main()* that will do the job. We will not step-wise refine this algorithm because the problem is relatively simple. Notice that the algorithm simply reads one character at a time, subtracts 32 from it, and writes the result to the uppercase file until the last character in the file has been processed. Notice that the pseudocode only shows the program logic, not the file manipulation details.

74

```
main()
BEGIN
    While (Read character from input file)
        Subtract 32 from character.
        Write the character to the uppercase file.
END
```

 # In-the-Lab

Coding the Program

✓Start Your Text Editor

Using your text editor, create a file of lowercase characters by simply typing your first and last name, as well as your institution name. Save the file as *lowcase*. If your text editor automatically adds an extension to files, you may have to rename your file after it is created and saved. In Microsoft Windows, you can enter *lowcase* within quotation marks in the save dialog window to keep an extension from being added automatically.

✓Start Your Compiler

Start your C++ program development environment.

✓Open a new File

Make sure that a new file (and project if required) is open.

✓Enter the Source Code

Using the given algorithm, complete the following program shell for the file I/O program. Refer to your textbood for the coding details. If you are using Staugaard's text, refer to Section 4-3.

```
// LAB 4-3 (L4_3.CPP)
// AUTHOR : type your name here
// DATE WRITTEN : type the date here

// PREPROCESSOR DIRECTIVES
```

```
int main()
{
// DEFINE AND INITIALIZE VARIABLES
```

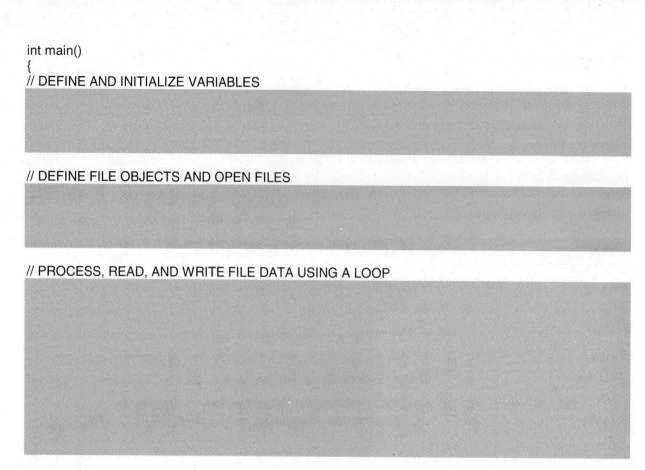

```
// DEFINE FILE OBJECTS AND OPEN FILES
```

```
// PROCESS, READ, AND WRITE FILE DATA USING A LOOP
```

```
//RETURN
    return 0;
} //END MAIN
```

✓ Save the Program

After you have entered the source code, you need to save the program. Name this program *L4_3.cpp*.

Testing and Debugging the Program

✓ Compile the Program

Now that you have entered and saved the program, compile it.

✓ Errors?

If there were any errors in the program you will have to edit the program code to fix the errors, and then compile the program again before you can link and run the program. Be sure to save the program again after you correct any errors.

✓ Link the Program

Once the program is successfully compiled, you need to link it with the C++ library files needed by the program.

✓ Run the Program

When the program is successfully compiled and linked, run it. If you are not getting the results you expect, make sure that the *lowcase* file created by your text editor is in your C++ working directory (this is usually the directory where your program writes the *upcase* file). Another alternative is to hardcode the *lowcase* file path when you define its file object.

✓ Check the Program Output

To check the program output, start your text editor and open the *upcase* file. You should find your name and the name of your institution in all uppercase characters.

What character was a space, or blank, converted to? _____

Explain why you get the above conversion for a blank character: _____

_____

Documenting Program

✓ Print the Source Code

Get a printout of the program source code and the *lowcase* and *upcase* files.

✓ Close the File

When you are finished with the program file, make sure that you have saved any final changes and then close the file (and project or workspace if required).

✓ Exit C++

When you are finished with the lab exercises, exit your C programming environment.

Using Standard Functions & Operations

OBJECTIVES

In this lab, you will . . .

- Use C++ arithmetic operations.
- Use C++ assignment operations.
- Use various standard C++ functions.

REQUIRED READING

Chapter 5: Structured & Object-Oriented Problem Solving Using C++, 3rd edition, by Andrew C. Staugaard, Jr.

INTRODUCTION

Arithmetic operations available in C++ include the common addition, subtraction, multiplication, and division operations. Table 5-1 lists these basic arithmetic operations and the C++ operators used to implement those operations. Refer to your text for information on using the C++ arithmetic operators and the order of priority of the operators.

TABLE 5-1 ARITHMETIC OPERATORS DEFINED IN C++

Operation	Operator
Add	+
Subtract	−
Multiply	*
Divide	/
Modulus (Remainder)	%

Assignment operators store a value in memory. Once the value is stored, the identifier on the left side of the assignment operator has access to the value on the right side of the assignment operator. Another way to say this is that the identifier on the left side of the operator is set to the value of the expression on the right side of the operator. Table 5-1 lists the C++ assignment operators. Refer to your text for information on using the assignment operators. Remember that the = operator does not mean "equal to." In C++, the identifier on the left side of the = is set to the value of the expression on the right side of the =.

TABLE 5-2 ASSIGNMENT OPERATORS USED IN C++

Operation	Symbol	Example	Equivalent to
Simple assignment	=	*value* = 1	*value* = 1
Addition/assignment	+=	*value* += 1	*value* = *value* + 1
Subtraction/assignment	–=	*value* -= 1	*value* = *value* – 1
Multiplication/assignment	*=	*value* *= 2	*value* = *value* * 2
Division/assignment	/=	*value* /= 2	*value* = *value* / 2
Modulus/assignment (integers only)	%=	*value* %= 2	*value* = *value* % 2

In Problem 1 you will develop a problem definition, a set of algorithms, and a user-friendly program to calculate and display the regular price and sale price of certain health and beauty aid items in Ma & Pa's General Store.

In Problem 2 you will develop a problem definition, a set of algorithms, and a user-friendly C++ program for Ma & Pa that will calculate their payroll and produce a formatted report.

Problem 3 is a challenge problem. In Problem 3, you will use math functions to calculate the distance to an object using triangulation.

PROBLEM SOLVING REVIEW

Here is a problem from Staugaard's text that is similar to what you will be asked to do in this project. Read it over carefully, and use it as a guide to complete the problems in this project.

PROBLEM

Following is a partial inventory listing of items in the sporting goods department of the CPP*Mart super center:

Item	Beginning Quantity	Units Sold This Month
Fishing line	132 spools	24 spools
Fish hooks	97 packages	45 packages
Sinkers	123 packages	37 packages
Fish nets	12 ea.	5 ea.

Write a program that will display a monthly report showing the item name, beginning quantity, units sold this month, ending quantity, and percent of quantity sold. The problem solution begins with the problem definition phase.

DEFINING THE PROBLEM

Output: The program must generate a monthly report of the item name, beginning quantity, units sold this month, ending quantity, and percent of quantity sold. Now is a good time to develop the output format. Suppose we use a tabular format, like

MONTH:

ITEM BEGIN QTY UNITS SOLD ENDING QTY % SOLD

Input: The sporting goods manager must enter the month of the report and inventory data shown in the preceding table, except for the ending quantity and percent sold, which will be calculated by our program. Therefore, the program must be very user friendly.

Processing: The program must use the input information to calculate two things: the ending quantity and the percent sold. The ending quantity is found by simply subtracting the units sold from the beginning quantity:

$$ending\ qty\ =\ begin\ qty\ -\ units\ sold$$

The percent sold is found by dividing the units sold by the beginning quantity and multiplying by 100 percent:

$$\%\ sold\ =\ (units\ sold\ /\ begin\ qty)\ \times\ 100\%$$

PLANNING THE SOLUTION

We must now construct a set of algorithms from the problem definition. Using a modular program design, we will divide the problem into individual subproblems to solve the overall problem. There are three major tasks that follow directly from the problem definition:

- Obtain the inventory data for a given item from the user.
- Calculate the ending quantity and percent sold for the given item.
- Display the item report.

Because we do not yet have a way of telling C++ to automatically repeat a task, the first two tasks must be repeated for each item in the inventory. The diagram in Figure 5-1 shows the modular structure required for the program.

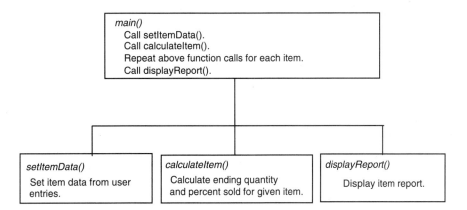

Figure 5-1   A problem solving diagram for the inventory problem.

81

The initial algorithm level, *main()*, will reflect the foregoing analysis and call the individual function modules.

Initial Algorithm

main()
BEGIN
    Call function to set the inventory data for a given item from user entries.
    Call function to calculate the ending quantity and percent sold.
    Repeat last two calls for each inventory item.
    Call function to display the item report.
END.

In developing the algorithm, you would quickly realize that the processing is the same for each sales item. As a result, we have used a single *repeat* statement rather than actually repeating the algorithm statements three more times. This has been done to make the algorithm more efficient.

The first level of refinement requires that we show a detailed algorithm for each task, or function, that we have identified. They are as follows:

First Level of Refinement

setItemData()
BEGIN
    Write a user prompt to enter the item name.
    Read *item*.
    Write a user prompt to enter the beginning quantity.
    Read *begin qty*.
    Write a user prompt to enter the number of units sold.
    Read *units sold*.
END.

calculateItem()
BEGIN
    Calculate *ending qty = begin qty – units sold*.
    Calculate *% sold = (units sold / begin qty) × 100 %*.
END.

displayReport()
BEGIN
    Display *item*, *begin qty*, *units sold*, *ending qty*, and *% sold* for each item.
END.

Given our problem definition, the foregoing collection of algorithms is straightforward. The first two functions must be executed for each of the items in the inventory. The last function is executed to display the composite report. The *setItemData()* function prompts and reads the item information from the user and assigns it to the item variables. The *calculateItem()* function will make the required calculations. Finally, the *displayReport()* function will display the item report.

Now the job is to code these algorithms in C++. With your present knowledge of C++, coding most of these algorithms should not present a problem. But what about the repeat statement at the end of the *main()* function algorithm? Well, notice that this statement requires that you go back and repeat many of the previous statements over and over until all the items are processed. Such a repeating operation is called an

82

iteration, or *looping*, operation. To date, you do not have the C++ tools to perform such an operation. Thus, we will have to repeat all of the processing steps for each of the sales items in the inventory. In Chapter 7, you will learn how to perform iterative operations in C++, making the code much more efficient.

Coding the Program

Here is the fully standards compliant code. Remember, that if you are using Visual C++ 6.0, the *getline()* function will require you to press the Enter key twice for each string entry. (The bug is a known issue as of Service Pack 5.) Listing 1 is fully standards compliant. Listing 2 uses older C-strings for compilers that have not yet implemented the string class. The Listing 1 code (ACT05_01.cpp) is available on Staugaard's text CD, or it can be downloaded from the text Web site at www.prenhall.com/staugaard. You may wish to compile and execute the code to observe its operation.

Listing 1: (ANSI/ISO Compliant Compilers)

```
/*
ACTION 5-1 (ACT05_01.cpp)

OUTPUT:    A MONTHLY REPORT OF THE
           ITEM NAME, BEGINNING QUANTITY,
           UNITS SOLD THIS MONTH, ENDING
           QUANTITY, AND PERCENT OF QUANTITY SOLD

INPUT:     MONTH OF REPORT, ITEM NAME, BEGIN QTY.
           UNITS SOLD THIS MONTH

PROCESSING: THE PROGRAM MUST CALCULATE TWO THINGS:
            ENDING QUANTITY AND THE PERCENT SOLD
*/

//PREPROCESSOR DIRECTIVES
#include <iostream>              //FOR cin AND cout
#include <string>               //FOR string CLASS

using namespace std;            //REQUIRED WHEN INCLUDING iostream

//MAIN FUNCTION
int main()
{
  //DEFINE AND INITIALIZE MONTH OBJECT
  string month = " ";           //MONTH OF REPORT

  //DEFINE AND INITIALIZE ITEM 1 OBJECTS AND VARIABLES
  string item1 = " ";           //SALES ITEM NAME
  double beginQty1 = 10.0;      //BEGINNING QUANTITY
  double unitsSold1 = 5.0;      //NUMBER OF UNITS SOLD
  double endQty1 = 0;           //ENDING QUANTITY
  double percentSold1 = 0.0;    //PERCENT OF SALES

  //DEFINE AND INITIALIZE ITEM 2 OBJECTS AND VARIABLES
  string item2 = " ";           //SALES ITEM NAME
  double beginQty2 = 0.0;       //BEGINNING QUANTITY
  double unitsSold2 = 0.0;      //NUMBER OF UNITS SOLD
  double endQty2 = 0;           //ENDING QUANTITY
  double percentSold2 = 0.0;    //PERCENT OF SALES
```

83

```cpp
//DEFINE AND INITIALIZE ITEM 3 OBJECTS AND VARIABLES
string item3 = " ";              //SALES ITEM NAME
double beginQty3 = 0.0;          //BEGINNING QUANTITY
double unitsSold3 = 0.0;         //NUMBER OF UNITS SOLD
double endQty3 = 0;              //ENDING QUANTITY
double percentSold3 = 0.0;       //PERCENT OF SALES

//DEFINE AND INITIALIZE ITEM 4 OBJECTS AND VARIABLES
string item4 = " ";              //SALES ITEM NAME
double beginQty4 = 0.0;          //BEGINNING QUANTITY
double unitsSold4 = 0.0;         //NUMBER OF UNITS SOLD
double endQty4 = 0;              //ENDING QUANTITY
double percentSold4 = 0.0;       //PERCENT OF SALES

//DISPLAY PROGRAM DESCRIPTION MESSAGE
cout << "\n\nDear Sporting Goods Manager\n"
     << "You will be asked to enter four sales items, one at\n"
     << "a time.  With each item you will be asked to enter\n"
     << "the item name, the beginning quantity, and the quantity\n"
     << "sold this month. The computer will then print a monthly\n"
     << "inventory report for the sales items." << endl;

 //SET MONTH FROM USER ENTRY
cout << "\nPlease enter the month in of this report: ";
cin >> month;

//SET ITEM 1 DATA FROM USER ENTRY
cout << "\nPlease enter the item name: ";
cin >> ws;
getline(cin,item1);
cout << "Please enter the beginning quantity of " << item1 << ": ";
cin >> beginQty1;
cout << "Please enter the quantity of " << item1 << " sold in "
     << month << ": ";
cin >> unitsSold1;

//CALCULATE ENDING QUANTITY AND PERCENT SOLD FOR ITEM 1
endQty1 = beginQty1 - unitsSold1;
percentSold1 = unitsSold1 / beginQty1 * 100;

//SET ITEM 2 DATA FROM USER ENTRY
cout << "\nPlease enter the item name: ";
cin >> ws;
getline(cin,item2);
cout << "Please enter the beginning quantity of " << item2 << ": ";
cin >> beginQty2;
cout << "Please enter the quantity of " << item2 << " sold in "
     << month << ": ";
cin >> unitsSold2;

//CALCULATE ENDING QUANTITY AND PERCENT SOLD FOR ITEM 2
endQty2 = beginQty2 - unitsSold2;
percentSold2 = unitsSold2 / beginQty2 * 100;
```

```cpp
//SET ITEM 3 DATA FROM USER ENTRY
cout << "\nPlease enter the item name: ";
cin >> ws;
getline(cin,item3);
cout << "Please enter the beginning quantity of " << item3 << ": ";
cin >> beginQty3;
cout << "Please enter the quantity of " << item3 << " sold in "
    << month << ": ";
cin >> unitsSold3;

//CALCULATE ENDING QUANTITY AND PERCENT SOLD FOR ITEM 3
endQty3 = beginQty3 - unitsSold3;
percentSold3 = unitsSold3 / beginQty3 * 100;

//SET ITEM 4 DATA FROM USER ENTRY
cout << "\nPlease enter the item name: ";
cin >> ws;
getline(cin,item4);
cout << "Please enter the beginning quantity of " << item4 << ": ";
cin >> beginQty4;
cout << "Please enter the quantity of " << item4 << " sold in "
    << month << ": ";
cin >> unitsSold4;

//CALCULATE ENDING QUANTITY AND PERCENT SOLD FOR ITEM 4
endQty4 = beginQty4 – unitsSold4;
percentSold4 = unitsSold4/ beginQty4 * 100;

//DISPLAY REPORT HEADER INFORMATION
cout << "\n\nMONTH:  " <<  month << endl;
cout << "\n\n\nITEM\tBEGIN QTY\tUNITS SOLD\tENDING QTY"
    << "\t% SOLD" << endl;
cout << "----\t---------\t----------\t----------\t------" << endl;

//DISPLAY ITEM REPORT
cout << item1 << "\t" << beginQty1 << "\t\t" << unitsSold1 << "\t\t" << endQty1
    << "\t\t" << percentSold1 << endl;
cout << item2 << "\t" << beginQty2 << "\t\t" << unitsSold2 << "\t\t" << endQty2
  << "\t\t" << percentSold2 << endl;
cout << item3 << "\t" << beginQty3 << "\t\t" << unitsSold3 << "\t\t" << endQty3
    << "\t\t" << percentSold3 << endl;
cout << item4 << "\t" << beginQty4 << "\t\t" << unitsSold4 << "\t\t" << endQty4
  << "\t\t" << percentSold4 << endl;

//RETURN
return 0;
} //END main()
```

Listing 2: (ANSI/ISO Noncompliant Compilers)

```
//OUTPUT:         A MONTHLY REPORT OF THE
//               ITEM NAME, BEGINNING QUANTITY,
//               UNITS SOLD THIS MONTH, ENDING
//               QUANTITY, AND PERCENT OF QUANTITY
//               SOLD
//INPUT:          MA OR PA ENTER THE INVENTORY DATA
//PROCESSING:  THE PROGRAM MUST CALCULATE TWO THINGS:
//               ENDING QUANTITY AND THE PERCENT SOLD


#include <iostream.h>     //FOR cin AND cout
#include <iomanip.h>      //FOR setw()


//DECLARE CONSTANTS
const int MONTH_SIZE = 8;      //SIZE OF MONTH ARRAY
const int ITEM_SIZE = 21;      //SIZE OF ITEM NAME ARRAY

int main()
{
    char month[MONTH_SIZE] = "\0";    //MONTH OF REPORT
    char item1[ITEM_SIZE] = "\0";     //SALES ITEM 1 NAME
    char item2[ITEM_SIZE] = "\0";     //SALES ITEM 2 NAME
    char item3[ITEM_SIZE] = "\0";     //SALES ITEM 3 NAME
    char item4[ITEM_SIZE] = "\0";     //SALES ITEM 4 NAME
    double beginQty1 = 0.0;           //BEGINNING QUANTITY FOR ITEM 1
    double beginQty2 = 0.0;           //BEGINNING QUANTITY FOR ITEM 2
    double beginQty3 = 0.0;           //BEGINNING QUANTITY FOR ITEM 3
    double beginQty4 = 0.0;           //BEGINNING QUANTITY FOR ITEM 4
    double unitsSold1 = 0.0;          //NUMBER OF UNITS SOLD FOR ITEM 1
    double unitsSold2 = 0.0;          //NUMBER OF UNITS SOLD FOR ITEM 2
    double unitsSold3 = 0.0;          //NUMBER OF UNITS SOLD FOR ITEM 3
    double unitsSold4 = 0.0;          //NUMBER OF UNITS SOLD FOR ITEM 4
    double endQty1 = 0.0;             //ENDING QUANTITY FOR ITEM 1
    double endQty2 = 0.0;             //ENDING QUANTITY FOR ITEM 2
    double endQty3 = 0.0;             //ENDING QUANTITY FOR ITEM 3
    double endQty4 = 0.0;             //ENDING QUANTITY FOR ITEM 4
    double percentSold1 = 0.0;        //PERCENT OF SALES FOR ITEM 1
    double percentSold2 = 0.0;        //PERCENT OF SALES FOR ITEM 2
    double percentSold3 = 0.0;        //PERCENT OF SALES FOR ITEM 3
    double percentSold4 = 0.0;        //PERCENT OF SALES FOR ITEM 4

    //DISPLAY PROGRAM DESCRIPTION MESSAGE
    cout << "Dear Ma or Pa\n\n"
         << "You will be asked to enter four sales items, one at\n"
         << "a time.  With each item you will be asked to enter\n"
         << "the item name, the beginning quantity, and the quantity\n"
         << "sold this month.  The computer will then print a monthly\n"
         << "inventory report for the sales items." << endl << endl;

    //SET MONTH FROM USER ENTRY
    cout << "Please enter the month in MM/YYYY format:  ";
    cin >> month;
```

```cpp
//SET ITEM DATA FROM USER ENTRIES
cout << "Please enter the item name:" << endl;
cin >> ws;
cin.getline(item1,ITEM_SIZE);
cout << "Please enter the beginning quantity of " << item1 << endl;
cin >> beginQty1;
cout << "Please enter the number of units of " << item1
   << " sold in " << month << endl ;
cin >> unitsSold1;

//CALCULATE ENDING QUANTITY AND PERCENT SOLD FOR ITEM
endQty1 = beginQty1 - unitsSold1;
percentSold1 = (unitsSold1 / beginQty1) * 100;

//SET ITEM DATA FROM USER ENTRIES
cout << "Please enter the item name:" << endl;
cin >> ws;
cin.getline(item2,ITEM_SIZE);
cout << "Please enter the beginning quantity of " << item2 << endl;
cin >> beginQty2;
cout << "Please enter the number of units of " << item2
   << " sold in " << month << endl ;
cin >> unitsSold2;

//CALCULATE ENDING QUANTITY AND PERCENT SOLD FOR ITEM
endQty2 = beginQty2 - unitsSold2;
percentSold2 = (unitsSold2 / beginQty2) * 100;

//SET ITEM DATA FROM USER ENTRIES
cout << "Please enter the item name:" << endl;
cin >> ws;
cin.getline(item3,ITEM_SIZE);
cout << "Please enter the beginning quantity of " << item3 << endl;
cin >> beginQty3;
cout << "Please enter the number of units of " << item3
   << " sold in " << month << endl ;
cin >> unitsSold3;

//CALCULATE ENDING QUANTITY AND PERCENT SOLD FOR ITEM
endQty3 = beginQty3 - unitsSold3;
percentSold3 = (unitsSold3 / beginQty3) * 100;

//SET ITEM DATA FROM USER ENTRIES
cout << "Please enter the item name:" << endl;
cin >> ws;
cin.getline(item4,ITEM_SIZE);
cout << "Please enter the beginning quantity of " << item4 << endl;
cin >> beginQty4;
cout << "Please enter the number of units of " << item4
   << " sold in " << month << endl ;
cin >> unitsSold4;

//CALCULATE ENDING QUANTITY AND PERCENT SOLD FOR ITEM
endQty4 = beginQty4 - unitsSold4;
percentSold4 = (unitsSold4 / beginQty4) * 100;
```

```cpp
//DISPLAY REPORT
cout.setf(ios::fixed);
cout.precision(2);
cout << "\n\nMONTH:  " << month << endl;
cout << "\n\n\n" << setw(15) << "ITEM" << setw(15) << "BEGIN QTY"
     << setw(15) << "UNITS SOLD" << setw(15) << "ENDING QTY"
     << setw(10) << "% SOLD" << endl;
cout << setw(15) << "----" << setw(15) << "---------"
     << setw(15) << "----------" << setw(15) << "----------"
     << setw(10) << "------" << endl;
cout << setw(15) << item1 << setw(15) << beginQty1
     << setw(15) << unitsSold1 << setw(15) << endQty1
     << setw(10) << percentSold1 << endl;
cout << setw(15) << item2 << setw(15) << beginQty2
     << setw(15) << unitsSold2 << setw(15) << endQty2
     << setw(10) << percentSold2 << endl;
cout << setw(15) << item3 << setw(15) << beginQty3
     << setw(15) << unitsSold3 << setw(15) << endQty3
     << setw(10) << percentSold3 << endl;
cout << setw(15) << item4 << setw(15) << beginQty4
     << setw(15) << unitsSold4 << setw(15) << endQty4
     << setw(10) << percentSold4 << endl;

return 0;
} //END main()
```

Using the sales data provided, this program will print the following inventory report:

MONTH: May

ITEM	BEGIN QTY	UNITS SOLD	ENDING QTY	%SOLD
Fishing Line	132	24	108	18.18
Fish Hooks	97	45	52	46.39
Sinkers	123	37	86	30.08
Fish Nets	12	5	7	41.67

Again, notice how a whole block of C++ code is repeated four times to process the four sales items? Wouldn't it be nice to simply code the processing steps once and then tell the computer to repeat these steps the required number of times? Such a repeating operation would make our coding much more efficient.

In this exercise you will develop a problem definition and a set of algorithms to calculate and display the regular price and sale price of certain items in Ma & Pa's General Store. You will then write the source code program that produces a formatted output. You will compile, link, run, test, and print your program. Finally, you will modify the program to allow Ma or Pa to enter any percentage of sales discount.

Pre-Lab

PROBLEM

Here is the inventory and price list of the Health and Beauty Aids department in Ma & Pa's General Store.

Item	Price
Grandma's Lye Soap	0.49
Bag Balm	1.29
Chicken Soup	0.29
Liniment	2.35
Baking Soda	0.63

Ma and Pa want to run a "big" sale and reduce all Health and Beauty Aid items by 5 percent. Write a program that will display a listing of all the Health and Beauty Aid items, showing the regular and sale price. Assume that Ma or Pa will enter the items and prices shown. Format your output, showing all of the items, regular prices, and sale prices.

Defining the Problem

Output: What output is needed according to the problem statement?

_____

Input: What input will be needed for processing to obtain the required output?

_____

Processing: What processing is required to calculate the sale prices?

_____

According to the problem statement, the output will be a formatted report showing the item, regular price, and sale price. The item name, regular price, and sale percentage are needed as input. The sale percentage can be hard-coded into the program as a constant. To calculate the sale price, you need to subtract the discount from the regular price. The discount is the regular price multiplied by the decimal equivalent of the sale percentage.

Planning the Solution

Write an algorithm to include the input, output, and processing that you developed in the problem definition.

Here is the initial algorithm for function *main()* developed from the problem definition. Notice that the problem can be refined according to the three major tasks relating to input, processing, and output. Your job is to write the algorithms required for the first level of refinement.

main()
BEGIN
    Set item name and regular price.
    Calculate item sale price.
    Repeat for each item on sale.
    Display a report of item names, regular prices, and sale prices.
END.

SET ITEM NAME AND PRICE FROM USER ENTRIES
BEGIN

END.

CALCULATE ITEM SALE PRICE
BEGIN

END.

DISPLAY ITEM REPORT
BEGIN

END.

 **In-the-Lab**

Coding the Program

✓ Start Your Editor

Start your C++ editor / IDE.

✓ Create a New Project

Make sure that a new file (and project if required) is open.

✓ Enter the Source Code

Make sure that a new file is open. Using the algorithm that you developed, complete the following program shell for the Ma & Pa sale program. (*Hint:* Declare *DISCOUNT* as a constant value of 0.05 and calculate the sale price as *salePrice = regularPrice * (1 – DISCOUNT)*).

In order to display a result table of all the sale items, you should define multiple variables/objects to hold each of the sales items, regular prices, and sale prices. Then, display the entire report at one time.

```
//LAB 5-1 (L5_1.CPP)
//AUTHOR : type your name here
//DATE WRITTEN : type the date here

//PREPROCESSOR DIRECTIVES




//DECLARE CONSTANTS


int main()
{
//DEFINE VARIABLES AND OBJECTS
```

//DISPLAY PROGRAM DESCRIPTION MESSAGE

//SET ITEM NAME AND PRICE FROM USER ENTRIES

//CALCULATE ITEM SALE PRICE

//REPEAT ABOVE FOR EACH SALE ITEM

```
   return 0;
} //END main()
```

✓ Save the Program

After you have entered the source code, you need to save the program. Name this program *L5_1.cpp*.

Testing and Debugging the Program

✓ Compile the Program

Now that you have entered and saved the program, compile it.

✓ Errors?

If there were any errors in the program, you will have to edit the program code to fix the errors, and then compile the program again before you can link and run the program. Be sure to save the program again after you correct any errors.

✓ Link the Program

If you used a "compile" option rather than a "build" or "make" option, you may have to explicitly tell your compiler to link your program after compiling it.

✓ Run the Program

When the program is successfully compiled and linked, run it to make sure that it does what it is supposed to do. Use the inventory information in the problem statement as input.

✓ Check the Program Output

Sample output screens of the sale program for Ma and Pa are shown in Figures 5-2 and 5-3. Your output screens should look similar to these. If your output does not look similar to the ones shown, edit your program code so that you obtain the correct output. You may need to adjust the *setf()*, *setw()* or *precision()* statements in your program to obtain similar results.

The example report shown in Figure 5-3 has been displayed on a blank screen. You may simply write it to the screen directly after the last line of input if you prefer; however, it would be a good programming challenge to look in your compiler documentation to find out how to clear the screen to display the report on an otherwise empty screen.

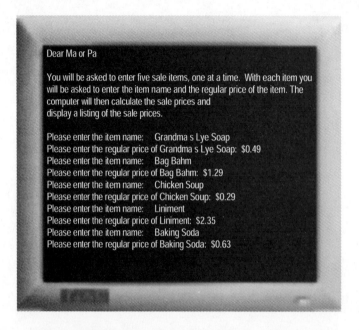

Figure 5-2 The input screen for the sale price program

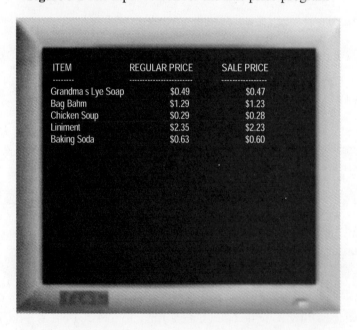

Figure 5-3 The output screen for the sale price program

94

Documenting the Program

✓ Test and Print a Sample Run of the Program

Get a printout of the program run. See *Printing Console Output From Microsoft Windows* in *Appendix A* if you are running Microsoft Windows and need help with this.

✓ Print the Source Code

Get a printout of the program source code.

Extra Credit Challenge

Revise your program to allow Ma or Pa to enter any percentage discount they desire, thus making the program more flexible. Compile, link, and run the program. Get a printout of the program output and source code if required by your instructor.

✓ Close the File

When you are finished with the program file, make sure that you have saved any final changes and then close the file (and project or workspace if required).

In this exercise you will develop a problem definition, a set of algorithms, and a user-friendly C++ program that will calculate payroll and produce a formatted payroll report.

 **Pre-Lab**

PROBLEM

Ma and Pa were so elated with the last program you wrote for them that they want to expand their computer operations to the payroll department. Write Ma and Pa a payroll program that will calculate the net pay for Herb (their only employee), given the following information:

> Employee's name
> Number of hours worked in a week
> Hourly rate of pay
> FICA (7.15%)
> Federal withholding (28%)
> State withholding (10%)

Ma or Pa should only be required to enter the first three items when running the program. Display a report using the following format:

        Employee Name: XXXXXXXXXXXXXXXXXXX

        Rate of Pay: $XXX.XX
        Hours Worked: XX.XX
        Gross Pay: $XXXX.XX
        Deductions:
                FICA $XXX.XX
                Fed. Withholding   XXX.XX
                State Withholding XXX.XX

                Total Deductions $XXX.XX

        Net Pay: $XXXX.XX

Defining the Problem

Output: What output is needed according to the problem statement?

_____

Input: What input will be needed for processing to obtain the required output?

_____

Can any of the values needed for processing be hard-coded as constants? If so, which values?

_____

Processing: What processing is needed to calculate the gross pay?

_____

What processing is needed to calculate the FICA?

_____

What processing is needed to calculate the federal withholdings?

_____

What processing is needed to calculate the state withholdings?

_____

What processing is needed to calculate the total deductions?

_____

What processing is needed to calculate the net pay?

_____

     The output of your program will be a formatted report showing the employee's name, rate of pay, hours worked, gross pay, itemized deductions, and net pay. The employee's name, pay rate, and hours worked are needed as input. These items cannot be hard-coded into the program as constants; they must be accepted as variable input from the keyboard. The FICA, federal withholding, and state withholding percentages can be declared as constants. To calculate the gross pay, you need to multiply the pay rate by the hours worked. The FICA, federal, and state withholding percentage values (in decimal form) each need to be multiplied by the gross pay. You must add the itemized deductions together to calculate the total deductions. The net pay is then calculated by subtracting the total deductions from the gross pay.

Planning the Solution

Here is the initial algorithm for function *main()* developed from the problem definition. Notice that the problem can be refined according to the three major tasks relating to input, processing, and output. Your job is to write the algorithms required for the first level of refinement.

main()
BEGIN
    Call function to set the employee's name, hours worked, and rate of pay from user entries.
    Call function to calculate the gross pay, individual deductions, total deductions, and net pay.
    Call function to display the payroll report in the required format.
END.

SET EMPLOYEE INFORMATION FROM USER ENTRIES
BEGIN

END.

MAKE THE PAYROLL CALCULATIONS
BEGIN

END.

DISPLAY PAYROLL REPORT
BEGIN

END.

 **In-the-Lab**

Coding the Program

✓ Start Your Editor

Start your C++ editor/IDE.

✓ Create a New Project

Make sure that a new file (and project if required) is open.

✓ Enter the Source Code

Make sure that a new file is open. Using the algorithms that you developed, complete the following program shell for the Ma & Pa payroll program:

```
//LAB 5-2 (L5_2.CPP)
//AUTHOR : type your name here
//DATE WRITTEN : type the date here

//PREPROCESSOR DIRECTIVES




//DECLARE CONSTANTS




int main()
{
//DEFINE VARIABLES AND OBJECTS
```

//DISPLAY PROGRAM DESCRIPTION MESSAGE

//SET EMPLOYEE INFORMATION FROM USER ENTRIES

//MAKE THE PAYROLL CALCULATIONS

//DISPLAY PAYROLL REPORT

```
  return 0;
} //END main()
```

✓ **Save the Program**

After you have entered the source code, you need to save the program. Name this program *L5_2.cpp*.

Testing and Debugging the Program

✓ **Compile the Program**

Now that you have entered and saved the program, compile it.

100

✓Errors?

If there were any errors in the program, you will have to edit the program code to fix the errors, and then compile the program again before you can link and run the program. Be sure to save the program again after you correct any errors.

✓Link the Program

If you used a "compile" option rather than a "build" or "make" option, you may have to explicitly tell your compiler to link your program after compiling it.

✓Run the Program

When the program is successfully compiled and linked, run it to make sure that it does what it is supposed to do. Use the inventory information in the problem statement as input.

✓Check the Program Output

Sample output screens of the sale program for Ma and Pa are shown in Figures 5-4 and 5-5. Your output screens should look similar to these. If your output does not look similar to the ones shown, edit your program code so that you obtain the correct output. You may need to adjust the *setf()*, *setw()* or *precision()* statements in your program to obtain similar results.

The example report shown in Figure 5-5 has been displayed on a blank screen. You may simply write it to the screen directly after the last line of input if you prefer; however, it would be a good programming challenge to look in your compiler documentation to find out how to clear the screen to display the report on an otherwise empty screen.

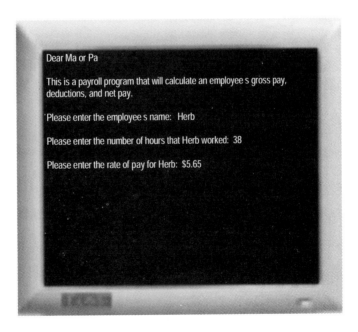

Figure 5-4 The input screen for Ma and Pa's payroll program

101

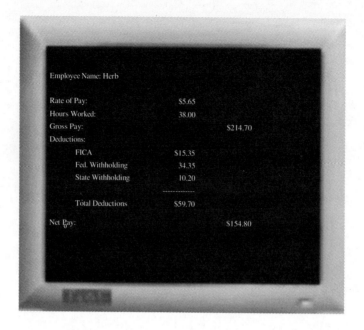

Figure 5-5 The output screen for Ma and Pa's payroll program

Documenting the Program

✓Test and Print a Sample Run of the Program

Run the program using the following test data:

Employee name	Hours worked	Rate of Pay
<your name>	44	10.00
Herb	0	7.34
Herb	24	13.71

Get a printout of each program run. See *Printing Console Output From Microsoft Windows* in *Appendix A* if you are running Microsoft Windows and need help with this.

✓Print the Source Code

Get a printout of the program source code.

✓Close the File

When you are finished with the program file make sure that you have saved any final changes and then close the file (and project or workspace if required).

In this problem, you will be presented with a problem definition and it will be up to you to work through the programmer's algorithm to create a user-friendly C++ program that solves the problem.

Table 5-3 lists some C++ math functions that you can use if you use a *#include* statement to include the <math.h> header file.

TABLE 5-3 SOME STANDARD MATHEMATICAL FUNCTIONS AVAILABLE IN C++

Function Name	Header File	Operation
abs()	math.h	Returns the absolute value of the argument.
acos()	math.h	Returns the arc cosine of the argument (radians).
asin()	math.h	Returns the arc sine of the argument (radians).
atan()	math.h	Returns the arc tangent of the argument (radians).
cos()	math.h	Returns the cosine of the argument (radians).
hypot(a,b)	math.h	Returns the hypotenuse of a right triangle whose sides are *a* and *b*.
log()	math.h	Returns the natural log of the argument.
log10()	math.h	Returns the base 10 log of the argument.
pow(x,y)	math.h	Returns *x* to the power of *y*.
pow10(y)	math.h	Returns 10 to the power of *y*.
rand()	math.h	Generates a random number between 0 and $2^{15}-1$.
srand()	math.h	Initializes the random-number generator and should be used prior to *rand()*.
sin()	math.h	Returns the sine of the argument (radians).
sqrt()	math.h	Returns the square root of the argument.
tan()	math.h	Returns the tangent of the argument (radians).

 # Pre-Lab

PROBLEM

Develop a problem definition, a set of algorithms, and a user-friendly C++ program to solve the triangulation problem illustrated in Figure 5-6.

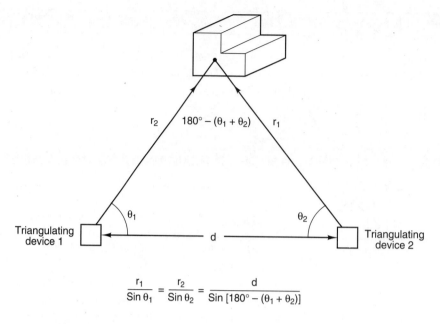

$$\frac{r_1}{Sin\ \theta_1} = \frac{r_2}{Sin\ \theta_2} = \frac{d}{Sin\ [180° - (\theta_1 + \theta_2)]}$$

Figure 5-6 A triangulation diagram for the math challenge

The diagram in Figure 5-6 illustrates how triangulation is used to find the distance to an object. Here's the idea: two triangulating devices are positioned a known distance apart, and both devices get a "fix" on an object (i.e. each device determines the angle between the other device and the object). The two triangulating devices and the object form a triangle whose leg d and two respective angles, $\theta1$ and $\theta2$, are known. The third angle is easily found by subtracting the two known angles from 180 degrees. The distance from each triangulating device to the object is then found using the Law of Sines, which states:

$$r1\ /\ \sin\ \theta1 = r2\ /\ \sin\ \theta2 = d\ /\ \sin\ (180 - (\theta1 + \theta2))$$

Write a user-friendly program to find the distance that the object is from each triangulating device. The user should enter the distance (d) between the devices and the two angles ($\theta1$ and $\theta2$) that the object makes with the triangulating devices.

Defining the Problem

Output: What output is needed according to the problem statement?

_____

Input: What input will be needed for processing to obtain the required output?

_____

Processing: What C++ math function will you use to solve this problem? What header file must you include to use the function?

_____

What processing is needed to calculate the two distances?

_____

Planning the Solution

Develop an initial algorithm for function *main()* from the problem definition, then write the algorithms required for the first level of refinement. Use the space provided.

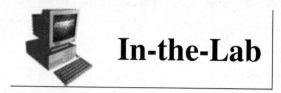

In-the-Lab

Coding the Program

✓ Start Your Editor

Start your C++ editor/IDE.

✓ Create a New Project

Make sure that a new file (and project if required) is open.

✓ Enter the Source Code

Make sure that a new file is open. Using the algorithms that you developed, write a program to solve the triangulation problem.

✓ Save the Program

After you have entered the source code, you need to save the program. Name this program *L5_3.cpp*.

Testing and Debugging the Program

✓ Compile the Program

Now that you have entered and saved the program, compile it.

✓ Errors?

If there were any errors in the program, you will have to edit the program code to fix the errors, and then compile the program again before you can link and run the program. Be sure to save the program again after you correct any errors.

✓ Link the Program

If you used a "compile" option rather than a "build" or "make" option, you may have to explicitly tell your compiler to link your program after compiling it.

✓ Run the Program

When the program is successfully compiled and linked, run it to make sure that it does what it is supposed to do. Use the inventory information in the problem statement as input.

✓ Check the Program Output

Make sure the program calculates a few inputs correctly by working them out by hand with a calculator.

Documenting the Program

✓ Test and Print a Sample Run of the Program

Get a printout of some program runs. See *Printing Console Output From Microsoft Windows* in *Appendix A* if you are running Microsoft Windows and need help with this.

✓ Print the Source Code

Get a printout of the program source code.

✓ Close the File

When you are finished with the program file, make sure that you have saved any final changes and then close the file (and project or workspace if required).

Decision Structures

In this lab, you will . . .

♦ Use the C++ **if**, **if/else** and **switch** statements for decision making.

♦ Use nested decision making.

Chapter 6: Structured & Object-Oriented Problem Solving Using C++, 3rd edition, by Andrew C. Staugaard, Jr.

In this project you will be using the C++ **if**, **if/else** and **switch** statements for decision making. The **if** and **if/else** statements are used to control the flow of your program based upon the outcome of a Boolean expression.

In a strict definition, a Boolean expression is a mathematical expression composed of operands (which may be mathematical expressions or *string* objects) and *relational operators* (which compare the two operands and produce a true/false result). Table 6-1 shows a list of relational operators used in C++. Boolean expressions also can be combined with other Boolean expressions using *logical operators*, which compare the two Boolean expressions and produce a true/false result. Table 6-2 shows a list of logical operators available in C++.

TABLE 6-1 THE SIX RELATIONAL OPERATORES USED IN C++

Mathematical Symbol	C++ Operator	Meaning
=	==	Equal to
≠	!=	Not equal to
<	<	Less than
≤	<=	Less than or equal to
>	>	Greater than
≥	>=	Greater than or equal to

TABLE 6-2 LOGICAL OPERATORS USED IN C++

Operation Name	Symbol
NOT	!
OR	‖
AND	&&

109

In C++, a logical false is equated to a 0, and a logical true is equated to a 1. (Actually, *any nonzero* value is considered true *when* applied to a Boolean operation in C++.) C++ does not limit Boolean expressions to the strict definition; therefore, any mathematical expression can be used in place of a Boolean expression. If the expression evaluates to 0, it will be treated as a logical false; otherwise, it will be considered a logical true.

When using the **if** statement, the statements that follow the **if** will be executed if the Boolean expression evaluates to true. Otherwise, if the condition is false, the statements following the **if** will be skipped. When using the **if/else** statement, the statements that follow the **if** will be executed if the condition is true. Otherwise, the statements following the **else** will be executed. The **if** and **if/else** statements perform one-way and two-way decisions, respectively.

You can achieve additional decision options by using nested **if** or **if/else** statements. A nested **if** or **if/else** statement is simply an **if** or **if/else** statement within another **if** or **if/else** statement. The Boolean expression in the nested **if** or **if/else** statement is not even evaluated if the block of code that it is contained in is not executed as a result of the *outer* **if** or **if/else** statement. Look at this example:

```
.
.
.
if ( y != 0)
{
    if( x / y > 5)
    {
        cout << "X is more than 5 times a large as y" << endl;
    } //END INNER IF
} //END OUTER IF
.
.
.
```

The Boolean expression in the *inner* (or nested) **if** statement will cause a run-time error if it is evaluated with *y* equal to 0. However, this code will never produce the error because the outer **if** statement prevents the inner **if** statement from being evaluated when *y* is equal to 0.

The **switch** statement enables the program to select one of many options, each listed with a **case** statement. A *selector variable* is evaluated and is compared (using the Boolean equality operator, ==) with a series of cases. If the selector value matches one of the **case** values, the program begins executing the statements after the **case**, jumping out of the **switch** structure only when encountering a **break** statement or the end of the **switch** statement (even if that means executing statements under the matching **case** statement).

A valuable protection feature to the **switch** statement is the **default** option that allows a series of statements to be executed if no match is found within the **switch** statement. For example, if the user enters incorrect input information, the **default** option allows you to notify the user that an error was made and that no match will be found. This feature is often used in menu-driven programs. If no match is made and no **default** statement exists, the program simply continues in a straight-line fashion, with the first statement following the close of the **switch** statement.

The selector variable in a **switch** statement must be an integral data type. By an *integral data type*, we mean a data type that is stored as an integer. This basically means that the selector variable must be defined as either an integer or a character. *You cannot use strings or floating point values as the selector variable in a **switch** statement.*

Here is a problem from Staugaard's text that is similar to what you will be asked to do in this project. Read it over carefully and use it as a guide to complete the problems in this project.

PROBLEM

The **switch** statement is often used to create menu-driven programs. We're sure you have seen a menu-driven program. It's one that asks you to select different options during the execution of the program. For instance, suppose you must write a menu-driven consumer loan calculator program that will allow the user to determine several things about a loan. The idea will be to generate a menu similar to the one shown in Figure 6-1 that gives the user four options, as follows:
- An option to calculate monthly loan payments.
- An option to calculate the total interest of the loan.
- An option to calculate the total amount of the loan.
- An option to quit the program.

We will assume that the user will enter the amount of the loan, the annual interest rate of the loan, and the term of the loan. The program should reject invalid entries.

```
This program will calculate a monthly loan
payment, total loan interest, or total loan amount.


        Enter P to get monthly payment
        Enter I to get total loan interest
        Enter T to get total loan amount
        Enter Q to quit

    Please enter your choice:
```

Figure 6-1   A menu for the consumer loan calculator problem.

Defining the Problem

Output: A program menu that prompts the user to select a monthly payment, total interest, or total loan amount calculation option.
The monthly loan payment, total loan interest, or total loan amount, depending on the program option that the user selects.
Invalid entry messages as required.

Input: A user response to the menu (P, I, T, or Q).
If P is selected, user enters the loan amount, interest rate, and term.
If I is selected, user enters the loan amount, interest rate, and term.
If T is selected, user enters the loan amount, interest rate, and term.
If Q is selected, terminate program.

Processing: Calculate the selected option as follows:

Case P: $payment = principle * rate/(1 - (1+rate)^{-term})$

Case I: $interest = term * payment - principle$

Case T: $total = principle + interest$

Case Q: Quit the program.

where: *principle* is the amount of the loan.

rate is a monthly interest rate in decimal form.

term is the number of months of the loan.

Planning the Solution

Using a modular program design, we will divide the problem into individual subproblems to solve the overall problem. There are two major tasks that follow directly from the problem definition:

- Display the menu and read the user choice.
- Perform the chosen calculation and display the results.

First, the program must display a menu of choices to the user. The user will enter his or her choice from the menu, and, depending on this choice, one of three calculations will be made to determine the required quantity. The problem-solving diagram in Figure 6-2 illustrates the design.

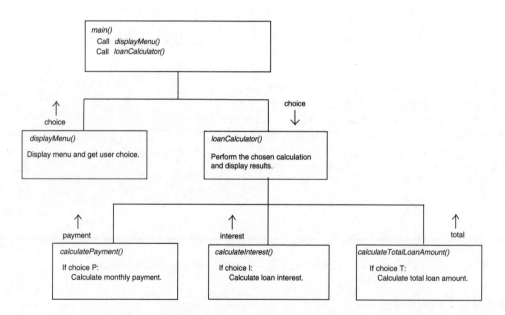

Figure 6-2   A problem-solving diagram for the loan problem.

Notice that there are now three levels to solving the problem. At the first level, *main()*, a function is called to display the menu and get the user choice. The *displayMenu()* function accomplishes this task and *returns* the user choice back to *main()*, as indicated on the diagram. Function *main()* will then *pass* the choice to a function called *loanCalculator()*, which will call one of three functions, depending on the choice, to perform the required calculation. This is the first time you have seen the *passing* of data between functions. This concept is central to both structured and object-oriented program design and the use of functions. From the problem-solving diagram you see that the user choice, *choice*, is *passed* from the *displayMenu()* function back to its calling function, *main()*. Then, when *main()* calls the *loanCalculator()* function, *choice* is passed from *main()* to *loanCalculator()*. The *loanCalculator()* function will then use

112

choice to determine which calculation function to call. Finally, each of the calculation functions will *return* the value it calculates back to the *loanCalculator()* function.

The initial algorithm reflects *main()*, which is used to call the *displayMenu()* and *loanCalculator()* functions, as follows:

Initial Algorithm

main()
BEGIN
    Call the *displayMenu()* function.
    Call the *loanCalculator()* function.
END.

The first level of refinement shows the contents of the *displayMenu()* and *loanCalculator()* functions, as follows:

First Level of Refinement

displayMenu()
BEGIN
    Display a program menu that prompts the user to choose a monthly payment (P), total interest (I), total loan amount (T), or quit (Q) option.
    Read *choice*.
    Return *choice*.
END.

loanCalculator()
BEGIN
    Case P: Call function *calculatePayment()* and display payment.
    Case I: Call function *calculateInterest()* and display interest.
    Case T: Call function *calculateTotalLoanAmount()* and display total
                loan amount.
    Case Q: Quit the program.
    Default: Write an invalid entry message and ask the user to select again.
END.

The *displayMenu()* function simply displays the menu and reads the user's choice. Notice that a *Return* statement is used to indicate that the function returns *choice* to the function that called it, *main()*. The The *loanCalculator()* function calls the required calculation function and displays the result, depending on the user's choice. In addition, the loanCalculator() function terminates the program if the user chooses to quit and writes an invalid entry message if the user's choice does not reflect one of the choice options.

Now, we need a second level of refinement to show the contents of the calculation functions. Here it is:

Second Level of Refinement

calculatePayment()
BEGIN
    Write a prompt to enter the amount of the loan.
    Read *principle*.
    Write a prompt to enter the annual interest rate.

113

Read *rate*.
Write a prompt to enter the term of the loan.
Read *term*.
If *rate* <= 0 OR *rate* > 100
 Write an invalid entry message.
Else
 Calculate *rate = rate*/12/100.
 Calculate *payment = principle * rate*/(1-(1+*rate*) –*term*).
 Return *payment*.
END.

calculateInterest()
BEGIN
 Write a prompt to enter the amount of the loan.
 Read *principle*.
 Write a prompt to enter the annual interest rate.
 Read *rate*.
 Write a prompt to enter the term of the loan.
 Read *term*.
 If *rate* <= 0 OR *rate* > 100
  Write an invalid entry message.
 Else
  Calculate *rate = rate*/12/100.
  Calculate *payment = principle * rate*/(1-(1+*rate*) –*term*).
  Calculate *interest = term * payment – principle*.
  Return *interest*.
END.

calculateTotalLoanAmount()
BEGIN
 Write a prompt to enter the amount of the loan.
 Read *principle*.
 Write a prompt to enter the annual interest rate.
 Read *rate*.
 Write a prompt to enter the term of the loan.
 Read *term*.
 If *rate* <= 0 OR *rate* > 100
  Write an invalid entry message.
 Else
  Calculate *rate = rate*/12/100.
  Calculate *payment = principle * rate*/(1-(1+*rate*) –*term*).
  Calculate *interest = term * payment – principle*.
  Calculate *total = principle + interest*.
  Return *total*.
END.

Each calculation function obtains the data required for the respective calculation. First, notice that each function employs an **if/else** statement to protect against an invalid interest rate entry. We will reject any interest rate that is less than or equal to 0 percent or greater than 100 percent as being invalid. If the interest rate is invalid, the user is notified. Otherwise, the function makes the respective calculation and *returns* the result. Notice also that the annual percentage interest rate must first be converted to a monthly decimal value for use in the subsequent payment calculation. Finally, you see that each function *returns* the result of its calculation to its calling function.

Coding the Program

Here is the code. This code (ACT06_02.cpp) is available on Staugaard's text CD or can be downloaded from the text Web site at www.prenhall.com/staugaard. You may wish to compile and execute the code to observe its operation.

```
/*
ACTION 6-2 (ACT06_02.CPP)
OUTPUT:  A PROGRAM MENU THAT PROMPTS THE USER TO SELECT A
         MONTHLY PAYMENT, TOTAL INTEREST, OR TOTAL LOAN AMOUNT
         CALCULATION OPTION.
         INVALID ENTRY MESSAGES AS REQUIRED.
         THE MONTHLY LOAN PAYMENT, TOTAL LOAN INTEREST,
         OR TOTAL LOAN AMOUNT, DEPENDING ON THE PROGRAM OPTION THAT THE
         USER SELECTS.
         INVALID ENTRY MESSAGES AS REQUIRED.

INPUT:   A USER RESPONSE TO THE MENU (P, I, T, OR Q).
         IF P IS SELECTED: USER ENTERS THE LOAN AMOUNT, INTEREST RATE, AND TERM.
         IF I IS SELECTED: USER ENTERS THE LOAN AMOUNT, INTEREST RATE, AND TERM.
         IF R IS SELECTED: USER ENTERS THE LOAN AMOUNT, INTEREST RATE, AND TERM.
         IF Q IS SELECTED: TERMINATE PROGRAM.

PROCESSING:  CALCULATE THE SELECTED OPTION AS FOLLOWS:
         CASE P: PAYMENT = PRINCIPLE * RATE/(1 - (1+RATE) –TERM)
         CASE I:  INTEREST = TERM * PAYMENT - PRINCIPLE
         CASE T: TOTAL = PRINCIPLE + INTEREST
         CASE Q: QUIT THE PROGRAM.

         WHERE:    PRINCIPLE IS THE AMOUNT OF THE LOAN.
                   RATE IS A MONTHLY INTEREST RATE IN DECIMAL FORM.
                   TERM IS THE NUMBER OF MONTHS OF THE LOAN.
*/

//PREPROCESSOR DIRECTIVES
#include <iostream.h>     //FOR cin AND cout
#include <math.h>         //FOR pow()

//MAIN FUNCTION
int main()
{
    //DEFINE AND INITIALIZE VARIABLES
    char choice = 'Q';          //USER MENU ENTRY
    double payment = 0.0;       //MONTHLY PAYMENT
    double interest = 0.0;      //TOTAL INTEREST FOR LIFE OF LOAN
    double total = 0.0;         //TOTAL LOAN AMOUNT
    double principle = 0.0;     //LOAN AMOUNT
    double rate = 0.0;          //INTEREST RATE
    int term = 0;               //TERM OF LOAN IN MONTHS
```

```
//SET OUTPUT FORMAT
cout.setf(ios::fixed);
cout.setf(ios::showpoint);
cout.precision(2);

//DISPLAY PROGRAM DESCRIPTION MESSAGE
cout   << "This program will calculate a monthly loan\n"
       << "payment, total loan interest, or total loan amount." << endl;

//displayMenu() FUNCTION
cout   << "\n\n\t\t\tEnter P to get monthly payment"
       << "\n\t\t\tEnter I to get total loan interest"
       << "\n\t\t\tEnter T to get total loan amount"
       << "\n\t\t\tEnter Q to quit" << endl;

 cout << "\n\n\tPlease enter your choice:  ";

//READ USER CHOICE
cin >> choice;

//loanCalculator() FUNCTION
switch (choice)
{
 case 'p':  //calculatePayment() FUNCTION
 case 'P' : cout << "\nEnter the amount of the loan: $";
            cin >> principle;
            cout << "\nEnter the duration of the loan in months: ";
            cin >> term;
            cout << "\nEnter the annual interest rate in percent: ";
            cin >> rate;

            //CHECK FOR INVALID ENTRY
            if ((rate <= 0) || (rate > 100))
               cout << "\n\nThis is an invalid entry. Please"
                    << " run the program again." << endl;
            else
            {
              rate = rate/12/100;
              payment = principle * rate/(1 - pow((1+rate), -term));
              cout << "\n\nThe monthly payment is $" << payment << endl;
            }//END ELSE
            break;

 case 'i':  //calculateInterest() FUNCTION
 case 'I' : cout << "\nEnter the amount of the loan: $";
            cin >> principle;
            cout << "\nEnter the duration of the loan in months: ";
            cin >> term;
            cout << "\nEnter the annual interest rate in percent: ";
            cin >> rate;
            //CHECK FOR INVALID ENTRY
            if ((rate <= 0) || (rate > 100))
                cout  << "\n\nThis is an invalid entry. Please"
                      << " run the program again." << endl;
```

```
                  else
                  {
                      rate = rate/12/100;
                      payment = principle * rate/(1-pow((1+rate), -term));
                      interest = term * payment - principle;
                      cout << "\n\nThe total interest is $" << interest << endl;
                  }//END ELSE
                  break;

    case 't':   //calculateTotalLoanAmount() FUNCTION
    case 'T':   cout << "\nEnter the amount of the loan: $";
                cin >> principle;
                cout << "\nEnter the duration of the loan in months: ";
                cin >> term;
                cout << "\nEnter the annual interest rate in percent: " ;
                cin >> rate;

                //CHECK FOR INVALID ENTRY
                if ((rate <= 0) || (rate > 100))
                    cout  << "\n\nThis is an invalid entry. Please"
                          << " run the program again." << endl;
                else
                {
                    rate = rate/12/100;
                    payment = principle * rate/(1-pow((1+rate), -term));
                    interest = term * payment - principle;
                    total = principle + interest;
                    cout << "\n\nThe total loan amount is $" << total << endl;
                }//END ELSE
                break;

    case 'q':   //QUIT THE PROGRAM
    case 'Q':   cout << "Program terminated" << endl;
                break;

    //DISPLAY INVALID ENTRY MESSAGE
    default : cout << "\n\nThis is an invalid entry. Please"
                   << " run the program again." << endl;
  } //END SWITCH

  //RETURN
  return 0;
} //END main()
```

First, notice how the functions from our design are embedded into this flat implementation. The comments show the location of our functions. Now look at the program closely, and you will find that it incorporates most of the things that you have learned in this chapter. In particular, you will find a **switch** statement that contains a **default** option. In addition, notice the **if/else** statements embedded within each **case**. You should observe the beginnings and endings of the various sections, along with the associated indentation and commenting scheme. As you can see, the program is very readable and self-documenting.

Now for the details. There are eight cases, two for each user-selected option. Notice that the first case in each option allows the user to enter a lowercase character. These cases do not have a **break** statement and, therefore, permit the program to *fall through* to the uppercase character case. This is done to allow the user to enter either a lower- or an uppercase character for each option. Notice that there is a **break** statement at the end of each uppercase case to terminate the **switch** once the **case** statements are executed.

If the user enters an invalid character from the main menu, the **default** statement is executed, which displays an error message and asks the user to run the program again. Likewise, if the user enters an invalid interest rate within a given case, it is caught by the **if/else** statement, which displays an error message and asks the user to run the program again. As you can see, we have used the **if** part of the **if/else** to catch the invalid entry and the **else** part to proceed with the calculation if the entry is valid. This logic is typical of the way that many programs are written. Finally, notice how that standard *pow()* function is to make the payment calculation.

The screen in Figure 6-3 displays the menu generated by the program, as well as a sample case execution.

```
This program will calculate a monthly loan
payment, loan interest, or loan amount.


        Enter P to get monthly payment
        Enter I to get total loan interest
        Enter T to get total loan amount
        Enter Q to quit

  Please enter your choice: p↵

Enter the amount of the loan: $1000↵

Enter the duration of the loan in months: 12↵

Enter the annual interest rate in percent: 12↵


The monthly payment is $88.85
```

Figure 6-3   A screen shot produced from the *Action06_02.C++* program.

In this exercise you will develop a problem definition and set of algorithms that employ nested **if/else** statements to convert a numeric score to a letter grade. You will then write the source code program that produces a user-friendly output. You will compile, run, test, and print your program.

 # Pre-Lab

PROBLEM

Use nested **if/else** statements to convert a numeric score to a letter grade according to the following scale:

90 – 100	A
80 – 89	B
70 – 79	C
60 – 69	D
Below 60	F

Write a user-friendly program that will accept a numeric score and then display the corresponding letter grade.

Defining the Problem

Output: What output is needed according to the problem statement?

_____

Input: What input will be needed for processing to obtain the required output?

_____

Processing: What processing is required to determine the letter grade?

_____

_____

_____

_____

_____

The output will report a letter grade. The student's numeric score is needed as input. To determine the letter grade, you will need to use nested **if/else** statements to make correspondence between the numeric score and the letter grade.

Planning the Solution

Here is the initial algorithm for function *main()* developed from the problem definition. Write the algorithms required for the first level of refinement.

main()
BEGIN
    Call function to set the numeric test score from a user entry.
    Call function to convert the numeric score to a letter grade.
    Call function to display the letter grade.
END.

SET NUMERIC SCORE FROM USER ENTRY
BEGIN

END.

CONVERT NUMERIC SCORE TO LETTER GRADE
BEGIN

END.

DISPLAY LETTER GRADE
BEGIN

END.

120

 **In-the-Lab**

Coding the Program

✓ Start Your Editor

Start your C++ editor/IDE.

✓ Create a New Project

Make sure that a new file (and project if required) is open.

✓ Enter the Source Code

Make sure that a new file is open. Using the algorithms that you developed, complete the following program shell for the score conversion sale program:

```
// LAB 6-1 (L6_1.CPP)
// AUTHOR : type your name here
// DATE WRITTEN : type the date here

// PREPROCESSOR DIRECTIVES



int main()
{
// DEFINE AND INITIALIZE VARIABLES








// DISPLAY PROGRAM DESCRIPTION MESSAGE


```

// SET NUMERIC SCORE FROM USER ENTRY

// CONVERT NUMERIC SCORE TO LETTER GRADE

// DISPLAY LETTER GRADE

return 0;

} // END main()

✓ Save the Program

After you have entered the source code, you need to save the program. Name this program *L6_1.cpp*.

Testing and Debugging the Program

✓ Compile the Program

Now that you have entered and saved the program, compile it.

✓ Errors?

If there were any errors in the program you will have to edit the program code to fix the errors, and then compile the program again before you can link and run the program. Be sure to save the program again after you correct any errors.

✓ Link the Program

If you used a "compile" option rather than a "build" or "make" option, you may have to explicitly tell your compiler to link your program after compiling it.

✓ Run the Program

When the program is successfully compiled and linked, run it to make sure that it does what it is supposed to do.

✓ Check the Program Output

Observe your program output. A sample output screen of the grade conversion program is shown in Figure 6-4. Your output screen should look similar to this. If it doesn't, edit your program code so that you obtain the correct output.

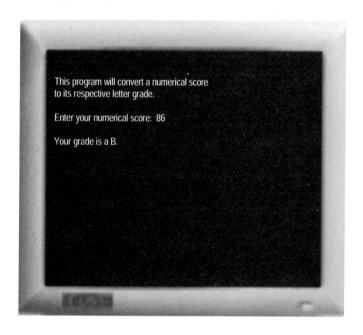

Figure 6-4 Sample run of the letter grade conversion program

Documenting the Program

✓ Observe the Program Execution with the Debugger

Use your debugger (if your environment has a debugger) to single-step the program execution and observe the operation of the **if/else** statements in your program. Set a watch on the score variable using a watch window. (If you are using Microsoft Visual C++ 6, see *Appendix B* for help with the debugger.)

✓ Test and Print a Sample Run of the Program

Get a printout of sample program runs with the following test data:

Numeric Score
83
50
74
95

See *Printing Console Output From Microsoft Windows* in *Appendix A* if you are running Microsoft Windows and need help with this.

✓ Print the Source Code

Get a printout of the program source code.

✓ Close the File

When you are finished with the program file, make sure you have saved any final changes and then close the file (and project or workspace if required).

In this exercise you will develop a problem definition, a set of algorithms, and a menu-driven program to determine electrical power, voltage, or current, depending on the user's choice.

 # Pre-Lab

PROBLEM

An engineer wants you to write a menu-driven program to determine electrical power, voltage, or current, given the other two quantities. The electrical power (in watts) of a direct current (dc) circuit is defined as the product of voltage and current. In symbols,

$$P = V \times I$$

where

      P is power in watts
      V is voltage in volts
      I is current in amperes

      The engineer also informs you that any of these quantities can be negative. Write a menu-driven program that will solve the engineer's problem.

Defining the Problem

Output: What output is needed according to the problem statement?

_____

Input: What input will be needed for processing to obtain the required output?

_____

Processing: What processing is required to calculate the power in watts, given the values of voltage and current?

_____

      What processing is required to calculate the voltage in volts, given the values of power and current?

_____

      What processing is required to calculate the current in amperes, given the values of power and voltage?

_____

According to the problem statement, the solution requires a menu-driven program to calculate power, voltage, or current, given the other two quantities. Therefore, the output must first include a program menu that prompts the user to select a power, voltage, or current calculation option. In addition, invalid entry messages and prompts should be generated as required. The final output must be a value for power, voltage, or current, depending on the program option that the user selects.

The input must be the user response to the menu (*P*, *V*, *I*, or *Q* for quit). If *P* is selected, the user must enter values for voltage and current. If *V* is selected, the user must enter values for power and current. If *I* is selected, the user must enter values for power and voltage. Finally, if *Q* is selected, the program must terminate.

The processing requires the application of the power equation, according to the user selection as follows:

Case P: *power = voltage × current*
Case V: *voltage = power / current*
Case I: *current = power / voltage*

Planning the Solution

Using modular program design, we will divide the problem into individual subproblems to solve the overall problem. There are two major tasks that follow directly from the problem definition:

- Display the menu and read the user choice.
- Perform the chosen calculation and display the results.

First, the program must display a menu of choices to the user. The user will enter a choice from the menu, and, depending on this choice, one of three calculations will be made to determine the required quantity. The problem-solving diagram in Figure 6-5 illustrates how this problem will be solved in a top-down fashion.

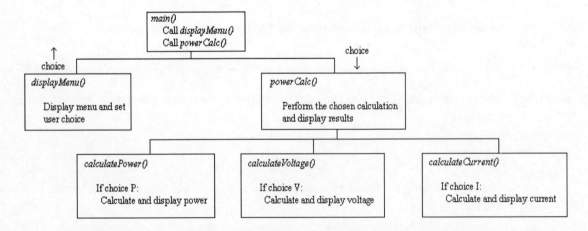

Figure 6-5   A problem-solving diagram for the engineer's power problem

Write an algorithm for the main function to perform the first two major tasks. (Remember, function *main()* will simply call functions to perform the two tasks.)

126

main()
BEGIN

END.

Now, perform the first level of refinement by writing algorithms for function *displayMenu()* and function *powerCalc()*. From the problem solving diagram, you see that function *displayMenu()* sets the user's choice and function *powerCalc()* receives the user's choice and calls upon one of three functions to perform the required calculation. (*Hint*: Use a **switch** statement, with the possible user choice's set up under different **case** statements.)

displayMenu()
BEGIN

END.

powerCalc()
BEGIN

END.

127

Finally, perform the second level of refinement by writing three algorithms to determine the power, voltage, or current, depending on the choice received by the *powerCalc()* function. Remember to protect against division by zero.

calculatePower()
BEGIN

END.

calculateVoltage()
BEGIN

END.

calculateCurrent()
BEGIN

END.

128

In-the-Lab

Coding the Program

✓ Start Your Editor

Start your C++ editor/IDE.

✓ Create a New Project

Make sure that a new file (and project if required) is open.

✓ Enter the Source Code

Make sure that a new file is open. Using the algorithms that you developed, complete the following program shell for the flat implementation of the engineer's power problem:

```
// LAB 6-2 (L6_2.CPP)
// AUTHOR : type your name here
// DATE WRITTEN : type the date here

// PREPROCESSOR DIRECTIVES




int main()
{
// DEFINE AND INITIALIZE VARIABLES





// DISPLAY PROGRAM DESCRIPTION MESSAGE



```

// displayMenu() FUNCTION

// powerCalc() FUNCTION

```
    return 0;

} // END main()
```

✓ Save the Program

After you have entered the source code, you need to save the program. Name this program *L6_2.cpp*.

Testing and Debugging the Program

✓ Compile the Program

Now that you have entered and saved the program, compile it.

✓ Errors?

If there were any errors in the program you will have to edit the program code to fix the errors, and then compile the program again before you can link and run the program. Be sure to save the program again after you correct any errors.

✓ Link the Program

If you used a "compile" option rather than a "build" or "make" option, you may have to explicitly tell your compiler to link your program after compiling it.

✓ Run the Program

When the program is successfully compiled and linked, run it to make sure it does what it is supposed to do.

✓ Check the Program Output

Test the program for each menu option, as well as zero entries for all values in all selected menu options. Sample screens are shown in Figure 6-6 and Figure 6-7. Your screen should be similar to these.

Documenting the Program

✓ Test and Print a Sample Run of the Program

Get a printout of several program runs. See *Printing Console Output From Microsoft Windows* in *Appendix A* if you are running Microsoft Windows and need help with this.

✓ Print the Source Code

Get a printout of the program source code.

✓ Close the File

When you are finished with the program file make sure that you have saved any final changes and then close the file (and project or workspace if required).

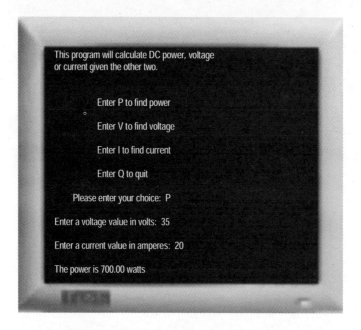

Figure 5-6 Sample menu and output for the engineer's power program

Figure 6-7 Sample menu and invalid entry message for the engineer's power program

Iteration Structures

In this lab, you will . . .

♦ Use the C++ **while**, **do/while** and **for** looping statements to perform repetitive operations.

♦ Write a menu-driven program using loops.

Chapter 7: Structured & Object-Oriented Problem Solving Using C++, 3rd edition, by Andrew C. Staugaard, Jr.

In this project, you will be controlling the flow of your programs using *iteration*. Iteration simply means to do something repeatedly. In programming, this is called *looping*.

It is important to provide a way to exit from a loop or the computer will perform the loop indefinitely. To prevent ***infinite loops***, all iteration control structures test a condition to determine when to exit the loop. ***Pretest*** loops test a condition each time before the loop statements are executed. If the test condition for a pretest loop if false the first time it is encountered, the loop body will never be executed. ***Posttest*** loops test a condition each time after the loop statements are executed; therefore, the loop body is always executed at least once, even if the test condition is false the first time it is encountered. ***Fixed repetition*** loops cause the loop statements to be executed a predetermined number of times.

Remember, an infinite loop, which occurs if the control test for a loop never becomes false, is a logic error. **The compiler will NOT detect an infinite loop condition.** For this reason, you should always desk-check your loop structures very closely prior to coding and execution. A little time desk-checking could save you a lot of time at the keyboard.

You will be using the C++ **while**, **do/while** and **for** statements to perform looping operations. The difference between these statements is found in the way they control the executing of the loop. The **while** is a pretest loop, the **do/while** is a posttest loop, and the **for** is a fixed repetition loop.

Here is a problem from Staugaard's text that is similar to what you will be asked to do in this project. Read it over carefully and use it as a guide to complete the problems in this project.

PROBLEM

In the last project, you saw that the **switch** statement is used to create menu-driven programs. It is often desirable to allow the user to select a menu option, perform the task associated with that option, then return to the menu to select another option without terminating the program until a quit option is chosen. Such a program would require the menu to be displayed repeatedly until the quit option is chosen. This is an ideal application for looping. We will encase our menu within a loop so that the menu and associated tasks will keep repeating until the user chooses to terminate the program. We will apply this technique to the menu-driven consumer loan solution developed in the last project. Let's revisit the problem through the problem definition.

Defining the Problem

Output: A program menu that prompts the user to select a monthly payment, total interest, or total loan amount calculation option.

The monthly loan payment, total loan interest, or total loan amount, depending on the program option that the user selects.

Invalid entry messages as required.

Input: A user response to the menu (P, I, T, or Q).

If P is selected, user enters the loan amount, interest rate, and term.

If I is selected, user enters the loan amount, interest rate, and term.

If T is selected, user enters the loan amount, interest rate, and term.

If Q is selected, terminate program.

Processing: Calculate the selected option as follows:

Case P: $payment = principle * rate/(1 - (1+rate)^{-term})$

Case I: $interest = term * payment - principle$

Case T: $total = principle + interest$

Case Q: Quit the program.

where: *principle* is the amount of the loan.

                 rate is a monthly interest rate in decimal form.

                 term is the number of months of the loan.

Repeat the menu until the user chooses to terminate the program.

Planning the Solution

Using the program design developed in the last chapter, we divided the problem into two subproblems to solve the overall problem:

- Display the menu and read user choice.
- Perform the chosen calculation and display results.

The problem-solving diagram for this solution is shown again in Figure 7-1.

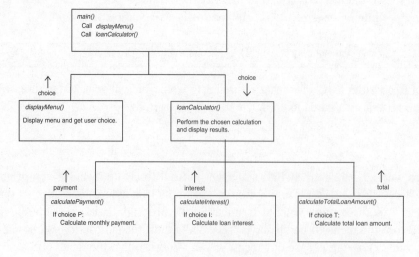

Figure 7-1   A problem-solving diagram for the loan problem.

Recall that there were three levels to solving the problem. At the first level, *main()*, a function is called to display the menu and get the user choice. The *displayMenu()* function accomplishes this task and sends the user choice back to *main()*, as indicated on the diagram. Function *main()* will then send the choice to a function called *loanCalculator()*, which will call one of three functions, depending on the choice, to perform and return the required calculation. Now, the process description requires that we add a loop control feature to the program. Here is the revised set of algorithms through the first level of refinement:

Initial Algorithm

main()
BEGIN
do
    Call *displayMenu()* function.
    Call *loanCalculator()* function.
while *choice* ≠ 'q' AND *choice* ≠ 'Q'
END.

First Level of Refinement

displayMenu()
BEGIN
    Display a program menu that prompts the user to choose a monthly payment (P), total interest (I), total loan amount (T), or quit (Q) option.
    Read *choice*.
END.

loanCalculator()
BEGIN
    Case P: Call function *calculatePayment()* and display payment.
    Case I: Call function *calculateInterest()* and display interest.
    Case T: Call function *calculateTotalLoanAmount()* and display total
             loan amount.
    Case Q: Terminate program.
    Default: Write an invalid entry message and ask the user to select again.
END.

Notice that the loop control feature is added to the initial algorithm level, *main()*. The *displayMenu()* and *loanCalculator()* algorithms at the first level of refinement have not changed much from our earlier solution. So, let's focus on the loop control in *main()*. Recall that the *displayMenu()* function obtains the user's menu choice. If the user enters a 'q' or 'Q' to quit the program, the loop will break, and the program terminates. But, is there something wrong here? We said if the "user enters a 'q' *or* 'Q' to quit the program ..."; however, the loop test employs the AND operation. So, why have we used the Boolean AND operation rather than the OR operation to perform this test? This is a classic candidate for desk-checking the algorithm logic *before* coding the program. Ask yourself, "When will the loop break?" Any C++ loop breaks when the condition being tested is false, right? Remember that the result of an AND operation is false when any one of its conditions is false. As a result, the loop will break when *choice* is a 'q' *or* a 'Q'. The loop will continue when both sides of the AND operation are true. Therefore, the loop will continue as long as *choice* is not a 'q' *and choice* is not 'Q'. Isn't this what we want to do? What would happen if you mistakenly used the OR operation in the foregoing loop test? An OR operation produces a true result when any one of its conditions is true. One of these conditions would always be true, because *choice* cannot be both a 'q' and a 'Q'. The result of this oversight would be an infinite loop.

Another point needs to be made here. This application is a classic candidate for a **do/while** loop rather than a **while** loop, because you always want the menu to be displayed at least once to allow for a user choice.

Coding the Program

Here is the code. This code (ACT07_01.cpp) is available on Staugaard's text CD or can be downloaded from the text Web site at www.prenhall.com/staugaard. You may wish to compile and execute the code to observe its operation.

Listing:

```
/*
ACTION 7-1 (ACT07_01.CPP)
OUTPUT:  A PROGRAM MENU THAT PROMPTS THE USER TO SELECT A
         MONTHLY PAYMENT, TOTAL INTEREST, OR TOTAL LOAN AMOUNT
         CALCULATION OPTION.
         INVALID ENTRY MESSAGES AS REQUIRED.
         THE MONTHLY LOAN PAYMENT, TOTAL LOAN INTEREST,
         OR TOTAL LOAN AMOUNT, DEPENDING ON THE PROGRAM OPTION THAT THE
         USER SELECTS.
         INVALID ENTRY MESSAGES AS REQUIRED.

INPUT:   A USER RESPONSE TO THE MENU (P, I, T, OR Q).
         IF P IS SELECTED: USER ENTERS THE LOAN AMOUNT, INTEREST RATE, AND TERM.
         IF I IS SELECTED: USER ENTERS THE LOAN AMOUNT, INTEREST RATE, AND TERM.
         IF R IS SELECTED: USER ENTERS THE LOAN AMOUNT, INTEREST RATE, AND TERM.
         IF Q IS SELECTED: TERMINATE PROGRAM.

PROCESSING:  CALCULATE THE SELECTED OPTION AS FOLLOWS:
         CASE V: PAYMENT = PRINCIPLE * RATE/(1 - (1+RATE) -TERM)
         CASE I:  INTEREST = TERM * PAYMENT - PRINCIPLE
         CASE T: TOTAL = PRINCIPLE + INTEREST
         CASE Q: QUIT THE PROGRAM.
         WHERE: PRINCIPLE IS THE AMOUNT OF THE LOAN.
                RATE IS A MONTHLY INTEREST RATE IN DECIMAL FORM.
                TERM IS THE NUMBER OF MONTHS OF THE LOAN.
*/

//PREPROCESSOR DIRECTIVES
#include <iostream.h>     //FOR cin AND cout
#include <math.h>         //FOR pow()

//MAIN FUNCTION
int main()
{
 //DEFINE AND INITIALIZE VARIABLES
char choice = 'Q';          //USER MENU ENTRY
double payment = 0.0;       //MONTHLY PAYMENT
double interest = 0.0;      //TOTAL INTEREST FOR LIFE OF LOAN
double total = 0.0;         //TOTAL LOAN AMOUNT = PRINCIPLE + INTEREST
double principle = 0.0;     //LOAN AMOUNT
double rate = 0.0;          //INTEREST RATE
int term = 0;               //TERM OF LOAN IN MONTHS
```

```cpp
//SET OUTPUT FORMAT
cout.setf(ios::fixed);
cout.setf(ios::showpoint);
cout.precision(2);

//DISPLAY PROGRAM DESCRIPTION MESSAGE
cout << "This program will calculate a monthly loan\n"
     << "payment, total loan interest, or total loan amount." << endl;

//MENU LOOP - DO UNTIL ENTRY 'q' OR 'Q'
do
{

    //displayMenu() FUNCTION
    cout  << "\n\n\t\t\tEnter P to get monthly payment"
          << "\n\t\t\tEnter I to get total loan interest"
          << "\n\t\t\tEnter T to get total loan amount"
          << "\n\t\t\tEnter Q to quit" << endl;

    cout << "\n\n\tPlease enter your choice:  ";

    //READ USER CHOICE
    cin >> choice;

    //loanCalculator() FUNCTION
    switch (choice)
    {
      case 'p':     //calculatePayment() FUNCTION
      case 'P' :    cout << "\nEnter the amount of the loan: $";
                           cin >> principle;
                    cout << "\nEnter the duration of the loan in months: ";
                    cin >> term;
                    cout << "\nEnter the annual interest rate: ";
                    cin >> rate;

                        //CHECK FOR INVALID RATE
                        while ((rate <= 0) || (rate > 100))
                        {
                          //DISPLAY INVALID ENTRY MESSAGE
                          cout << "\n\nThis is an invalid entry." << endl;
                          cout << "\nEnter the annual interest rate: ";
                          cin >> rate;
                        }//END WHILE

                        //CALCULATE AND DISPLAY PAYMENT
                        rate = rate/12/100;
                        payment = principle * rate/(1 - pow((1+rate), -term));
                        cout << "\n\nThe monthly payment is $" << payment << endl;
                        break;

      case 'i':     //calculateInterest() FUNCTION
      case 'I' :    cout << "\nEnter the amount of the loan: $";
                    cin >> principle;
                    cout << "\nEnter the duration of the loan in months: ";
                    cin >> term;
                    cout << "\nEnter the annual interest rate: ";
                    cin >> rate;
```

137

```cpp
                    //CHECK FOR INVALID RATE
                    while ((rate <= 0) || (rate > 100))
                    {
                        //DISPLAY INVALID ENTRY MESSAGE
                        cout << "\n\nThis is an invalid entry." << endl;
                        cout << "\nEnter the annual interest rate: ";
                        cin >> rate;
                    }//END WHILE

                    //CALCULATE AND DISPLAY INTEREST
                    rate = rate/12/100;
                    payment = principle * rate/(1-pow((1+rate), -term));
                    interest = term * payment - principle;
                    cout << "\n\nThe total interest is $" << interest << endl;
                    break;

    case 't':       //calculateTotalLoanAmount() FUNCTION
    case 'T':       cout << "\nEnter the amount of the loan: $";
                    cin >> principle;
                    cout << "\nEnter the duration of the loan in months: ";
                    cin >> term;
                    cout << "\nEnter the annual interest rate: ";
                    cin >> rate;

                    //CHECK FOR INVALID RATE
                    while ((rate <= 0) || (rate > 100))
                    {
                        //DISPLAY INVALID ENTRY MESSAGE
                        cout << "\n\nThis is an invalid entry." << endl;
                        cout << "\nEnter the annual interest rate: ";
                        cin >> rate;
                    }//END WHILE

                    //CALCULATE AND DISPLAY TOTAL
                    rate = rate/12/100;
                    payment = principle * rate/(1-pow((1+rate), -term));
                    interest = term * payment - principle;
                    total = principle + interest;
                    cout << "\n\nThe total loan amount is $" << total << endl;
                    break;

    case 'q':       //QUIT THE PROGRAM
                    case 'Q': cout << "Program terminated" << endl;
                    break;

//DISPLAY INVALID ENTRY MESSAGE
default : cout << "\n\nThis is an invalid entry. Please"
            << " select again." << endl;
    } //END SWITCH
    }//END WHILE
    while ((choice != 'q') && (choice != 'Q'));

    //RETURN
    return 0;
} //END main()
```

138

The major change here is the **do/while** loop control feature that we added in our solution planning. Notice how the conditional loop test is coded at the end of the program. The entire test must be within parentheses. The variable *choice* is tested twice; both tests must be enclosed within parentheses. The results of both tests are combined via the Boolean AND (&&) operation.

We have added another feature to the program which uses a **while** loop to check for invalid user entries. Notice how the *rate* is obtained from the user. The *rate* is read using a *cin* statement; then, a **while** loop test is made to see if the *rate* is less than or equal to 0 or greater than 100. If it is, the body of the loop executes displaying an invalid entry message and requiring the user to enter another value for *rate*. The **while** loop will force the user to enter a value that is between 0 and 100, exclusive, because the loop will not terminate until the user does so. This is a classic example of where you would use a **while** loop rather than a **do/while** loop. You must use the **while** loop because you do not want the loop to execute at all if the user enters a *rate* that is within the specified range. Of course, because the **while** loop is a pretest loop, you must obtain a value for *rate* before the loop test is made, right? Using a **while** loop like this to force a user to enter correct data is a much better technique than using an **if/else** statement as we did in the last lab project. (Of course, we didn't have the **while** loop at our disposal in the last project.)

In this exercise, you will develop a problem definition, algorithm, and program that employs a **while** loop to average any number of test scores. You will write the source code program that produces a user-friendly output. You will compile, link, run, test, and print your program. You will revise the algorithm and program to employ a **do/while** loop to solve the problem and then revise the algorithm and program again using a **for** loop.

 # Pre-Lab

PROBLEM

Write a user-friendly program using a **while** loop to compute the average of any number of test scores and report the result to the user.

Defining the Problem

Output: What output is needed according to the problem statement?

_____

Input: What input will be needed for processing to obtain the required output?

_____

Processing: What processing is required to calculate the test score average?

_____

_____

_____

     The output will report the average of the test scores. The number of tests and the test score values are needed as input. You need to prompt the user for the number of tests to average. You need this number in your program to control the number of loop iterations. A **while** loop will be used to read the scores and accumulate a total. To determine the average of the test scores, you will need to divide this total by the number of test scores entered after all the scores have been entered and totaled by the loop.

Planning the Solution

Here is the initial algorithm for function *main()* developed from the problem definition. Write the algorithms required for the first level of refinement.

main()
BEGIN
    Call function to set the number of test scores from a user entry.
    Call function to loop to read the individual scores from the user and accumulate a total.
    Call function to calculate the test average.
    Call function to report the test average.
END.

SET THE NUMBER OF TEST SCORES FROM A USER ENTRY
BEGIN

END.

LOOP TO READ THE INDIVIDUAL SCORES FROM THE USER AND ACCUMULATE A TOTAL
BEGIN

END.

CALCULATE THE TEST AVERAGE
BEGIN

END.

REPORT THE TEST AVERAGE
BEGIN

END.

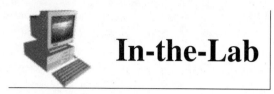 **In-the-Lab**

Coding the Program

✓Start Your Editor

Start your C++ editor / IDE.

✓Create a New Project

Make sure that a new file (and project if required) is open.

✓Enter the Source Code

Using the algorithms that you developed, complete the following program shell for the test score average program:

```
// LAB 7-1a (L7_1a.CPP)
// AUTHOR : type your name here
// DATE WRITTEN : type the date here

// PREPROCESSOR DIRECTIVES




int main()
{
// DEFINE AND INITIALIZE VARIABLES AND OBJECTS












// DISPLAY PROGRAM DESCRIPTION MESSAGE


```

// SET NUMBER OF TEST SCORES FROM USER ENTRY

// LOOP TO GET INDIVIDUAL SCORES FROM USER AND ACCUMULATE A TOTAL

// CALCULATE TEST AVERAGE

// REPORT THE TEST AVERAGE

return 0;

} //END main()

✓ Save the Program

After you have entered the source code, you need to save the program. Name this program *L7_1a.cpp*.

Testing and Debugging the Program

✓ Compile the Program

Now that you have entered and saved the program, compile it.

143

✓Errors?

If there were any errors in the program, you will have to edit the program code to fix the errors, and then compile the program again before you can link and run the program. Be sure to save the program again after you correct any errors.

✓Link the Program

If you used a "compile" option rather than a "build" or "make" option, you may have to explicitly tell your compiler to link your program after compiling it.

✓Run the Program

When the program is successfully compiled and linked, run it to make sure that it does what it is supposed to do.

✓Check the Program Output

Observe your program output. A sample output screen of the grade conversion program is shown in Figure 7-2. Your output screen should look similar to this. If it doesn't, edit your program code so that you obtain the correct output.

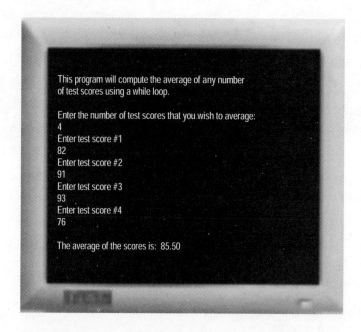

Figure 7-2 Sample output for the test score average program

Documenting the Program

✓Observe the Program Execution with the Debugger

Use your debugger (if your environment has a debugger) to single step the program execution and observe the operation of the **while** loop in your program. Set a watch on your loop counter, test score, and sum

144

variables using a watch window. (If you are using Microsoft Visual C++ 6, see *Appendix B* for help with the debugger.)

✓Test and Print a Sample Run of the Program

Get a printout of sample program runs with the following test data:

Numeric Grade	Test Scores
3	83 79 94
0	(You will have to decide how to handle this case)
7	53 72 91 82 75 62 94
4	74 98 89 93

See *Printing Console Output From Microsoft Windows* in *Appendix A* if you are running Microsoft Windows and need help with this.

✓Print the Source Code

Get a printout of the program source code.

✓Close the File

When you are finished with the program file, make sure you have saved any final changes and then close the file (and project or workspace if required).

Revise the program from Problem 1a to employ a **do/while** loop to accept the test scores, instead of the **while** loop. This version of the program should not look or act any differently from a user's standpoint; however, the programming logic will be slightly different.

✓ Save, Compile, and Link the Program

After you have revised the source code, you need to save the modified program. Name this program *L7_1b.cpp*. Now that you have saved the program, it is time to compile it, correcting any syntax errors that arise. If you used a "compile" option rather than a "build" or "make" option, you may have to explicitly tell your compiler to link your program after compiling it.

✓ Run the Program

When the program is successfully compiled and linked, run it to make sure that it does what it is supposed to do.

✓ Check the Program Output

Check the program output to see the results of the program run.

✓ Test and Print Sample Runs of the Program

Get a printout of sample program runs with the following test data:

Numeric Grade	Test Scores						
3	83	79	94				
0	(You will have to decide how to handle this case)						
7	53	72	91	82	75	62	94
4	74	98	89	93			

See *Printing Console Output From Microsoft Windows* in *Appendix A* if you are running Microsoft Windows and need help with this.

✓ Print the Source Code

Get a printout of the program source code.

✓ Close the File

When you are finished with the program file make sure that you have saved any final changes and then close the file (and project or workspace if required).

Revise the program from Problem 1a to employ a **for** loop to accept the test scores, instead of the **while** loop. This version of the program should not look or act any differently from a user's standpoint; however, the programming logic will be slightly different from problems 1a and 1b.

✓ Save, Compile, and Link the Program

After you have revised the source code, you need to save the modified program. Name this program *L7_1c.cpp*. Now that you have saved the program, it is time to compile it, correcting any syntax errors that arise. If you used a "compile" option rather than a "build" or "make" option, you may have to explicitly tell your compiler to link your program after compiling it.

✓ Run the Program

When the program is successfully compiled and linked, run it to make sure that it does what it is supposed to do.

✓ Check the Program Output

Check the program output to see the results of the program run.

✓ Test and Print Sample Runs of the Program

Get a printout of sample program runs with the following test data:

Numeric Grade	Test Scores
3	83 79 94
0	(You will have to decide how to handle this case)
7	53 72 91 82 75 62 94
4	74 98 89 93

See *Printing Console Output From Microsoft Windows* in *Appendix A* if you are running Microsoft Windows and need help with this.

✓ Print the Source Code

Get a printout of the program source code.

✓ Close the File

When you are finished with the program file, make sure that you have saved any final changes and then close the file (and project or workspace if required).

In this exercise you will develop a problem definition, a set of algorithms, and a user-friendly C++ program that will generate a menu to allow the user to calculate either the total resistance in a series circuit or the total resistance in a parallel circuit.

Pre-Lab

PROBLEM

Develop a menu-driven program that will calculate and report the total resistance of any number of resistors in a series or a parallel circuit. Provide for loop control of the menu-driven program so that the program does not terminate until the user chooses a quit option from the menu.

Defining the Problem

Output: What output is needed according to the problem statement?

_____

Input: What input will be needed for processing to obtain the required output?

_____

Processing: What processing is required to determine the total resistance of a series circuit?

_____

What processing is required to determine the total resistance of a parallel circuit?

_____

The output will be the total resistance for a series or a parallel circuit. In addition, a menu must be displayed as well as the individual resistance values. The input required is the user response to the menu choices, the number of resistors in the circuit, and the individual resistance values. The processing required for this problem depends on the user's choice from the menu. If the user selects the series resistance option, you must add the individual resistance values to get the total resistance as follows:

$$R_{total} = R_1 + R_2 + R_3 + \ldots + R_n$$

If the user selects the parallel option, you can use the *product-over-sum rule* to find the total resistance. The product-over-sum rule calculates the total resistance by dividing the product of the first two resistance's by their sum, then repeating the calculation using this result and the third resistance value, then repeating the calculation using this result and the fourth resistance value, and so on, until all resistance values have been used in the calculation. (See *Problem Solving in Action: Parallel Resistor Circuit*

Analysis in Chapter 7 of Staugaard's text for more details.) Thus, each time a resistor value, R, is entered, the total parallel resistance is recalculated using the product-over-sum rule like this:

Initial R_{equiv}: $\qquad R_{equiv} = (R_1 \times R_2) / (R_1 + R_2)$

Subsequent R_{equiv}'s: $\qquad R_{equiv} = (R_{equiv} \times R_{next}) / (R_{equiv} + R_{next})$

$\qquad\qquad\qquad\qquad$ where R_{next} is the next resistance (i.e. $R_3, R_4, \ldots, R_n$)

Planning the Solution

Here is the initial algorithm for function *main()* developed from the problem definition. Write a set of algorithms for the first and second levels of refinement.

main()
BEGIN
$\quad$ do
$\qquad$ Call function to generate a menu for the user and set the user's *choice*.
$\qquad$ Call function to switch on the *choice*.
$\qquad$ Case S: $\quad$ Call function to calculate and display total series resistance.
$\qquad$ Case P: $\quad$ Call function to calculate and display total parallel resistance.
$\qquad$ Case Q: $\quad$ Quit the program.
$\qquad$ Default: $\quad$ Invalid entry message.
$\quad$ while *choice* $\neq$ 'q' and *choice* $\neq$ 'Q'
END.

Now, write the algorithms for the first level of refinement.

GENERATE MENU FOR USER AND SET USER CHOICE
BEGIN

END.

SWITCH ON THE CHOICE
BEGIN

149

END.

Now, write the algorithms for the second level of refinement.

CALCULATE AND DISPLAY TOTAL SERIES RESISTANCE
BEGIN

END.

CALCULATE AND DISPLAY TOTAL PARALLEL RESISTANCE
BEGIN

END.

 **In-the-Lab**

Coding the Program

✓Start Your Editor

Start your C++ editor / IDE.

✓Create a New Project

Make sure that a new file (and project if required) is open.

✓Enter the Source Code

Make sure that a new file is open. Using the algorithms that you developed, complete the following program shell for the flat implementation of the resistance problem:

```
// LAB 7-2 (L7_2.CPP)
// AUTHOR : type your name here
// DATE WRITTEN : type the date here

// PREPROCESSOR DIRECTIVES




int main()
{
// DEFINE AND INITIALIZE VARIABLES AND OBJECTS




// DISPLAY PROGRAM DESCRIPTION MESSAGE
```

// GENERATE MENU ANG SET USER CHOICE USING A LOOP TO CONTROL PROGRAM TEXT

// SWITCH STATEMENT TO SELECT AND PERFORM APPROPRIATE CALCULATION

return 0;

} // END main()

✓ Save the Program

After you have entered the source code, you need to save the program. Name this program *L7_2.cpp*.

152

Testing and Debugging the Program

✓ Compile the Program

Now that you have entered and saved the program, compile it.

✓ Errors?

If there were any errors in the program, you will have to edit the program code to fix the errors, and then compile the program again before you can link and run the program. Be sure to save the program again after you correct any errors.

✓ Link the Program

If you used a "compile" option rather than a "build" or "make" option, you may have to explicitly tell your compiler to link your program after compiling it.

✓ Run the Program

When the program is successfully compiled and linked, run it to make sure that it does what it is supposed to do.

✓ Check the Program Output

Figure 7-3 shows a sample run for the series option, and Figure 7-4 shows a sample run for the parallel option. Your screen should be similar to these.

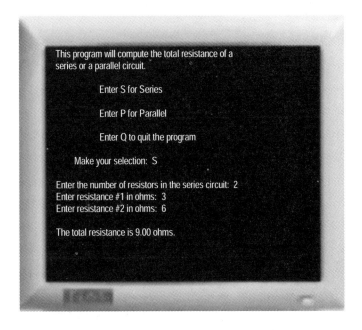

Figure 7-3 Menu and series option for the resistance program

153

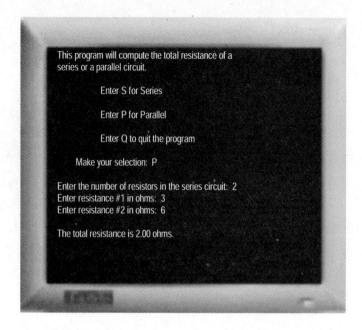

Figure 7-4 Menu and parallel option for the resistance program

Documenting the Program

✓ Test and Print Sample Runs of the Program

Get a printout of program runs using the table that follows. See *Printing Console Output From Microsoft Windows* in *Appendix A* if you are running Microsoft Windows and need help with this.

Menu Selection	Number of Resistors	Resistor Value(s)	Expected Result
R	N/A	N/A	Invalid entry, regenerate menu
q	N/A	N/A	Terminate Program
Q	N/A	N/A	Terminate Program
S	0	N/A	Regenerate menu
S	2	0 ohms and 6 ohms	6.00 ohms
S	2	3 ohms and 6 ohms	9.00 ohms
P	0	N/A	Regenerate menu
P	2	0 ohms and 6 ohms	0.00 ohms
P	2	3 ohms and 6 ohms	2.00 ohms
P	3	2 ohms, 2 ohms, and 2 ohms	0.67 ohms

Did your program handle all of these above cases correctly? If not, rewrite your algorithms and program so that your program produces the expected result.

✓ Print the Source Code

Get a printout of the program source code.

✓ Close the File

When you are finished with the program file, make sure that you have saved any final changes and then close the file (and project or workspace if required).

154

LAB PROJECT #8

Functions

OBJECTIVES

In this lab, you will . . .
♦ Design modular, well-structured programs.
♦ Create and employ programmer-defined functions.
♦ Use value and reference parameters.
♦ Learn the importance of a function prototype.
♦ Use recursive functions.

REQUIRED READING

Chapter 8: Structured & Object-Oriented Problem Solving Using C++, 3rd edition, by Andrew C. Staugaard, Jr.

If not using an ANSI/ISO compatible compiler, read about C-strings in Chapter 9 of Structured & Object-Oriented Problem Solving Using C++, 3rd edition by Andrew C. Staugaard, Jr.

INTRODUCTION

In this project, you will be creating and employing programmer-defined functions to write modular, well-structured C++ programs. The programs that you have been working with so far have consisted of one large section defined by function *main()*. Although you have been creating structured designs, you have been implementing your designs by using a nonstructured, or flat, implementation. It is now time to learn how to implement your structured designs, using structured programming.

Functions that you create yourself are called ***programmer-defined*** functions. Functions eliminate the need for duplicate statements within a program. If you have a task that needs to be performed more than once, the statements can be written just once in a function. Then, the function is given a name and ***called***, or ***invoked***, by using its name each time its task is to be performed within the ***calling program***. All programmer-defined functions are defined after the closing brace of *main()*. Using functions adds to the clarity and readability of your program code. And, most importantly, the use of functions allows you to solve very large complex problems, using a top/down structured programming approach.

The function ***header*** defines a function ***interface***. The header dictates what types of data the function will accept from the calling program and what types of data the function will return to the calling program. The header forms a common boundary between the function and its calling program and therefore defines the function interface.

Data passed to a function when the function is called are referred to as ***arguments***. ***Parameters*** are defined within the function header and take on the value(s) of the arguments when the function is called. When parameters are required for evaluation by the function, they must be listed in the function header in one of two ways: as ***value parameters*** or as ***reference parameters***. Value parameters allow for *one-way communication* of data from the calling program to the function. Another way to think of it is that the parameter receives a *copy* of the argument value. When the function operates on a value parameter, it is operating on a copy rather than on the original value in the calling program. Thus, the argument value in

155

the calling program is protected from being accidentally changed by the function. The important thing to remember when using value parameters is that any manipulation of the parameters within the function does not affect the argument values used for the function call. Reference parameters differ from value parameters in that they provide two-way communication between the calling program and the function. The argument values are passed to the parameters in the function, and then the parameter values are passed back to the arguments. This allows the function to change the argument values in the calling program. Recall that a *value parameter* is simply a copy of the argument value; therefore, any operations on the parameter within the function have no effect on its original argument value. On the other hand, a *reference parameter* represents the *address* in memory of an argument variable. As a result, any changes made to the reference parameter within the function will change what's stored at that address. This obviously changes the original value of the argument variable in the calling program. To create a reference parameter, you simply insert an ampersand, &, prior to the appropriate parameter identifiers in the function heading.

One way to determine whether a parameter needs to be value or reference is to ask yourself if the respective argument within the function call needs to be changed by the function. If so, then the parameter should be a reference parameter. If you do not want the argument changed by the function, the parameter should be a value parameter. You can use Table 8-1 to help you decide whether a function parameter should be a value parameter or a reference parameter.

TABLE 8-1 FUNCTION PARAMETERS

Accepts/Returns	Parameter
Nothing accepted	none
Accepts without returning (one-way)	value
Accepts and returns (two-way)	reference

There are two ways that functions can supply data to a calling program: by returning a single value, or by modifying a variable argument that is passed by reference. Functions that send a single *return value* to the calling program are known as *non-void* functions. Non-void functions can be called within an expression in the calling program, and the return value of the function will be evaluated and inserted into the expression in place of the function call. Functions that do not send a return value to the calling program, are called *void* functions. A **void** function call cannot be used within an expression in the calling program because it does not send a return value back to the calling program. This does NOT mean that a **void** function cannot send data back to the calling program. In fact, **void** functions can send multiple values back to the calling program by modifying variable arguments that have been passed by reference. You can use Table 8-2 to help you decide whether a function should be a non-void function or a void function.

TABLE 8-2 FUNCTION RETURN TYPES

Returns	Return Data Type
A single value	non-void type
Nothing	void
Multiple Values	void

156

A *function prototype*, sometimes referred to as a *function declaration*, is a model of the interface to the function that is used by the compiler to check calls to the function for the proper number of arguments and correct data types of the arguments. A function prototype is required by C++ for each function used in your program. The function prototype can simply be a copy of the function header followed by a semicolon. It must appear prior to function *main()*.

A recursive function is a function that calls itself until a primitive state is reached. There must always be a primitive state to terminate a recursive function call. Otherwise, a run-time error will occur. Recursive operations can be performed as part of an **if/else** statement. The primitive state forms the **if** clause, while the recursive call is part of the **else** clause of the statement. All recursive operations can also be performed by using iteration. (*Note*: Recursion eats up time and memory compared to iteration, so you should consider recursion only when a simple iterative solution is not possible and when the execution and memory efficiency of the solution are within acceptable limits).

Here is a problem from Staugaard's text that is similar to what you will be asked to do in this project. Read it over carefully and use it as a guide to complete the problems in this project.

PROBLEM

In the previous project, we developed a loop-controlled, menu-driven loan program. However, although we developed a modular design, we employed a flat implementation when coding the design. It is now time to do it right and employ modular programming via functions to implement the modular design. Here is the problem definition that we developed earlier

Defining the Problem

Output: A program menu that prompts the user to select a monthly payment, total interest, or total loan amount calculation option.
The monthly loan payment, total loan interest, or total loan amount, depending on the program option that the user selects.
Invalid entry messages as required.

Input: A user response to the menu (P, I, T, or Q).
If P is selected, user enters the loan amount, interest rate, and term.
If I is selected, user enters the loan amount, interest rate, and term.
If T is selected, user enters the loan amount, interest rate, and term.
If Q is selected, terminate program.

Processing: Calculate the selected option as follows:
Case P: *payment = principal * rate/(1 − (1+rate)$^{-term}$)*
Case I: *interest = term * payment − principal*
Case T: *total = principal + interest*
Case Q: Quit the program.
where: *principal* is the amount of the loan.
rate is a monthly interest rate in decimal form.
term is the number of months of the loan.
Repeat the menu until the user chooses to terminate the program.

Planning the Solution

The problem-solving diagram we developed earlier is shown again in Figure 8-1. Now, here is the set of algorithms we developed earlier:

Initial Algorithm

main()
BEGIN
do
    Call *displayMenu()* function.
    Call *loanCalculator()* function.
while *choice* ≠ 'q' AND *choice* ≠ 'Q'
END.

First Level of Refinement

displayMenu( )
BEGIN
    Display a program menu that prompts the user to choose a monthly payment (P), total interest (I), total loan amount (T), or quit (Q) option.
    Read *choice*.
END.

loanCalculator( )
BEGIN
    Case P: Call function *calculatePayment( )* and display payment.
    Case I: Call function *calculateInterest( )* and display interest.
    Case T: Call function *calculateTotalLoanAmount( )* and display total
                 loan amount.
    Case Q: Terminate program.
    Default: Write an invalid entry message, and ask the user to select again.
END.

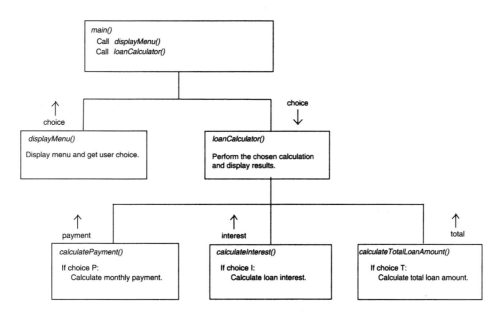

Figure 8-1   A problem-solving diagram for the loan problem.

Coding the Program

Now, to implement the design, we need to construct the functions. The main task here is to develop the function interfaces, or headers. To do this, we must develop a problem definition for *each* function. The problem definition developed earlier addresses output, input, and processing for the overall application program, *main( )*. This is still needed to define the problem for the program as a whole. However, to construct the function interfaces, we must address problem definition from the perspective of the function. In other words, we must consider the output, input, and processing of each individual function. The *input* to the function is what the function must accept in order to perform its designated task, the *output* from the function is what the function *returns*, and the *processing* is the task, or algorithm, the function will perform.

We will start with the *displayMenu()* function. You must ask yourself two questions: 1) "What does the function need to *accept* (input) to perform its designated task?" and 2) "What does the function need to *return* (output) to the calling program?" The task of the *displayMenu()* function is to display the menu and return the user's choice to its calling function, *main()*. This function does not need to accept anything from *main()* to perform its task, but it needs to return a single value to *main()*, which is the user's menu choice. This is shown in the problem-solving diagram by the variable *choice* coming out of *displayMenu()*. Notice that nothing is going into this function. Here is the problem definition from the perspective of this function:

Function *displayMenu()*: Display menu and get user entry.
Accepts: Nothing.
Returns: Menu choice obtained from user.

The function definition describes the function interface. The first decision you need to make is whether to use a void function or a non-void function. Use a non-void function if the function produces a single value that is returned to the calling program. Use a void function if the function returns *more than* one value or does not return anything to the calling program. In other words, if the problem-solving diagram indicates that a single value is being produced by the function, use a non-void function. If the problem-solving diagram indicates that more than one value or nothing is being returned by the function, use a void function. These guidelines are summarized in Table 8-2. Because our *displayMenu()* function accepts nothing, but returns the user's menu choice, it must be a non-void function. So, the return type must be **char** because the user's choice will be a character from the menu.

Next, we must decide the function parameters. Table 8-1 provides the guidelines for determining whether a given parameter must be a value or a reference parameter.

No parameters are required for *displayMenu()*, because it does not accept anything. The function interface is simply

```
char displayMenu()
```

Now, we simply place the *displayMenu()* code developed earlier inside the function. Here is the complete function:

```
//DISPLAY MENU FUNCTION
char displayMenu()
{
    //DEFINE LOCAL CHOICE VARIABLE
    char choice = 'Q';
    cout << "\n\n\t\t\tEnter P to get monthly payment"
        << "\n\t\t\tEnter I to get total loan interest"
        << "\n\t\t\tEnter T to get total loan amount"
        << "\n\t\t\tEnter Q to quit" << endl;

    cout << "\n\n\tPlease enter your choice:  ";

    //READ USER CHOICE
    cin >> choice;

    //RETURN CHOICE
    return choice;
} //END displayMenu()
```

Notice that our *choice* variable is now defined as a local variable inside the function. In addition, a **return** statement is placed at the end of the function to return *choice* to its calling program, in this case *main()*.

Next, let's develop the *loanCalculator()* function. We begin by developing the function interface. From the problem-solving diagram, it is easy to see the following:

Function *loanCalculator()*:   Perform chosen calculation and display results.
Accepts: Menu entry, *choice*, obtained from the *main()*.
Returns: Nothing.

From the interface description, it is easy to see that we must use a **void** function because nothing is returned by the function. Even though the function is displaying the result, it *is not* returning any values to its calling function, *main()*. However, this function needs to accept the menu choice from *main()*. This means that we need a function parameter and the parameter will be a value parameter because it only needs to be passes one way to the function. The required parameter is a character, so the function interface becomes

    void loanCalculator(char choice)

Now, after inserting our **switch** statement code into the body of the function, the complete function becomes:

```
//LOAN CALCULATOR FUNCTION
void loanCalculator(char choice)
{
    switch (choice)
    {
    case 'p':   //CALL calculatePayment() FUNCTION
    case 'P':   cout << "The monthly loan payment is $"
                     << calculatePayment() << endl;
                break;

    case 'i':   //CALL calculateInterest() FUNCTION
    case 'I':   cout << "The monthly loan payment is $"
                     << calculateInterest() << endl;
                break;

    case 't':   //CALL calculateTotalLoanAmount() FUNCTION
    case 'T':   cout << "The total loan amount is $"
                     << calculateTotalLoanAmount() << endl;
                break;

    case 'q':   //QUIT THE PROGRAM
    case 'Q':   cout << "Program terminated" << endl;
                break;

    default :   //DISPLAY INVALID ENTRY MESSAGE
                cout << "\n\nThis is an invalid entry." << endl;
    } //END SWITCH
} //END loanCalculator()
```

Notice that the body of the function employs our earlier **switch** statement, which acts on the user choice, *choice*, received as a parameter from the calling function, *main()*. Next, you see that each **case** calls another function as part of a *cout* statement to calculate the required loan payment, interest, or total loan amount, depending on the value of *choice*. Each function will return a single value of monthly payment, interest, or total loan amount depending on which **case** is executed. Does this give you a hint as to what type of function these will be (void or non-void)? Finally, notice that there is no **return** statement in our *loanCalculator()* function, because it is a void function.

Next, here are the interface descriptions for each of the loan functions:

Function *calculatePayment()*:	Set loan principal, rate, and term from user entries and calculate loan payment.
Accepts:	Nothing.
Returns:	Loan payment.
Function *calculateInterest()*:	Set loan principal, rate, and term from user entries and calculate the loan interest.
Accepts:	Nothing.
Returns:	Loan interest.
Function *calculateTotalLoanAmount()*:	Set loan principal, rate, and term from user entries and calculate the total loan amount.
Accepts:	Nothing.
Returns:	Loan amount.

Each of these functions will have the same interface, except, of course, for the function name. Each function will be a non-void function because a single value is being produced and returned by the function. No parameters are required, because none of the functions need to accept any data from the calling function, *loanCalculator()*. You are probably thinking that each function needs the three unknown quantities to make the required calculation, right? However, these quantities will be obtained from the user within each of the functions and not from the calling function. As a result, these values are *not* passed to any of the functions. Here are the resulting function interfaces:

```
double calculatePayment()
double calculateInterest()
double calculateTotalLoanAmount()
```

Now, here is each complete function implementation:

```
//CALCULATE PAYMENT FUNCTION
double calculatePayment()
{
    //DEFINE LOCAL VARIABLES
    double principle = 0.0;    //LOAN PRINCIPLE
    double rate = 0.0;         //ANNUAL INTEREST RATE
    int term = 0;              //TERM OF LOAN

    //GET LOAN DATA FROM USER
    cout << "\nEnter the amount of the loan:  $";
    cin >> principle;
    cout << "\nEnter the duration of the loan in months:  ";
    cin >> term;
    cout << "\nEnter the annual interest rate:  ";
    cin >> rate;

    //CHECK FOR INVALID RATE
    while ((rate <= 0) || (rate > 100))
    {
        //DISPLAY INVALID ENTRY MESSAGE
        cout << "\n\nThis is an invalid entry." << endl;
        cout << "\nEnter the annual interest rate:  ";
```

```cpp
        cin >> rate;
    } //END while

    //CALCULATE PAYMENT
    rate = rate/12/100;
    return principle * rate/(1-pow((1+rate),-term));
} //END calculatePayment()

//CALCULATE INTEREST FUNCTION
double calculateInterest()
{
    //DEFINE LOCAL VARIABLES
    double payment = 0.0;      //MONTHLY PAYMENT
    double principle = 0.0;    //LOAN PRINCIPLE
    double rate = 0.0;         //ANNUAL INTEREST RATE
    int term = 0;              //TERM OF LOAN

    //GET LOAN DATA FROM USER
    cout << "\nEnter the amount of the loan:  $";
    cin >> principle;
    cout << "\nEnter the duration of the loan in months:  ";
    cin >> term;
    cout << "\nEnter the annual interest rate:  ";
    cin >> rate;

    //CHECK FOR INVALID RATE
    while ((rate <= 0) || (rate > 100))
    {
        //DISPLAY INVALID ENTRY MESSAGE
        cout << "\n\nThis is an invalid entry." << endl;
        cout << "\nEnter the annual interest rate:  ";
        cin >> rate;
    } //END while

    //CALCULATE INTEREST
    rate = rate/12/100;
    payment = principle * rate/(1-pow((1+rate),-term));
    return term * payment - principle;
} //END calculateInterest()

//CALCULATE TOTAL LOAN AMOUNT FUNCTION
double calculateTotalLoanAmount()
{
    //DEFINE LOCAL VARIABLES
    double payment = 0.0;      //MONTHLY PAYMENT
    double interest = 0.0;     //TOTAL INTEREST FOR LIFE OF LOAN
    double principle = 0.0;    //LOAN PRINCIPLE
    double rate = 0.0;         //ANNUAL INTEREST RATE
    int term = 0;              //TERM OF LOAN

    //GET LOAN DATA FROM USER
    cout << "\nEnter the amount of the loan:  $";
    cin >> principle;
    cout << "\nEnter the duration of the loan in months:  ";
    cin >> term;
    cout << "\nEnter the annual interest rate:  ";
    cin >> rate;
```

163

```
    //CHECK FOR INVALID RATE
    while ((rate <= 0) || (rate > 100))
    {
        //DISPLAY INVALID ENTRY MESSAGE
        cout << "\n\nThis is an invalid entry." << endl;
        cout << "\nEnter the annual interest rate:  ";
        cin >> rate;
    } //END while

    //CALCULATE TOTAL LOAN AMOUNT
    payment = principle * rate/(1-pow((1+rate),-term));
    interest = term * payment - principle;
    return principle + interest;
} //END calculateTotalLoanAmount ()
```

Notice that each function obtains the data required for the calculation from the user. The interest rate value is tested. If it is invalid, a loop is entered that writes an invalid entry message and continues to iterate until the user enters a valid interest rate.

We are now ready to combine everything into a complete program. The fully standards-compliant listing is shown below. Remember, depending on the standards compliance of your compiler, you may need to add a ".h" to the header files and drop the *using namespace std* line. This code (ACT08_01.cpp) is available on Staugaard's text CD or can be downloaded from the text Web site at www.prenhall.com/staugaard. You may wish to compile and execute the code to observe its operation.

```
/*
ACTION 8-1 (ACT08_01.CPP)
OUTPUT:    A PROGRAM MENU THAT PROMTS THE USER TO SELECT A
           MONTHLY PAYMENT, TOTAL INTEREST, OR TOTAL LOAN
           AMOUNT CALCULATION OPTION.
           THE MONTHLY LOAN PAYMENT, TOTAL LOAN INTEREST,
           OR TOTAL LOAN AMOUNT, DEPENDING ON THE PROGRAM OPTION THAT THE
           USER SELECTS.
           INVALID ENTRY MESSAGES AS REQUIRED.

INPUT:     A USER RESPONSE THE MENU (P, I, T, OR Q)
           IF P IS SELECTED:  USER ENTERS THE LOAN AMOUNT, INTEREST RATE,
                              AND TERM.
           IF I IS SELECTED:  USER ENTERS THE LOAN AMOUNT, INTEREST RATE,
                              AND TERM.
           IF R IS SELECTED:  USER ENTERS THE LOAN AMOUNT, INTEREST RATE,
                              AND TERM.
           IF Q IS SELECTED:  TERMINATE PROGRAM.

PROCESSING: CALCULATE THE SELECTED OPTION AS FOLLOWS:
           CASE P:    PAYMENT = PRINCIPLE * RATE/(1 - (1 + RATE) - TERM)
           CASE I:    INTEREST = TERM * PAYMENT - PRINCIPLE
           CASE T:    TOTAL = PRINCIPLE + INTEREST
           CASE Q:    QUIT THE PROGRAM
*/

//PREPROCESSOR DIRECTIVES
#include <iostream>   //FOR cin AND cout
#include <math.h>     //FOR pow()

using namespace std;
```

```cpp
//FUNCTION PROTOTYPES
char displayMenu();
void loanCalculator(char choice);
double calculatePayment();
double calculateInterest();
double calculateTotalLoanAmount();

//MAIN FUNCTION
int main()
{
    //DEFINE VARIABLES
    char choice = 'Q';      //USER MENU ENTRY

    //DISPLAY PROGRAM DESCRIPTION MESSAGE
    cout << "\nThis program will calculate a monthly loan interest\n"
        << "payment, total loan interest, or total loan amount." << endl;

    //MENU CONTROL LOOP
    do
    {
        choice = displayMenu();
        loanCalculator(choice);
    } //END do/while
    while ((choice != 'q') && (choice != 'Q'));

    //RETURN
    return 0;
} //END main()

//DISPLAY MENU FUNCTION
char displayMenu()
{
    //DEFINE LOCAL CHOICE VARIABLE
    char choice = 'Q';
    cout << "\n\n\t\t\tEnter P to get monthly payment"
        << "\n\t\t\tEnter I to get total loan interest"
        << "\n\t\t\tEnter T to get total loan amount"
        << "\n\t\t\tEnter Q to quit" << endl;

    cout << "\n\n\tPlease enter your choice:  ";

    //READ USER CHOICE
    cin >> choice;

    //RETURN CHOICE
    return choice;
} //END displayMenu()

//LOAN CALCULATOR FUNCTION
void loanCalculator(char choice)
{
    switch (choice)
    {
    case 'p': //CALL calculatePayment() FUNCTION
    case 'P': cout << "The monthly loan payment is $"
                << calculatePayment() << endl;
            break;
```

165

```
        case 'i':   //CALL calculateInterest() FUNCTION
        case 'I':   cout << "The monthly loan payment is $"
                        << calculateInterest() << endl;
                break;

        case 't':   //CALL calculateTotalLoanAmount() FUNCTION
        case 'T':   cout << "The total loan amount is $"
                        << calculateTotalLoanAmount() << endl;
                break;

        case 'q':   //QUIT THE PROGRAM
        case 'Q':   cout << "Program terminated" << endl;
                break;

        default :   //DISPLAY INVALID ENTRY MESSAGE
                    cout << "\n\nThis is an invalid entry." << endl;
        } //END SWITCH
} // END loanCalculator()

//CALCULATE PAYMENT FUNCTION
double calculatePayment()
{
    //DEFINE LOCAL VARIABLES
    double principle = 0.0;     //LOAN PRINCIPLE
    double rate = 0.0;          //ANNUAL INTEREST RATE
    int term = 0;               //TERM OF LOAN

    //GET LOAN DATA FROM USER
    cout << "\nEnter the amount of the loan:  $";
    cin >> principle;
    cout << "\nEnter the duration of the loan in months:  ";
    cin >> term;
    cout << "\nEnter the annual interest rate:  ";
    cin >> rate;

    //CHECK FOR INVALID RATE
    while ((rate <= 0) || (rate > 100))
    {
        //DISPLAY INVALID ENTRY MESSAGE
        cout << "\n\nThis is an invalid entry." << endl;
        cout << "\nEnter the annual interest rate:  ";
        cin >> rate;
    } //END while

    //CALCULATE PAYMENT
    rate = rate/12/100;
    return principle * rate/(1-pow((1+rate),-term));
} //END calculatePayment()

//CALCULATE INTEREST FUNCTION
double calculateInterest()
{
    //DEFINE LOCAL VARIABLES
    double payment = 0.0;       //MONTHLY PAYMENT
    double principle = 0.0;     //LOAN PRINCIPLE
    double rate = 0.0;          //ANNUAL INTEREST RATE
    int term = 0;               //TERM OF LOAN
```

166

```
    //GET LOAN DATA FROM USER
    cout << "\nEnter the amount of the loan:  $";
    cin >> principle;
    cout << "\nEnter the duration of the loan in months:  ";
    cin >> term;
    cout << "\nEnter the annual interest rate:  ";
    cin >> rate;

    //CHECK FOR INVALID RATE
    while ((rate <= 0) || (rate > 100))
    {
        //DISPLAY INVALID ENTRY MESSAGE
        cout << "\n\nThis is an invalid entry." << endl;
        cout << "\nEnter the annual interest rate:  ";
        cin >> rate;
    } //END while

    //CALCULATE INTEREST
    rate = rate/12/100;
    payment = principle * rate/(1-pow((1+rate),-term));
    return term * payment - principle;
} //END calculateInterest()

//CALCULATE TOTAL LOAN AMOUNT FUNCTION
double calculateTotalLoanAmount()
{
    //DEFINE LOCAL VARIABLES
    double payment = 0.0;      //MONTHLY PAYMENT
    double interest = 0.0;     //TOTAL INTEREST FOR LIFE OF LOAN
    double principle = 0.0;    //LOAN PRINCIPLE
    double rate = 0.0;         //ANNUAL INTEREST RATE
    int term = 0;              //TERM OF LOAN

    //GET LOAN DATA FROM USER
    cout << "\nEnter the amount of the loan:  $";
    cin >> principle;
    cout << "\nEnter the duration of the loan in months:  ";
    cin >> term;
    cout << "\nEnter the annual interest rate:  ";
    cin >> rate;

    //CHECK FOR INVALID RATE
    while ((rate <= 0) || (rate > 100))
    {
        //DISPLAY INVALID ENTRY MESSAGE
        cout << "\n\nThis is an invalid entry." << endl;
        cout << "\nEnter the annual interest rate:  ";
        cin >> rate;
    } //END while

    //CALCULATE TOTAL LOAN AMOUNT
    payment = principle * rate/(1-pow((1+rate),-term));
    interest = term * payment - principle;
    return principle + interest;
} //END calculateTotalLoanAmount ()
```

Among the first things you see at the top of the program are the function prototypes. These are simply copied from the function headers, with a semi-colon added to the end of each. Remember that C++ requires a prototype for each function so that it can check the correctness of the function calls. Next, you should be impressed by the simplicity of function *main()*. All that needs to be done here is to write a program description message and call our two functions within a program control loop. Most of the real work of the program is being done within the functions. The rest of the program contains each of the functions that we discussed earlier.

In this exercise you will revise the problem definition, algorithms, and program you developed for Ma and Pa's payroll in Problem 2 of Lab Project #5 to use functions.

 Pre-Lab

PROBLEM

Revise the previously written payroll program to use functions. Recall that the payroll program will calculate Herb's net pay when given the following information:

> Employee's name
> Number of hours worked in a week
> Hourly rate of pay
> FICA (7.15%)
> Federal withholding (28%)
> State withholding (10%)

Ma or Pa should not be required to enter more than the first three items when running the program. Display a report using the following format:

Employee Name: XXXXXXXXXXXXXXXXXXXX

Rate of Pay:	$XXX.XX	
Hours Worked:	XX.XX	
Gross Pay:		$XXXX.XX
Deductions:		
FICA	$XXX.XX	
Fed. Withholding	XXX.XX	
State Withholding	XXX.XX	

Total Deductions	$XXX.XX	
Net Pay:		$XXXX.XX

Defining the Problem

Output: What output is needed according to the problem statement?

169

Can a function be used to produce the output? _____

Input: What input will be needed for processing to obtain the required output?

_____

Can you create a function to accept the needed input from the user? _____

Processing: What processing is required to calculate the gross pay?

_____

What processing is required to calculate the FICA tax?

_____

What processing is required to calculate the federal withholding tax?

_____

What processing is required to calculate the state withholding tax?

_____

What processing is required to calculate the total deductions?

_____

What processing is required to calculate the net pay?

_____

Can a function be used for processing? _____

According to the problem statement, the output will be a formatted report showing the employee's name, rate of pay, hours worked, gross pay, itemized deductions, and net pay. The employee's name, pay rate, and hours worked are needed as input. These items *cannot* be hard-coded into the program as constants and must be accepted as variable input from the keyboard.

The FICA, federal withholding percentage, and state withholding percentage can be declared as constants. To calculate the gross pay, you need to multiply the pay rate by the hours worked. The FICA, federal, and state withholding values each need to be multiplied by the gross pay to calculate the corresponding itemized deductions. Add the itemized deductions together to calculate the total deductions. The net pay is simply the gross pay minus the total deductions. The input, processing, and output can be programmed, using functions that are called by the payroll program.

Planning the Solution

Write a set of algorithms to perform each of the three tasks listed in the following initial algorithm.

main()
BEGIN
    Call a *setData()* function to set the required input data variables with information from the user.
    Call a *calculate()* function to calculate the payroll values.
    Call a *display()* function to generate the payroll report.
END.

    Notice that each function is called by *main()* to perform its designated task. Therefore the "calling program" is *main()* for each function. Now, write the algorithm required for the *setData()* function in the space provided.

setData()
BEGIN

END.

Complete the following questions to determine the *setData()* function interface.

Function *setData()*. What does this function do?

_____

Accepts: What data items must this function accept from *main()* to perform its designated task?

_____

Returns: What data items must this function return to *main()*?

_____

Will this function be a void function or a non-void function? _____

List any required parameters and designate each parameter as value or reference.

_____

Write a prototype/header for this function.

Note: If you are working on a compiler that does not support the C++ **string** class, the function must accept and return a C-string (character array) to get the employee's name. To make the function accept and return an array, you simply provide an array definition in your function header. For example, suppose that you define a C-string in *main()* to hold your name, as follows:

char name[MAX];

To accept this array from *main()* and return it to *main()*, you simply repeat the array definition in your function header, like this:

setData(char name[MAX], ...)

Of course, the function return type and additional parameters required for this function must be added to the header.

Write the algorithm required for the *calulate()* function in the space provided.

calculate()
BEGIN

END.

Complete the following questions to determine the *calculate()* function interface.

Function *calculate()*. What does this function do?

_____

Accepts: What data items must this function accept from *main()* to perform its designated task?

_____

Returns: What data items must this function return to *main()*?

_____

Will this function be a void function or a non-void function? _____

172

List any required parameters and designate each parameter as value or reference.

_____

Write a prototype/header for this function.

_____

Write the algorithm required for the *display()* function in the space provided.

display()
BEGIN

END.

Complete the following questions to determine the *display()* function interface definition.

Function *display()*. What does this function do?

_____

Accepts: What data items must this function accept from *main()* to perform its designated task?

_____

Returns: What data items must this function return to *main()*?

_____

Will this function be a void function or a non-void function? _____

List any required parameters and designate each parameter as value or reference.

_____

Write a prototype/header for this function.

_____

 **In-the-Lab**

Coding the Program

✓ Start Your Editor

Start your C++ editor/IDE.

✓ Create a New Project

Make sure that a new file (and project if required) is open.

✓ Enter the Source Code

Use the set of algorithms and function interfaces that you developed to complete the following program shell.

```
// LAB 8-1 (L8_1.CPP)
// AUTHOR : type your name here
// DATE WRITTEN : type the date here

// PREPROCESSOR DIRECTIVES




// CONSTANT DECLARATIONS




// FUNCTION PROTOTYPES





int main()
{

// DEFINE VARIABLES AND OBJECTS
```

```
// DISPLAY PROGRAM DESCRIPTION MESSAGE




// CALL FUNCTION setData()


// CALL FUNCTION calculate()


// CALL FUNCTION display()


return 0;
} // END main()

// setData():  THIS FUNCTION WILL OBTAIN THE EMPLOYEE DATA FROM THE USER

{




} //END setData()

// calculate(): THIS FUNCTION WILL PERFORM THE PAYROLL CALCULATIONS

{




} //END calculate()
```

```
// display(): THIS FUNCTION WILL DISPLAY THE PAYROLL REPORT
{
```

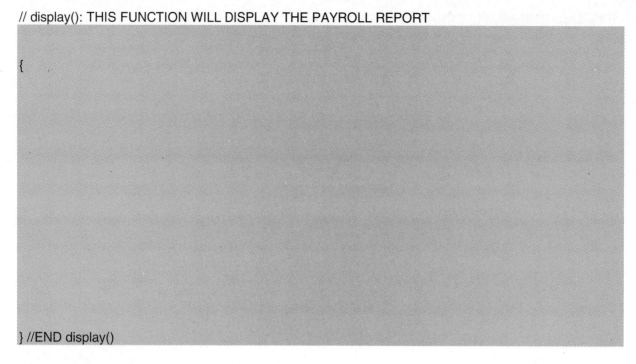

```
} //END display()
```

✓ Save the Program

After you have entered the source code, you need to save the program. Name this program *L8_1.cpp.*

Testing and Debugging the Program

✓ Compile the Program

Now that you have entered and saved the program, compile it.

✓ Errors?

If there were any errors in the program, you will have to edit the program code to fix the errors, and then compile the program again before you can link and run the program. Be sure to save the program again after you correct any errors.

✓ Link the Program

If you used a "compile" option rather than a "build" or "make" option, you may have to explicitly tell your compiler to link your program after compiling it.

✓ Run the Program

When the program is successfully compiled and linked, run it to make sure that it does what it is supposed to do.

✓ Check the Program Output

A sample of the input screen from the payroll program is shown in Figure 8-2, and a sample is shown in Figure 8-3. Your input and output should look similar to these. If not, edit your program code so that you obtain the correct output.

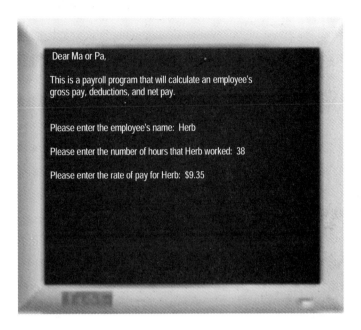

Dear Ma or Pa,

This is a payroll program that will calculate an employee's gross pay, deductions, and net pay.

Please enter the employee's name: Herb

Please enter the number of hours that Herb worked: 38

Please enter the rate of pay for Herb: $9.35

Figure 8-2 Sample input screen for the payroll program.

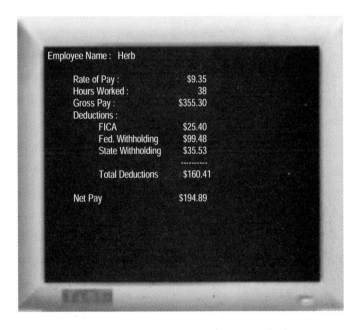

Employee Name : Herb

Rate of Pay :	$9.35
Hours Worked :	38
Gross Pay :	$355.30
Deductions :	
FICA	$25.40
Fed. Withholding	$99.48
State Withholding	$35.53

Total Deductions	$160.41
Net Pay	$194.89

Figure 8-3 Sample output for the payroll program.

Documenting the Program

✓ Observe the Program Execution with the Debugger

Use your debugger (if your environment has a debugger) to single-step the program execution and observe the operation of the functions in your program. Pay specific attention to the difference between stepping *into*, stepping *out of*, and stepping *over* function calls within the debugger. (If you are using Microsoft Visual C++ 6, see *Appendix B* for help with the debugger.)

✓ Test and Print a Sample Run of the Program

Get a printout of sample program runs of the payroll program. See *Printing Console Output From Microsoft Windows* in *Appendix A* if you are running Microsoft Windows and need help with this.

✓ Print the Source Code

Get a printout of the program source code.

✓ Close the File

When you are finished with the program file, make sure that you have saved any final changes and then close the file (and project or workspace if required).

In this exercise you will develop a problem definition, set of algorithms, and C++ program that will use a recursive function to generate a Fibonacci sequence of numbers to some position *n* entered by the user. You will also develop an algorithm and program that employ an iterative function to generate a Fibonacci sequence to some position *n* entered by the user. And, finally, you will time both programs to evaluate their execution efficiency.

Pre-Lab

PROBLEM

A Fibonacci sequence of numbers is defined as follows:

$$F_0 = 0$$
$$F_1 = 1$$
$$F_n = F_{n-1} + F_{n-2}, \text{ for } n > 1$$

This says that the first two numbers in the sequence are 0 and 1. Then, each additional Fibonacci number is the sum of the two previous numbers in the sequence. Thus, if the value of *n* is 9, the Fibonacci sequence is

$$0, 1, 1, 2, 3, 5, 8, 13, 21, 34$$

Here, we say that the first number occupies position 0 in the sequence, the second number position 1 in the sequence, and so on. Thus, the last position in a ten-number sequence is position 9.

Develop a problem definition, set of algorithms, and program that employs a *recursive* function to generate a Fibonacci sequence of all numbers up to some position, *n*, entered by the user.

Defining the Problem

Output: What output is needed according to the problem statement?

_____

Can a function be used to produce the output? _____

Input: What input will be needed for processing to obtain the required output?

_____

Can you create a function to accept the needed input from the user? _____

Processing: The processing for a Fibonacci sequence can be divided into three cases depending on the position, *n*, of the last number in the sequence.

CASE 1: What processing is required if *n* is 0?

CASE 2: What processing is required if *n* is 1?

CASE 3: What processing is required for values of *n* greater than 1?

According to the problem statement, the output will be a display showing the Fibonacci sequence generated up to some position value of *n*. The final position, *n*, is needed as input from the user. A recursive function that uses the definition of a Fibonacci sequence given in the problem statement will be called repeatedly to generate each number in the sequence, from position 0 to position *n*.. If *n* is 0, the sequence is 0. If *n* is 1, the sequence is 0, 1. If *n* is greater than 1, the sequence is 0, 1, (the sum of the two previous numbers in the sequence up to position *n*).

Planning the Solution

Here is the initial algorithm that we will use:

main()
BEGIN
    Call a *setData()* function to set the last desired sequence position (*n*) from a user input.
    Call a *display()* function to generate the Fibonacci sequence (*Note*: This function will repeatedly call function *fib()* to generate each number in the sequence up to position *n*).
END.

Write an algorithm for the *setData()* function in the space provided.

setData()
BEGIN

END.

Complete the following questions to determine the *setData()* function interface.

Function *setData()*. What does this function do?

_____

Accepts: What data items must this function accept from its calling program to perform its designated task?

_____

Returns: What data items must this function return to its calling program?

_____

Will this function be a void function or a non-void function? _____

List any required parameters and designate each parameter as value or reference.

_____

Write a prototype/header for this function.

_____

fib() (*Note*: This function will be a recursive function that returns a Fibonacci number for a sequence position received by the function. It will be called repeatedly by the *display()* function for the arguments from 0 to *n* to generate the entire sequence.)

Write an algorithm for function *fib()* in the space provided. (*Hint:* Use a nested *if/else* statement for the two terminating conditions (0 and 1) and the recursive call.

fib()
BEGIN

END.

Complete the following questions to determine the *fib()* function interface.

Function *fib()*. What does this function do?

_____

Accepts: What data items must this function accept from its calling program to perform its designated task?

_____

Returns: What data items must this function return to its calling program?

_____

Will this function be a void function or a non-void function? _____

List any required parameters and designate each parameter as value or reference.

_____

Write a prototype/header for this function. (*Hint:* Use *long double* as the data type for the value returned by the *fib()* function. This will decrease the possibility that a given value will cause an overflow error.)

_____

display(): This function will repeatedly call the *fib()* function to generate the Fibonacci sequence from position 0 to position *n*.

Write an algorithm for function *display()* in the space provided. (*Hint:* Use a loop to repeatedly call the *fib()* function and display its returned value from position 0 to position *n* to generate the sequence. Insert commas and spacing between the Fibonacci numbers.)

display()
BEGIN

END.

182

Complete the following questions to determine the *display()* function interface definition.

Function *display()*. What does this function do?

_____

Accepts: What data items must this function accept from its calling program to perform its designated task?

_____

Returns: What data items must this function return to its calling program?

_____

Will this function be a void function or a non-void function?   _____

List any required parameters and designate each parameter as value or reference.

_____

Write a prototype/header for this function.

_____

 In-the-Lab

Coding the Program

✓ Start Your Editor

Start your C++ editor/IDE.

✓ Create a New Project

Make sure that a new file (and project if required) is open.

✓ Enter the Source Code

Using the algorithms that you developed, complete the following program shell for the Fibonacci sequence program:

```
// LAB 8-2 (L8_2.CPP)
// AUTHOR : type your name here
// DATE WRITTEN : type the date here
```

```
//PREPROCESSOR DIRECTIVES




// FUNCTION PROTOTYPES




int main()
{

// DEFINE VARIABLES




// CALL FUNCTION TO SET THE LAST SEQUENCE POSITION, n, FROM USER ENTRY




// CALL FUNCTION TO DISPLAY FIBONACCI SEQUENCE




return 0;
} // END MAIN

// setData(): THIS FUNCTION WILL SET THE LAST SEQUENCE POSITION FROM THE USER ENTRY

{




} // END setData()

// fib(): THIS RECURSIVE FUNCTION WILL RETURN THE FIBONACCI NUMBER FOR THE
// POSITION IT RECEIVES

{




} // END fib()
```

```
// display(): THIS FUNCTION WILL DISPLAY THE FIBONACCI SEQUENCE BY REPEATEDLY
// CALLING THE fib() FUNCTION

{




} // END display()
```

✓ Save the Program

After you have entered the source code, you need to save the program. Name this program *L8_2.cpp*.

Testing and Debugging the Program

✓ Compile the Program

Now that you have entered and saved the program, compile it.

✓ Errors?

If there were any errors in the program, you will have to edit the program code to fix the errors, and then compile the program again before you can link and run the program. Be sure to save the program again after you correct any errors.

✓ Link the Program

If you used a "compile" option rather than a "build" or "make" option, you may have to explicitly tell your compiler to link your program after compiling it.

✓ Run the Program

When the program is successfully compiled and linked, run it to make sure that it does what it is supposed to do.

✓ Check the Program Output

Test the program for the value $n = 35$, then try larger values of n. Notice that each successive number in the sequence takes more and more time to generate. Why is this? In fact, it may take longer than you expect to generate the entire sequence. Why does it take so long for large values of n?

Figure 8-4 shows a sample Fibonacci sequence generated by the program for $n = 35$. If your output is not similar, edit the program code so that it produces correct results.

Figure 8-4 Output generated by the Fibonacci sequence with 35 as the last sequence position.

Documenting the Program

✓Test and Print Sample Runs of the Program

Print out the program results. See *Printing Console Output From Microsoft Windows* in *Appendix A* if you are running Microsoft Windows and need help with this.

✓Print the Source Code

Get a printout of the program source code.

✓Fibonacci Using Iteration

Develop a set of algorithms and program that generates a Fibonacci sequence of all numbers up to some position, *n*, entered by the user *without* using recursion. You may look up the non-recursive formula for the Fibonacci sequence in a mathematics book, or you can use a couple of local variables and a little ingenuity in your *fib()* function to generate a number in the sequence using a loop rather than recursion.

The earlier recursive solution is more elegant and easier to program, but the iterative solution takes a little more thought from a programming standpoint. This is why we often prefer to use recursion over iteration, because a recursive solution is often much simpler from the programmer's perspective than its iterative counterpart.

Code your algorithms and name this program *L8_3.cpp*. Compile, link, run, test, and print this program. The output you get from this program should be identical to that obtained from the *L8_2.cpp* program.

Run the *L8_2.cpp* program again. Measure and record below the amount of time it takes this program to generate a Fibonacci sequence for a value of *n* = 50. Now run the *L8_3.cpp* program again. Measure and record below the amount of time it takes this program to generate a Fibonacci sequence for a value of *n* = 50.

L8_2.cpp execution time: _____

L8_3.cpp execution time: _____

186

What do you conclude about the speed of recursion versus iteration?

_____

_____

Why does the recursive program take so long? Think about it! There is a lot going on here. This is why we say that recursion is *elegant*. It is relatively easy to program, but there is a lot going on underneath within the compiler.

_____

_____

✓ Close the Files

When you are finished with the program files, make sure that you have saved any final changes, and then close the files (and projects or workspaces if required).

One-Dimensional Arrays

In this lab, you will . . .

♦ Define, fill, manipulate, and display one-dimensional arrays.

♦ Pass arrays to user-defined functions for manipulation.

♦ Sort array elements.

♦ Search an array for given elements.

♦ Use the STL vector class.

Chapter 9: Structured & Object-Oriented Problem Solving Using C++, 3rd edition, by Andrew C. Staugaard, Jr.

In this project, you will be working with the array data structure. Arrays provide an organized means for locating and storing data, just as the post office boxes in the post office lobby provide an organized means of locating and storing mail. The array data structure can be used to store just about any type of data, including integers, floats, characters, arrays, objects, and pointers. Arrays are so versatile that they can be used to implement other data structures, such as stacks, queues, linked lists, and binary trees. The array provides a convenient means of storing large amounts of data in primary, or user, memory.

There are both one-dimensional and multi-dimensional arrays. In this lab project, you will be using the one-dimensional array; in a later lab project, you will expand into multi-dimensional arrays.

The two major components of any array are the ***elements*** stored in the array and the ***indices*** that locate the stored elements. The elements of an array are the data stored in the array. The elements can be of any data type that you have studied so far. There is one major restriction to the array elements: *The elements in a given array must all be of the same data type*. The array indices locate the array elements. The C++ compiler automatically assigns integer indices to the array element list, beginning with index 0. The last element in an array is at some integer *n*. Because the indices begin with 0 and go to *n*, there are *n* + 1 elements in the array.

All arrays in C++ must be defined. You must specify the type of the data elements, the name of the array, and the size of the array in the definition. Refer to your text for more information on defining arrays.

To access the array elements, you must use direct assignment statements, read/write statements, or loops. The **for** loop structure is the most common way of accessing multiple array elements.

You can pass an entire array to a function or pass a single array element to a function. The important thing to remember is that, to pass the entire array, you must pass the address of the array. In C++, the ***array name*** always references the address of the array.

Searching and sorting are common operations performed on arrays. You will be using a ***binary search*** and a ***insertion sort*** in this lab project.

In Problem 1, you will develop a problem definition, a set of algorithms, and program code that defines a set of arrays to store the user's name, street address, city, state, zip code, and telephone number. You will use functions to fill and display the arrays. In Problem 2, you will develop a problem definition, a set of algorithms, and program code that sorts and searches an array of integers. In both problems, you will write the source code program that accepts the required input and produces an output report. You will compile, link, run, test, and print your programs.

In Problem 3, you will explore the C++ Standard Template Library's (STL) functionality by re-coding Project 2, using STL vectors in place of an array and the STL *sort()* and *find()* functions in place of the programmer-defined insertion sort and binary search functions. You can find more information on the STL vector class in Chapter 9 of Staugaard's text.

PROBLEM SOLVING REVIEW

Here is a problem from Staugaard's text that is similar to what you will be asked to do in this project. Read it over carefully and use it as a guide to complete the problems in this project.

PROBLEM

Develop a function that can be called to sequentially search an array of integers for a given element value and return the index of the element if it is found in the array.

Defining the Problem

Because we are dealing with a function, the problem definition will focus on the function interface. As a result, we must consider what the function will accept and what the function will return. Let's call the function *seqSearch()*. Now, from the problem statement, you find that the function must search an array of integers for a given element value. Thus, the function needs two things to do its job: (1) the array to be searched, and (2) the element for which to search. These will be our function parameters. Do these need to be value or reference parameters? Well, the function will not be changing the array or the element being searched for, right? Therefore, the parameters will be value parameters.

Next, we need to determine what the function is to return to the calling program. From the problem statement, you see that the function needs to return the index of the element being searched for if it is found in the array. All array indices in C++ are integers, so the function will return an integer value. But, what if the element being searched for is not found in the array? We need to return some integer value that will indicate this situation. Because array indices in C++ range from 0 to some finite positive integer, let's return the integer -1 if the element is not found in the array. Thus, we will use -1 to indicate the "not-found" condition, because no array index in C++ can have this value. Here is the function interface description:

Function *seqSearch()*: Searches an integer array for a given element value.

Accepts: An array of integers and the element for which to search.
Returns: The array index of the element if found, or the value -1
             if the element is not found.

The preceding function interface description provides all the information required to write the function interface. Here it is:

```
int seqSearch(int array[SIZE], int element)
```

The interface dictates that the function will accept two things: (1) an array of *SIZE* integer elements, and (2) an integer value, called *element*, that will be the value for which to search. The next task is to develop the sequential search algorithm.

190

Planning the Solution

Sequential search does exactly what it says: It *sequentially* searches the array, from one element to the next, starting at the first array position and stopping either when the element is found or when it reaches the end of the array. Thus, the algorithm must test the element stored in the first array position, then the second array position, then the third, and so on until the element is found or it runs out of array elements. This is obviously a repetitive task of testing an array element, then moving to the next element and testing again, and so on. Consider the following algorithm that employs a **while** loop to perform the repetitive testing operation:

seqSearch() **Algorithm**

```
seqSearch()
BEGIN
   Set found = false.
   Set index = first array index.
   While (element is not found) AND (index <= last array index)
      If (array[index] == element)
        Set found = true.
      Else
         Increment index.
   If (found == true)
      Return index.
   Else
      Return –1.
END.
```

The idea here is to employ a Boolean variable, called *found*, to indicate whether the element was found during the search. The variable *found* is initialized to false, and a variable called *index* is initialized to the index of the first element in the array. Notice the **while** loop test. Because of the use of the **AND** operator, the loop will continue as long as the element is not found *and* the value of *index* is less than or equal to the last index value of the array. Another way to say this is that the loop will repeat until the element is found *or* the value of *index* exceeds the last index value of the array. Think about it! Inside the loop, the value stored at location [*index*] is compared to the value of *element*, received by the function. If the two are equal, the Boolean variable *found* is set to true. Otherwise, the value of *index* is incremented to move to the next array position.

When the loop terminates, the element either was found or was not found. If the element was found, the value of *found* will be true, and the value of *index* will be the array position, or index, at which the element was found. Thus, if *found* is true, the value of *index* is returned to the calling program. If the element was not found, the value of *found* will still be false from its initialized state, and the value –1 is returned to the calling program. That's all there is to it!

Coding the Program

Here is the C++ code that reflects the foregoing algorithm:

```
/*
ACTION 9-1 (ACT09_01.CPP)
SEQUENTIAL SEARCH FUNCTION
*/
```

```
int seqSearch(int array[SIZE], int element)
{
  bool found = false;          //INITIALIZE found TO FALSE
  int i = 0;                   //ARRAY INDEX VARIABLE

//SEARCH ARRAY UNTIL FOUND OR REACH END OF ARRAY
  while ((!found) && (i < SIZE))
  {
    if (array[i] == element)   //TEST ARRAY ELEMENT
      found = true;            //IF EQUAL, SET found TO TRUE
    else                       //ELSE INCREMENT ARRAY INDEX
      ++i;
  } //END WHILE

//IF ELEMENT FOUND, RETURN ELEMENT POSITION IN ARRAY
//ELSE RETURN –1.
  if (found)
    return i;
  else
    return –1;
} //END seqSearch()
```

There should be no surprises in this code. At the top of the function, you see a header that is identical to the function interface developed earlier. The variable *found* is defined as a Boolean variable and set to false. We will use the variable *i* as our array index variable. This variable is defined as an integer and set to the first array index, 0. Remember that arrays in C++ always begin with index 0. The **while** loop employs the **AND** (&&) operator to test the values of *found* and *i*. The loop will repeat as long as the element is not found (!*found*) and the value of *i* is less than the size of the array, *SIZE*. Remember that, when the size of the array is *SIZE*, the last array index is *SIZE* – 1. So, when *i* exceeds the maximum array index, *SIZE* – 1, the loop breaks. When the loop is broken, the value of *found* is tested. If *found* is true, the value of *i* is returned; if *found* is false, the value –1 is returned to indicate that the element was not found in the array.

This code (ACT09_01.cpp) is available on Staugaard's text CD or can be downloaded from the text Web site at www.prenhall.com/staugaard. You may wish to compile and execute the code to observe its operation.

In this exercise, you will use C-string arrays to store the name, street address, city, state, zip code, and telephone number of the program user. You will develop a function to fill all the C-string arrays and a second function to display the arrays.

 # Pre-Lab

PROBLEM

Write a program that uses six character arrays to store the user's name, street address, city, state, zip code, and telephone number. Provide one function to fill the arrays and another to display the array contents in proper addressing format.

Defining the Problem

Output: What output is needed according to the problem statement?

_____

            Can a function be used to produce the output? _____

Input: What input will be needed for processing to obtain the required output?

_____

            Can a function be used to accept the input? _____

Processing: What processing is required to obtain the output?

_____

            Can a function be used to do the processing? _____

According to the problem statement, the output will be a properly formatted display showing the user's name, street address, city, state, zip code, and telephone number. The name, street address, city, state, zip code, and telephone number are needed as input. These items must be accepted as variable input from the keyboard. There is no processing required after the input data is accepted from the user. The input information will be stored in C-strings and simply echoed back out to the display. The input and output can be programmed, using functions that are called by *main()*.

Planning the Solution

Here is an initial algorithm for function *main()*.

main()
BEGIN
       Call a *fillArrays()* function to read the address information into the arrays.
       Call a *displayArrays()* function to display the address information stored in the arrays.
END.

       Notice that each function is called by *main()* to perform its designated task. Therefore the "calling program" is *main()*. Now, write the algorithm required for the *fillArrays()* function in the space provided.

fillArrays()
BEGIN

END.

Complete the following questions to determine the *fillArrays()* function interface definition.

Function *fillArrays()*. What does this function do?

_____

Accepts: What data items must this function accept to perform its designated task?

_____

Returns: What data items must this function return to the calling program?

_____

Will this function be a void function or a non-void function? _____

List any required parameters and designate each parameter as value or reference.

_____

Write a prototype/header for this function.

_____

Write the algorithm required for the *displayArrays( )* function in the space provided.

displayArrays( )
BEGIN

END.

Complete the following questions to determine the *displayArrays( )* function interface definition.

Function *displayArrays( )*. What does this function do?

_____

Accepts: What data items must this function accept to perform its designated task?

_____

Returns: What data items must this function return to the calling program?

_____

Will this function be a void function or a non-void function?   _____

List any required parameters and designate each parameter as value or reference.

_____

Write a prototype/header for this function.

_____

In-the-Lab

Coding the Program

✓ Start Your Editor

Start your C++ editor/IDE.

✓ Create a New Project

Make sure that a new file (and project if required) is open.

✓ Enter the Source Code

Using the algorithms and prototypes that you developed, complete the following program shell. (*Hint:* Use the C-string *getline()* function available in *iostream.h* to fill the arrays from the user entries.)

```
// LAB 9-1 (L9_1.CPP)
// AUTHOR : type your name here
// DATE WRITTEN : type the date here

//PREPROCESSOR DIRECTIVES




// DECLARE GLOBAL CONSTANTS FOR ARRAY SIZES




// FUNCTION PROTOTYPES




int main()
{
// DEFINE ARRAYS



```

// CALL FUNCTION TO FILL ARRAYS FROM USER ENTRIES

// CALL FUNCTION TO DISPLAY ARRAYS

return 0;

} // END main()

// fillArrays() THIS FUNCTION WILL FILL THE ARRAYS FROM USER ENTRIES

{

} // END fillArrays()

// displayArrays(): THIS FUNCTION WILL DISPLAY THE CONTENTS OF THE ADDRESS ARRAYS

{

} // END displayArrays()

✓ Save the Program

After you have entered the source code, you need to save the program. Name this program *L9_1.cpp*.

Testing and Debugging the Program

✓ Compile the Program

Now that you have entered and saved the program, compile it.

✓ Errors?

If there were any errors in the program, you will have to edit the program code to fix the errors, and then compile the program again before you can link and run the program. Be sure to save the program again after you correct any errors.

✓ Link the Program

If you used a "compile" option rather than a "build" or "make" option, you may have to explicitly tell your compiler to link your program after compiling it.

✓ Run the Program

When the program is successfully compiled and linked, run it to make sure that it does what it is supposed to do.

✓ Check the Program Output

A sample of the screen from the address program is shown in Figure 9-1. Your input and output should look similar to this. If not, edit your program code so that you obtain the correct output.

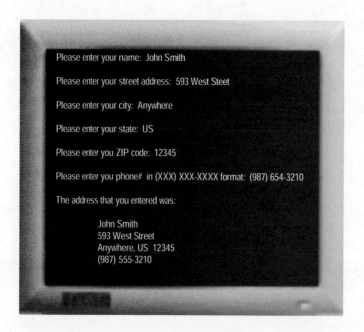

Figure 9-1 Sample screen for the address program.

Documenting the Program

✓ Observe the Program Execution with the Debugger

Use your debugger (if your environment has a debugger) to single-step the program execution and observe how the address arrays are filled during the execution of your program. Use a watch window to set a watch on the arrays so that you can observe them. (If you are using Microsoft Visual C++ 6, see *Appendix B* for help with the debugger.)

✓ Test and Print a Sample Run of the Program

Get print-outs of sample program runs for documentation. See *Printing Console Output From Microsoft Windows* in *Appendix A* if you are running Microsoft Windows and need help with this.

✓ Print the Source Code

Get a print-out of the program source code.

✓ Close the File

When you are finished with the program file, make sure that you have saved any final changes, and then close the file (and project or workspace if required).

In this exercise, you will develop a problem definition, a set of algorithms, and C++ program code that will randomly fill an integer array. You will then sort and search the array to find a value specified by the user.

 Pre-Lab

PROBLEM

Write a program that uses functions to fill an integer array with random values between 0 and 99, sort the array by using the insertion sort algorithm, prompt the user for an element to find within the sorted array (an integer element between 0 and 99), and finally, search for the specified element in the sorted array, using the recursive binary search algorithm. Display the following:

> appropriate messages to the user;
> the unsorted array;
> the sorted array;
> a message to the user that indicates whether the element was found in the search;
> the element and its index position, if the element was found.

Defining the Problem

Output: What output is needed according to the problem statement?

_____

Can a function be used to produce the output? _____

Input: What input will be needed for processing to obtain the required output?

_____

Can a function be used to accept the input? _____

Processing: What processing is required to obtain the specified output?

_____

_____

_____

Can functions be used to do the processing? If so, how? _____

_____

According to the problem statement, the output will be a display showing the unsorted integer array, the sorted array, the specified element, and its index position in the array. The array can be filled by using the standard *srand()* and *rand()* functions. (Consult your compiler's documentation or Chapter 5 in Staugaard's text for an explanation of *srand()* and *rand()*.) You will employ a function that uses the insertion sort algorithm for sorting the array and a function that uses the recursive binary search algorithm to search for the specified element. The binary search requires that the array be sorted prior to the search. It keeps dividing the array in half, directing itself to the half where the value is likely to be found.

Planning the Solution

Here is an initial algorithm for function *main()* using the input, output, and processing developed in the problem definition. Write an algorithm and prototype for each function.

BEGIN
        Call a *fillArray()* function to fill the array with random integer values.
        Call a *displayArray()* function to display the unsorted array.
        Call a *insertSort()* function to sort the array.
        Call a *displayArray()* function to display the sorted array
        Get a search element from the user.
        Call a *binSearch()* function to search the array for the element and display the element's position
        if found or a message that the element was not found.
END.

Write an algorithm for the *fillArray()* function to fill an array with random integer values from 0 to 99.

fillArray()
BEGIN

END.

Complete the following questions to determine the *fillArray()* function interface definition.

Function *fillArray()*. What does this function do?

_____

Accepts: What data items must this function accept to perform its designated task?

_____

Returns: What data objects must this function return to the calling program?

_____

Will this function be a void function or a non-void function? _____

List any required parameters and designate each parameter as value or reference.

_____

Write a prototype/header for this function.

_____

Write an algorithm for the *exchange()* function that will exchange any two variable values. This function will be called by *insertSort()* to exchange two integer elements.

exchange()
BEGIN

END.

Complete the following questions to determine the *exchange()* function interface definition.

Function *exchange()*. What does this function do?

_____

Accepts: What data items must this function accept to perform its designated task?

_____

Returns: What data items must this function return to the calling program?

_____

Will this function be a void function or a non-void function? _____

List any required parameters and designate each parameter as value or reference.

_____

Write a prototype/header for this function.

_____

Write an algorithm for the *insertSort()* function that will sort an array, using the insertion sort method. Make sure to call the *exchange()* function when two elements need to be exchanged.

insertSort( )
BEGIN

END.

Complete the following questions to determine the *insertSort()* function interface definition.

Function *insertSort()*. What does this function do?

_____

Accepts: What data items must this function accept to perform its designated task?

_____

Returns: What data items must this function return to the calling program?

_____

Will this function be a void function or a non-void function?   _____

List any required parameters and designate each parameter as value or reference.

_____

Write a prototype/header for this function.

_____

Write an algorithm for the *binSearch()* function that will search an array for a given value, using the recursive binary search method.

binSearch( )
BEGIN

END.

Complete the following questions to determine the *binSearch()* function interface definition.

Function *binSearch()*. What does this function do?

_____

Accepts: What data items must this function accept to perform its designated task?

_____

Returns: What data items must this function return to the calling program?

_____

Will this function be a void function or a non-void function? _____

List any required parameters and designate each parameter as value or reference.

_____

Write a prototype/header for this function.

_____

Write an algorithm for the *displayArray()* function that will display an integer array of a given size.

displayArray( )
BEGIN

END.

Complete the following questions to determine the *displayArray()* function interface definition.

Function *displayArray()*. What does this function do?

_____

Accepts: What data items must this function accept to perform its designated task?

_____

Returns: What data items must this function return to the calling program?

_____

Will this function be a void function or a non-void function? _____

List any required parameters and designate each parameter as value or reference.

_____

Write a prototype/header for this function.

_____

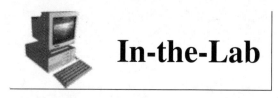

In-the-Lab

Coding the Program

✓ Start Your Editor

Start your C++ editor / IDE.

✓ Create a New Project

Make sure that a new file (and project if required) is open.

✓ Enter the Source Code

Make sure that a new file is open. Using the above algorithms and prototypes, complete the following program shell for filling, sorting, searching, and displaying the array. Make sure that you report whether the element being searched for was found in the array. If it is found, report the array index of the element.

```
// LAB 9-2 (L9_2.CPP)
// AUTHOR : type your name here
// DATE WRITTEN : type the date here

// PREPROCESSOR DIRECTIVES



// GLOBAL CONSTANT FOR ARRAY SIZE


// FUNCTION PROTOTYPES




int main()
{
// DEFINE ARRAYS AND VARIABLES



```

```
// CALL FUNCTION TO FILL THE ARRAY WITH RANDOM INTEGERS


// CALL FUNCTION TO DISPLAY THE RANDOM ARRAY


// CALL INSERTION SORT FUNCTION TO SORT THE ARRAY


// CALL FUNCTION TO DISPLAY THE SORTED ARRAY


// GET ELEMENT TO SEARCH FOR FROM THE USER




// CALL BINARY SEARCH FUNCTION AND DISPLAY ELEMENT POSITION IF FOUND AND
// MESSAGE IF NOT FOUND



return 0;

} // END main()

// fillArray():  THIS FUNCTION WILL FILL THE ARRAY WITH RANDOM NUMBERS

{




} // END fillArray()

// exchange(): THIS FUNCTION WILL EXCHANGE TWO INTEGER VALUES

{



} // END exchange()
```

```
// insertSort(): THIS FUNCTION WILL SORT THE ARRAY

{



} // END insertSort()
```

```
// binSearch(): THIS FUNCTION WILL SEARCH FOR A GIVEN ELEMENT

{



} // END binSearch()
```

```
// displayArray(): THIS FUNCTION WILL DISPLAY THE ARRAY CONTENTS

{



} // END displayArray()
```

✓ Save the Program

After you have entered the source code, you need to save the program. Name this program *L9_2.cpp*.

Testing and Debugging the Program

✓ Compile the Program

Now that you have entered and saved the program, compile it.

208

✓Errors?

If there were any errors in the program, you will have to edit the program code to fix the errors, then compile the program again before you can link and run the program. Be sure to save the program again after you correct any errors.

✓Link the Program

If you used a "compile" option rather than a "build" or "make" option, you may have to explicitly tell your compiler to link your program after compiling it.

✓Run the Program

When the program is successfully compiled and linked, run it to make sure that it does what it is supposed to do.

✓Check the Program Output

Figure 9-2 shows a sample screen from the sort and search program. If your output is not similar, edit the program code so that it produces correct results.

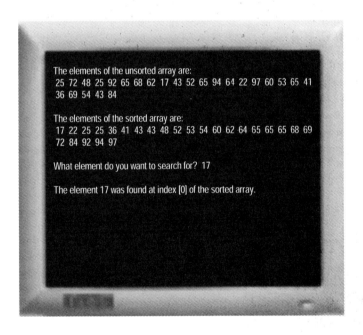

Figure 9-2 Array search and sort output.

Documenting the Program

✓Test and Print Sample Runs of the Program

Get a printout of sample program runs for documentation. See *Printing Console Output From Microsoft Windows* in *Appendix A* if you are running Microsoft Windows and need help with this.

✓ Print the Source Code

Get a printout of the program source code.

✓ Close the File

When you are finished with the program file, make sure that you have saved any final changes, and then close the file (and project or workspace if required).

In this exercise, you will be walked through the development of a problem definition, a set of algorithms, and a C++ program code that will randomly fill a Standard Template Library (STL) vector. You will be shown how to use the standard *sort()* function to sort the vector and the *find()* function to look for an element in the vector. Basically, you will see how to use the STL to create a program that runs identically to the program in Problem 2 from a user's standpoint, but it will take advantage of built-in C++ functionality.

Even though you will be sorting the vector with the *sort()* function before you search for an element with the *find()* function, the *find()* function does *not* require the vector to be sorted before you call it. This is in contrast to the *binSearch()* algorithm that you wrote in Problem 2, which required that the array be sorted before being searched.

***** *Note: Older compilers may not yet support the STL* *****

Pre-Lab

PROBLEM

Write a program that uses functions to fill a vector with random integer values between 0 and 99, sort the vector, prompt the user for an element to find within the sorted vector (an integer element between 0 and 99), and finally, search for the specified element in the sorted vector. Display the following:

appropriate messages to the user;
the unsorted vector;
the sorted vector;
a message to the user that indicates whether the element was found in the search;
if the element was found, the element and its index position.

Defining the Problem

Output: What output is needed, according to the problem statement?

_____

Can a function be used to produce the output? _____

Input: What input will be needed for processing to obtain the required output?

_____

Can a function be used to accept the input? _____

Processing: What processing is required to obtain the specified output?

_____

_____

_____

Can functions be used to do the processing? If so, how? _____

_____

According to the problem statement, the output will be a display showing the unsorted integer vector contents, the sorted vector contents, the specified element, and its index position in the sorted vector. The vector can be filled by using the standard *srand()* and *rand()* functions. (Consult your compiler's documentation or Chapter 5 in Staugaard's text for an explanation of *srand()* and *rand()*.) You will employ the C++ *sort()* function for sorting the vector and the C++ *find()* function to search the vector for the specified element.

Planning the Solution

Here is an initial algorithm for function *main()* using the input, output, and processing developed in the problem definition.

main()
BEGIN
    Call a *fillVector()* function to fill the vector with random integer values.
    Call a *displayVector()* function to display the unsorted vector.
    Call the standard C++ *sort()* function to sort the vector.
    Call a *displayVector()* function to display the sorted array
    Get a search element from the user.
    Call the standard C++ *find()* function to search the array for the element and display the element's
    position (if found) or a message that the element was not found.
END.

As you can see from the *main()* algorithm, there are really only two functions that you must write in this version of the program: *fillVector()* to fill the vector with random integers, and *displayVector()* to display a vector's contents. The *sort()* and *find()* functions already exist in the *algorithms* header file. Notice also that the *exchange()* function that was used in Problem 2 is no longer needed.

Here is an algorithm for the *fillVector()* function.

fillVector()
BEGIN
    For *i* = 0 to 9
        Call standard C++ vector *push_back()* function to insert a random integer (0-99) into the vector.
END.

The *fillVector()* function takes a vector and inserts 10 random numbers between 0 and 99 into it. It must accept the empty vector and return the filled vector; therefore, the vector object must be passed to the function by reference so that the changes made within the function are reflected in *main()*. The return type will be **void**, because, the data is being returned by way of the reference parameter. Here is a function prototype for *fillVector()*:

    void fillVector(vector <int> &v);

Next, here is an algorithm for our *displayVector()* function:

displayVector()
BEGIN
      For *vIterator*=first position in vector to last position in vector
         Write the contents of *vIterator*.
END

The *displayVector()* function takes a vector and displays its contents on the screen. It must accept the vector, and it does not return anything; therefore, the vector object must be passed to the function by value. The return type will be **void**, because no data are being returned. The variable *vIterator* refers to an iterator, which will be explained in more detail toward the end of this problem. Here is a function prototype for *displayVector()*.

    void displayVector(vector <int> v);

These algorithms look a little different from what you are used to seeing. Algorithms are written in pseudocode, so they typically are language independent, but these algorithms reference functions and data classes that are specific to C++. This is necessary in this particular case because we are writing the algorithm with the C++ Standard Template Library in mind.

 **In-the-Lab**

Coding the Program

✓ Start Your Editor

Start your C++ editor/IDE.

✓ Create a New Project

Make sure that a new file (and project if required) is open.

Make sure that a new file is open. Enter the following program, which was developed from the problem definition and algorithms above.

```cpp
// LAB 9-3 (L9_3.CPP)
// AUTHOR : type your name here
// DATE WRITTEN : type the date here

// PREPROCESSOR DIRECTIVES
#include <iostream>        //FOR cin AND cout
#include <algorithm>       //FOR sort() AND find()
#include <vector>          //FOR vector AND vector::iterator
using namespace std;

// FUNCTION PROTOTYPES
void fillVector(vector <int> &v);
void displayVector(vector <int> v);
int main()
{
    // DEFINE ARRAY AND VARIABLE OBJECTS
    vector <int> integerVector;                   //THIS IS THE VECTOR TO FILL, SORT,
                                                  //DISPLAY, AND SEARCH
    vector <int>::iterator integerVectorIterator; //THIS IS TO REFERENCE THE VECTOR
                                                  //ELEMENTS
                                                  //IT IS SIMILAR TO USING AN INTEGER INDEX
                                                  //TO REFERENCE AN ELEMENT OF AN ARRAY
    int searchNum;                                //THE NUMBER TO SEARCH FOR

    // CALL FUNCTION TO FILL THE ARRAY WITH RANDOM INTEGERS
    fillVector(integerVector);

    // CALL FUNCTION TO DISPLAY THE RANDOM ARRAY
    cout << "\nThe elements of the unsorted array are:" << endl;
    displayVector(integerVector);

    // CALL INSERTION SORT FUNCTION TO SORT THE ARRAY
    sort(integerVector.begin(),integerVector.end());
    cout << "\nThe elements of the sorted array are:" << endl;

    // CALL FUNCTION TO DISPLAY THE SORTED ARRAY
    displayVector(integerVector);

    // GET ELEMENT TO SEARCH FOR FROM THE USER
    cout << "\nWhat element do you want to search for?  ";
    cin >> searchNum;

    // CALL BINARY SEARCH FUNCTION AND DISPLAY ELEMENT POSITION IF FOUND AND
    // MESSAGE IF NOT FOUND
    integerVectorIterator = find(integerVector.begin(), integerVector.end(), searchNum);

    if(integerVectorIterator != integerVector.end())
    {
        cout << "\nThe element " << searchNum << " was found at index ["
            << integerVectorIterator - integerVector.begin() << "] of the sorted array" << endl;
    }
```

```
        else
        {
            cout << "\n" << searchNum << " was not found in the vector." << endl;
        }


        return 0;
} // END main()

// THIS FUNCTION WILL FILL THE ARRAY WITH RANDOM NUMBERS
void fillVector(vector <int> &v)
{
        //INITIALIZE RANDOM NUMBER GENERATION
        //NOTE: USING A CONSTANT NUMBER LIKE THIS MAY
        //   CAUSE THE PROGRAM TO GENERATE THE SAME
        //   SET OF NUMBER FOR EVERY RUN
        srand(1);

        //USE A FOR LOOP TO FILL THE VECTOR WITH 10 NUMBERS
        for(int loopCounter = 0; loopCounter < 10; ++loopCounter)
        {
            //CALL FUNCTION TO INSERT AN INTEGER INTO THE VECTOR
            //GENERATE THE RANDOM NUMBER AND SEND IT AS A PARAMETER
            v.push_back(rand() % 100);
        } //END for
}

// THIS FUNCTION WILL DISPLAY THE ARRAY CONTENTS
void displayVector(vector <int> v)
{
        vector<int>::iterator i;          //THIS IS FOR TRAVERSING THE VECTOR

        //LOOP THROUGH THE VECTOR UNTIL THE LAST ELEMENT IS REACHED
        for(i=v.begin();i!=v.end();i++)
        {
            //DISPLAY THE ELEMENT OF THE VECTOR IN ITERATOR POSITION i
            cout << *i << " ";
        }
        cout << endl;
}
```

In examining this code, you will notice some unfamiliar things. First, *vector* and *algorithm* have been included. These header files contain the vector class definition and the *sort()* and *find()* algorithms. The vector object is defined with the name of the class followed by the data type that the vector will contain enclosed in angle brackets, like this: < int >. The vector class is a **template** class, which means that you can define it to store any type of data you want simply by enclosing the type in the angle brackets when defining an object.

The iterator type (defined by *vector <int>::iterator*) is an example of a **pointer**. What this means is that it contains no data of its own; instead, it contains the memory address of some data that belongs to a different object—in this case, the vector. For this reason, when the *displayVector()* function uses an iterator to write a vector element to the screen, an asterisk (*) is placed in front of the iterator object so that the program **dereferences** the object. That is, rather than displaying the actual value of the object, it reads the value, which is a memory address, looks at that memory address, and displays the value that it finds at the memory address. Pointers are covered in depth in Chapter 13 of Staugaard's text, and programs dealing more specifically with pointers can be found in Project 13 of this lab manual.

Another area in the program where an iterator is used is at the *find()* function call. The *find()* function returns an iterator that references an element in the vector that matched the find criteria, or it references an area that is not actually part of the vector range that was searched. The latter case indicates that the element was not found.

The vector's *push_back()* function (used in *fillVector()*) inserts an element at the end of the vector. Its only parameter is the value to insert. The vector's *begin()* function returns an iterator that references the first element in the vector, and the *end()* function returns an iterator that references the element that, while not officially *in* the vector, is in the position directly after the last element of the vector. The *sort()* and *find()* functions both accept two iterators that define the range to sort or search within. Function *find()* also accepts the element for which to search. Sending *integerVector.begin()* and *integerVector.end()* to these functions tells the functions to operate on the entire vector.

The iterator can be used as the "counter" in the **for** loop within *displayVector()*, because the iterator's ++ operator will cause the iterator to reference the element in the vector that directly follows the element that it currently references. Therefore, it will start at the first element and traverse its way through the vector until it is equal to *v.end()* and terminates the **for** loop. It is also possible to use an integer variable as an index/loop counter to access elements by using the same syntax (*v[i]*) that you would use to access an array. In this case, the loop would terminate when *i* is equal to the size of the vector (*i<v.size()*). This is illustrated in Chapter 9 of Staugaard's text.

The iterator that references the found element in *main()* can also be used to find the position in the vector where the element resides by subtracting the iterator returned by the vector's *begin()* function. The difference between the two iterators' actual values (which, remember, are simply memory addresses) will be the position in the vector that the *find()* function has located.

✓Save the Program

After you have entered the source code, you need to save the program. Name this program *L9_3.cpp*.

Testing and Debugging the Program

✓Compile the Program

Now that you have entered and saved the program, compile it.

✓Errors?

If there were any errors in the program, you will have to edit the program code to fix the errors,
And then compile the program again before you can link and run the program. Be sure to save the program again after you correct any errors.

✓Link the Program

If you used a "compile" option rather than a "build" or "make" option, you may have to explicitly tell your compiler to link your program after compiling it.

✓Run the Program

When the program is successfully compiled and linked, run it to make sure that it does what it is supposed to do.

✓ Check the Program Output

Figure 9-3 shows a sample screen from the sort and search program. If your output is not similar, edit the program code so that it produces correct results.

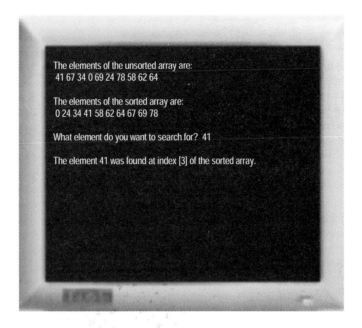

The elements of the unsorted array are:
41 67 34 0 69 24 78 58 62 64

The elements of the sorted array are:
0 24 34 41 58 62 64 67 69 78

What element do you want to search for? 41

The element 41 was found at index [3] of the sorted array.

Figure 9-3 Array search and sort output.

Documenting the Program

✓ Test and Print Sample Runs of the Program

Get a printout of sample program runs for documentation. See *Printing Console Output From Microsoft Windows* in *Appendix A* if you are running Microsoft Windows and need help with this.

✓ Print the Source Code

Get a printout of the program source code.

✓ Close the File

When you are finished with the program file, make sure that you have saved any final changes, and then close the file (and project or workspace if required).

✓ Compare Problem 2 and Problem 3

Look over the algorithms and code for lab problems 2 and 3. Notice that the main algorithm is basically the same. The actual implementation is different. Problem 3 is much nicer and cleaner, but it requires more knowledge of C++; Problem 2 requires only a basic understanding of the algorithms and could be implemented in any language.

Classes & Objects

OBJECTIVES

In this lab, you will . . .
- ♦ Declare classes and define objects for the classes.
- ♦ Implement class member functions to manipulate class data members.
- ♦ Develop an object-oriented application program.
- ♦ Create multi-file programs.

REQUIRED READING

Chapter 10: Structured & Object-Oriented Problem Solving Using C++, 3rd edition, by Andrew C. Staugaard, Jr.

INTRODUCTION

Object-oriented programs are developed from the inside out by expanding on simple classes. The fundamental components of any object-oriented program are the *class* and its *objects*. A given class provides the foundation for creating specific objects, each of which shares the general characteristics and behavior of the class.

At the abstract level, a class can be described as an interface, because it defines the behavior common to all of its objects. At the implementation level, a class is a programming construct that describes a set of data and related operations that are common to its objects. The abstract level provides an outside view of a class, while the implementation level provides the inside view of the class, disclosing its behavioral secrets.

At the implementation level, a class is comprised of a private section and a public section, each with members. Any item declared within a class is called a class *member*. To implement a class, you create public members and private members. Each of the public and private sections can consist of member functions and/or member data. The public member functions and data can be accessed anywhere within the scope of a given class. Public member data can be changed and member functions can be called from outside the class, as long as the class is visible at the time of access. The private member data and functions are accessible only by the member functions defined for the class. This means that the private member data can be changed only by the class's member functions and that private member functions can be called only by the public or other private member functions. The private class members are hidden from the outside; they can be accessed from outside the class only by using the public member functions of the class. This arrangement provides for *information hiding* within the class.

Encapsulation is the idea of packaging things together in a well-defined programming unit. A class in C++ is encapsulated, because it consists of a collection of data members and related function members. The class provides information hiding through its private member declarations.

An object is an instance of a class that can be manipulated in a program. Objects defined for a class share the fundamental framework of the class. Thus, an object of a given class has the structure and behavior defined by the class. You define an object for a class just as you define a variable for a simple data type. When the object is defined, memory is allocated to store the class for which the object is defined.

The format for declaring a class is shown here:

```
class class name
{
public:
  Public class member functions

private:
  Private class member data
  Private class member functions (utility functions)

};
```

Object-oriented programs normally are constructed by using a multifile approach. Class declarations are placed in separate header files. All the member function implementations for a given class are placed in a separate file that includes the class header file. Finally, the application program is placed in a separate file that includes all the class header files. The individual files are edited and compiled separately, then linked together to form an executable file. Most C++ IDE's include a project manager that facilitates the multifile approach to building programs. If you are using a command-line compiler, however, you will probably need to learn how to use a *makefile*. A makefile contains information that instructs the compiler about which files to include when compiling and linking all files together to form a single executable file. Consult your compiler documentation or a knowledgeable programmer for help in using makefiles.

In Problem 1, you will create an employee class and object; in Problem 2, you will create an invoice class and object. In both problems, you will declare the class in a header file, create an implementation file for the member functions, and develop an application program that defines an object for the class and tests the function implementations. You will then build a project file, linking the files that you have developed. You will compile, debug, run, test, and print the project files.

Here is a problem from Staugaard's text that is similar to what you will be asked to do in this project. Read it over carefully and use it as a guide to complete the problems in this project.

PROBLEM

Defining the Problem

Professional baseball has heard about C++ and they have hired you to write a simple program for their pitchers. The program must store the pitcher's name, team, wins, losses, winning percentage, and earned run average (ERA). In addition, a provision must be provided for the user to enter a given pitcher's stats as well as display a given pitcher's stats. Develop such a program using classes and objects.

The first thing to be done when developing an object-oriented program is to identify the nouns and verbs in the problem statement. Remember, the nouns suggest private data for the class and the verbs suggest functions for the class. Here is the problem statement again with the important nouns and verbs underlined:

The program must store the pitcher's <u>name</u>, <u>team</u>, <u>wins</u>, <u>losses</u>, <u>winning percentage</u>, and <u>ERA</u>. In addition, provision must be provided for the user to <u>enter</u> a given pitcher's data as well as <u>display</u> a given pitcher's data.

From the nouns and verbs, we develop a class specification as follows:

Class: *Pitcher*
      Function Members: *setStats()*
                         getStats()

      Data Members: *name*
                         team
                         wins
                         losses
                         winPercent
                         era

After analyzing the class members, a UML diagram can be constructed, as is shown in Figure 10-1. Notice how the UML diagram dictates that the constructor will initialize all the private members with the exclusion of *winPercent,* which will be calculated by the private *calculateWinPercent()* function shown at the bottom of the diagram. More about this shortly.

221

```
                              Pitcher

          -name:string
          -team:string
          -wins:int
          -losses:int
          -winPercent:double
          -era:double

          +Pitcher(in n:string = " ", in t:string = " ", in w:int = 0,
                     in l:int = 0, in era:double = 0.0)
          +setStats()
          +getStats()
          -calculateWinPercent()
```

Figure 10-1 A UML class diagram for the *Pitcher* class.

From the UML class diagram, we are ready to code the class. Here it is:

```
class Pitcher
{
//PUBLIC MEMBERS
public:

   //CONSTRUCTOR THAT INITIALIZES ALL PITCHER DATA EXCEPT WIN %
   Pitcher(string n = " ",string t = " ", int w = 0, int l = 0, double era = 0.0);

   //SET PITCHER STATS TO USER ENTRIES
   void setStats();

//GET AND DISPLAY STATS
void getStats();

//PRIVATE MEMBERS
private:
   string name;        //PITCHER'S NAME
   string team ;       //PITCHER'S TEAM
   int wins;           //NUMBER OF WINS
   int losses;         //NUMBER OF LOSSES
   double winPercent;  //WIN PERCENTAGE
   double era;         //EARNED RUN AVERAGE

   //UTILITY FUNCTION TO CALCULATE winPercent
   void calculateWinPercent();
}; // END Pitcher CLASS
```

First, look at the function members of the class. The first thing you see is a constructor. The constructor defines default parameters for each of the data members, except the winning percentage. Thus, you have the option of providing no arguments when defining an object for the class, or providing initializing values for each argument. If you do not supply any arguments, the default values will be used. If you supply arguments, the argument values are assigned to their respective data members. The remaining public members are the *setStats()* and *getStats()* function members that will obtain the pitcher stats from the user and display the pitcher stats, respectively.

222

Next, look at the data members of the class. Here you see all the data members that we found in the problem statement. In addition, you see a private function member called *calculateWinPercent()*. This function calculates the winning percentage, using the *wins* and *losses* data members. Such a function is called a **utility function** and must be called within a public function. This is an ideal application for a utility function, because it will be called only within the class, to calculate the *winPercent* data member, and does not need to be called from outside the class. You will see that our constructor function and *setStats()* function both call this function to initialize the *winPercent* data member.

Now, here are the function implementations:

```
//CONSTRUCTOR THAT INITIALIZES ALL PITCHER DATA EXCEPT
//WIN %
Pitcher :: Pitcher(string n,string t, int w, int l, double era)
{
    name = n;
    team = t;
    wins = w;
    losses = l;
    this -> era = era;
    calculateWinPercent();
}//END Pitcher(string,string,int,int,double)

//SET PITCHER STATS TO USER ENTRIES
void Pitcher :: setStats()
{
    //PROMPT AND READ PITCHER STATS
    cout << "Enter the pitcher's name: ";
    cin >> ws;
    getline(cin,name);
    cout << "Enter the pitcher's team: ";
    cin >> ws;
    getline(cin,team);
    cout << "Enter the number of wins for " << name << ": ";
    cin >> wins;
    cout << "Enter the number of losses for " << name << ": ";
    cin >> losses;
    cout << "Enter the era " << name << ": ";
    cin >> era;
    calculateWinPercent();
}//END setStats()

//GET AND DISPLAY STATS
void Pitcher :: getStats()
{
    cout << "\nPitcher name: " << name << endl;
    cout << "\tTeam: " << team << endl;
    cout << "\tNumber of wins: " << wins << endl;
    cout << "\tNumber of losses: " << losses << endl;
    cout << "\tWinning percentage: " << winPercent << endl;
    cout << "\tERA: " << era << endl;
}//END getStats()

void Pitcher :: calculateWinPercent()
{
    if ((wins + losses) == 0)
      winPercent = 0.0;
    else
      winPercent = (double)wins/(wins + losses) * 100;  //TYPE CASTING
}//END calculateWinPercent
```

As you can see, the constructor does its job of initializing the private data members. In particular, notice how the constructor calls the private *calculateWinPercent()* function to initialize the winning percentage. The next function, *setStats()*, prompts the user and reads the user entries for the private members. Again, notice that the *calculateWinPercent()* function is called to determine *winPercent* member value after the *wins* and *losses* have been set by the user. The *getStats()* function simply displays the pitcher data stored by the private data members of the class. Now, look at the *calculateWinPercent()* function. This is a private function, so it cannot be called from outside the class and must be called by a public function member of the class. You see that it contains an **if/else** statement. Why? Because if both *wins* and *losses* were zero, a run-time error would occur and the program would crash. So, the **if/else** statement protects against division by zero. Last, you see something that you have not seen before. The statement

```
winPercent = (double)wins/(wins + losses) * 100;  //TYPE CAST
```

includes what is called a ***type cast***. A type cast temporarily converts data of one type to a different type. The type cast is created by the code (double) in the preceding statement. Without the type cast to double, the calculation would always be 0. Why? Because *wins* and *losses* are both integers. When you divide two integers, you get an integer. Since (wins + losses) will always be greater than *wins*, integer division will always give you a result of 0. The type cast forces a double floating-point result, which is what we need for our *winPercent* member. Remember this little trick, because it often comes in handy. We should caution you, however, that type casting should be used only when really necessary, as it is in the above application. If you find yourself doing a lot of type casting, then you have probably not data-typed your variables properly when they were defined. This is why we have not discussed type casting until now.

Now, the last thing to do is to create an application program to exercise our *Pitcher* class. Here is the complete program:

```
/*
ACTION 10-1(ACT10_01.CPP)
*/

//PREPROCESSOR DIRECTIVES
#include <iostream>      //FOR cin AND cout
#include <string>        //FOR string CLASS

using namespace std;     //REQUIRED WHEN INCLUDING iostream

//PITCHER CLASS DECLARATION
class Pitcher
{
//PUBLIC MEMBERS
public:

  //CONSTRUCTOR THAT INITIALIZES ALL PITCHER DATA EXCEPT WIN %
  Pitcher(string n = " ",string t = " ", int w = 0, int l = 0, double era = 0.0);

  //SET PITCHER STATS TO USER ENTRIES
  void setStats();

  //GET AND DISPLAY STATS
  void getStats();

  //PRIVATE MEMBERS
  private:
    string name;      //PITCHER'S NAME
```

```cpp
    string team ;      //PITCHER'S TEAM
    int wins;        //NUMBER OF WINS
    int losses;      //NUMBER OF LOSSES
    double winPercent; //WIN PERCENTAGE
    double era;        //EARNED RUN AVERAGE

   //UTILITY FUNCTION TO CALCULATE winPercent
   void calculateWinPercent();
}; // END Pitcher CLASS

//MAIN FUNCTION
int main()
{
    //DEFINE PITCHER OBJECT
    Pitcher JohnSmoltz;

    //CALL PITCHER FUNCTIONS
    JohnSmoltz.setStats();
    JohnSmoltz.getStats();

    //RETURN
    return 0;

}//END main()

//PITCHER CLASS FUNCTION IMPLEMENTATIONS

//CONSTRUCTOR THAT INITIALIZES ALL PITCHER DATA EXCEPT
//WIN %
Pitcher :: Pitcher(string n,string t, int w, int l, double era)
{
    name = n;
    team = t;
    wins = w;
    losses = l;
    this -> era = era;
    calculateWinPercent();
}//END Pitcher(string,string,int,int,double)

//SET PITCHER STATS TO USER ENTRIES
void Pitcher :: setStats()
{
    //PROMPT AND READ PITCHER STATS
    cout << "Enter the pitcher's name: ";
    cin >> ws;
    getline(cin,name);
    cout << "Enter the pitcher's team: ";
    cin >> ws;
    getline(cin,team);
    cout << "Enter the number of wins for " << name << ": ";
    cin >> wins;
    cout << "Enter the number of losses for " << name << ": ";
    cin >> losses;
    cout << "Enter the era " << name << ": ";
    cin >> era;
    calculateWinPercent();
}//END setStats()
```

```
//GET AND DISPLAY STATS
void Pitcher :: getStats()
{
    cout << "\nPitcher Name: " << name << endl;
    cout << "\tTeam: " << team << endl;
    cout << "\tNumber of wins: " << wins << endl;
    cout << "\tNumber of losses: " << losses << endl;
    cout << "\tWinning percentage: " << winPercent << endl;
    cout << "\tERA: " << era << endl;
}//END getStats()

void Pitcher :: calculateWinPercent()
{
    if ((wins + losses) == 0)
      winPercent = 0.0;
    else
      winPercent = (double)wins/(wins + losses) * 100;  //TYPE CASTING
}//END calculateWinPercent
```

The application program is called *act10_01.cpp*. Notice that a *JohnSmoltz* object is defined for our *Pitcher* class, inside *main()*. The default initializing values will be used because no arguments are provided with the object definition. The *JohnSmoltz* object is then used to call the *setStats()* and *getStats()* functions to allow the user to enter the pitcher data and display the data, respectively. That's it! Now you are ready to build your own object-oriented programs. Here, we have placed all the code in one file. In the problems that follow, you will place the class code in a separate header file, the function code in a separate implementation file, and the code for *main()* in a separate application file. You will then use your compiler's project manager, or a makefile if you are using a command-line compiler, to compile and link all three files. Consult your compiler documentation on how to do this. You can refer to *Appendix B* if you are using Visual C++.

This code (act10_01.cpp) is available on Staugaard's text CD or can be downloaded from the text Web site at www.prenhall.com/staugaard. You may wish to compile and execute the code to observe its operation.

In this exercise, you will declare an employee class in a header file, create an implementation file for the member functions, and develop an application program that defines an object for the employee class and tests the function implementations. You will compile, debug, run, test, and print the project files.

 # Pre-Lab

PROBLEM

Write an application program that defines an object for an employee class and tests the required functions to produce an employee's payroll report including the employee's name, hourly rate, hours worked, and weekly pay. Assume that overtime is paid at a "time and a half" rate for any weekly hours worked over 40.

Defining the Problem

The following problem definition will be used when creating the functions for this problem.

Output: What output is needed, according to the problem statement?

_____

Can a function be used to produce the output? _____

Input: What input will be needed for processing to obtain the required output?

_____

Can a function be used to accept the input? _____

Processing: What processing is required to obtain the output?

_____

Can a function be used to do the processing? _____

According to the problem statement, the output will be a display showing the employee's name, hourly rate, hours worked, and weekly pay. The employee's name, hourly rate, and hours worked are needed as input. To process the weekly pay, you will test the hours to determine whether they are less than, equal to, or greater than 40. If the hours are less than or equal to 40, the weekly pay will simply be hours worked multiplied by the hourly rate. If the hours worked are greater than 40, the weekly pay will be 40 multiplied by the hourly rate for regular pay and any hours over 40 multiplied by 1.5 times the hourly rate for overtime pay.

Defining the Problem for the Employee Class

What will you name this class? _____

List the members that need to be declared public in this class:

_____

List the members that need to be declared private in this class:

_____

Planning the Solution for the Employee Class

Following is a list of functions required for implementing the members of the employee class. Write algorithms for these functions from the information you developed in the problem definition. Remember, if class function members are operating directly on class data members, the data members are not passed or returned by the functions.

- Constructor function to initialize the private data members.
- Function to set the employee name, hourly rate, and hours worked from user entries..
- Function to calculate the weekly pay.
- Function to get and display the employee name, hourly rate, hours worked, and weekly pay.

CONSTRUCTOR FUNCTION TO INITIALIZE THE PRIVATE DATA MEMBERS.
   BEGIN

   END.

What will you name this function? _____

What does this function do? _____

Which class data members are operated on by this function? _____

_____

Does this function need to accept or return any data from outside of the class? _____ If so, list the required data items: _____

Write a function header using the scoping operator, ::, to make the connection between the class and function.

_____

228

FUNCTION TO SET THE EMPLOYEE NAME, HOURLY RATE, AND HOURS WORKED FROM
USER ENTRIES
    BEGIN

    END.

What will you name this function? _____

What does this function do? _____

Which class data members are operated on by this function? _____

_____

Does this function need to accept or return any data from outside of the class? _____ If so, list the
required data items: _____

Write a function header using the scoping operator, ::, to make the connection between the class and
function.

_____

FUNCTION TO CALCULATE THE WEEKLY PAY
    BEGIN

    END.

What will you name this function? _____

What does this function do? _____

Which class data members are operated on by this function? _____

_____

Does this function need to accept or return any data from outside of the class? _____ If so, list the
required data items: _____

Write a function header using the scoping operator, ::, to make the connection between the class and function.

_____

FUNCTION TO DISPLAY THE EMPLOYEE NAME, HOURLY RATE, HOURS WORKED, AND WEEKLY PAY

BEGIN

END.

What will you name this function? _____

What does this function do? _____

Which class data members are operated on by this function? _____

_____

Does this function need to accept or return any data from outside of the class? _____ If so, list the required data items: _____

Write a function header using the scoping operator, ::, to make the connection between the class and function.

_____

Construct a UML class diagram for the employee class, using the member descriptions you developed above.

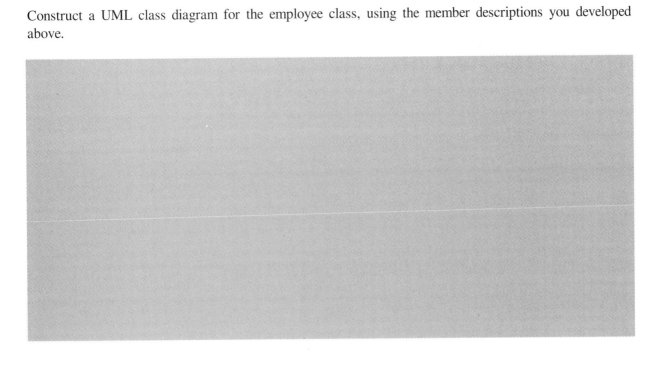

Planning the Solution for the Application Program

Write the algorithm for the steps to be carried out by function *main()* in the application program. Remember, *main()* must define an employee object, then use this object to call the public class functions.

main()
BEGIN

END.

In-the-Lab

Coding the Program

✓ Start Your Editor

Start your C++ editor/IDE.

✓ Create a New Project

Make sure that a new file (and project if required) is open.

✓ Write the Program

Employee Class Header File
Using the class UML diagram that you developed, complete the following header file shell.

```
// LAB 10_1 (EMPLOYEE.H)
// AUTHOR : type your name here
// DATE WRITTEN : type the date here

#ifndef EMPLOYEE_H
#define EMPLOYEE_H

// DECLARE EMPLOYEE CLASS
class
{
public:




private:




};
#endif
```

After you have entered the source code for the class declaration, save the header file with the name *employee.h*.

Employee Class Implementation File
Open a new file for the function implementation file. Using the function headers and algorithms that you developed, complete the following implementation file shell.

```
// LAB 10-1 (EMPLOYEE.CPP)
// AUTHOR : type your name here
// DATE WRITTEN : type the date here
```

//PREPROCESSOR DIRECTIVES

#include "employee.h"   // USE THE " " TO INCLUDE THE EMPLOYEE HEADER FILE
                          // SINCE IT IS LOCATED IN THE WORKING DIRECTORY.

// CONSTRUCTOR IMPLEMENTATION

// IMPLEMENTATION OF FUNCTION TO SET DATA FROM USER ENTRIES

// IMPLEMENTATION OF FUNCTION TO CALCULATE WEEKLY PAY

// IMPLEMENTATION OF FUNCTION TO GET AND DISPLAY DATA

After you have entered the source code for the function implementation, save the file with the name *employee.cpp*.

Application File

Open a new file for the application program. Using the *main()* algorithm that you developed, complete the following application program shell to define an object for the employee class and test the implementation functions that you have written.

```
// LAB 10-1 (L10_1.CPP)
// AUTHOR : type your name here
// DATE WRITTEN : type the date here

//PREPROCESSOR DIRECTIVES



#include "employee.h"    // USE THE " " TO INCLUDE THE EMPLOYEE HEADER FILE
                         // SINCE IT IS LOCATED IN THE WORKING DIRECTORY.

int main ()
{
// DEFINE Employee OBJECT



//CALL FUNCTION TO SET VALUES FROM USER ENTRIES
```

//CALL FUNCTION TO DISPLAY EMPLOYEE PAYROLL INFORMTION

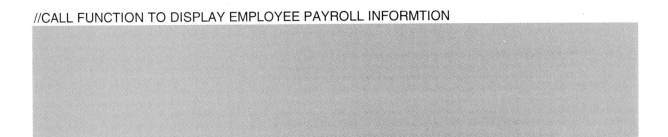

return 0;

} // END main()

After you have entered the source code for the application program, save the file with the name *L10_1.cpp*.

✓ Compile the Program

Now that you have entered and saved all the files, compile your program. Depending on your environment, the method to do this may vary. Most IDE's have a "Make" or "Build" option that will compile all of the files at one time. If you are working with a command line compiler, you may have to develop a makefile. Consult your compiler documentation or a knowledgeable programmer for instructions on how to do this for your particular compiler. Consult *Appendix B* if you are using Visual C++.

✓ Errors?

If there were any errors in the program, you will have to edit the program code to fix the errors, then compile the program again before you can link and run the program. Remember that, when your header file contains a syntax error (such as forgetting a semi-colon after closing a class definition) compilers often register the error in the implementation file rather than in the header file. If you have a tough time getting your entire program to compile at once, try compiling it one file at a time. Be sure to save any files that you change *before* you try to compile again.

✓ Link the Program

If you used a "compile" option rather than a "build" or "make" option, you may have to explicitly tell your compiler to link your program after compiling it.

Testing and Debugging the Program

✓ Run the Program

When the program is successfully compiled and linked, run it to make sure that it does what it is supposed to do.

✓ Check the Program Output

A sample of the screen from the employee payroll project is shown in Figure 10-2. Your program should look similar to this.

Figure 10-2 Sample output for the test score average program

Documenting the Program

✓ Test and Print a Sample Run of the Program

Get sample print-outs of the program runs for documentation. See *Printing Console Output From Microsoft Windows* in *Appendix A* if you are running Microsoft Windows and need help with this.

✓ Print the Source Code

Print a source code listings of your program files, including the header file, function implementation file, and application program file.

✓ Close the File

When you are finished with the program file, make sure that you have saved any final changes, and then close the file (and project or workspace if required).

In this exercise, you will declare an invoice class in a header file, create an implementation file for the member functions, and develop an application program that defines an object for the invoice class and tests the function implementations. Finally, you will build a project file linking the files that you have developed. You will compile, debug, run, test, and print the project file.

 # Pre-Lab

PROBLEM

Write an application program that defines an object for an invoice class and tests the required functions to produce an invoice report. Assume that the invoice must include the following data and functions:

> *Data:*
> Quantity Ordered
> Quantity Shipped
> Part Number
> Part Description
> Unit Price
> Extended Price
> Sales-Tax Rate
> Sales-Tax Amount
> Shipping
> Total

> *Functions:*
> - A constructor function to initialize all the data items to 0 except the sales tax rate, which should be initialized to 5%.
> - A function to allow the user to initialize the data items from the keyboard.
> - A function to calculate the extended price of the item.
> - A function to calculate the sales tax amount of the item.
> - A function to calculate the total amount of the invoice.
> - A function to display the invoice data with header information in a business-like format.

Defining the Problem

Output: What output is needed according to the problem statement?

_____

Can a function be used to produce the output? _____

Input: What input will be needed for processing to obtain the required output?

_____

                      Can a function be used to accept the input? _____

Processing: What processing is required to calculate the extended price of the item?

_____

_____

                      What processing is required to calculate the sales tax amount?

_____

_____

                      What processing is required to calculate the total amount on the invoice?

_____

_____

                      Can functions be used to do the processing? _____

According to the problem statement, the output will be a display of the invoice data in a business-like format. Because the quantity ordered might be different than the quantity shipped, you should display any quantity backordered. The part number, part description, unit price, quantity ordered, quantity shipped, and amount of shipping are needed as input. To process the extended price, the quantity shipped must be multiplied by the unit price. To process the amount of sales tax on the order, multiply the extended price by the sales-tax rate. The invoice total is simply the sum of the extended price, the sales tax amount, and the amount of shipping.

Before you can develop an application program, you need to declare an invoice class in a header file and develop the implementations for the required functions in an implementation file. Finally, you can create a project to combine the separate files into a working application.

PROBLEM STATEMENT FOR THE CLASS

Declare an invoice class as part of a header file. The class is to have data members to store the following:

        Quantity Ordered
        Quantity Shipped
        Part Number
        Part Description
        Unit Price
        Extended Price
        Sales-Tax Rate
        Sales-Tax Amount
        Shipping
        Total

The class is to have member functions to perform the following tasks:

- A constructor function to initialize all the data items to 0, except the sales-tax rate, which should be initialized to 5%.
- A function to allow the user to initialize the data items from the keyboard.
- A function to calculate the extended price of the item.
- A function to calculate the sales tax amount of the item.
- A function calculate the total amount of the invoice.
- A function to display the invoice data with header information in a business-like format.

Defining the Problem for the Invoice Class

What will you name this class? _____

List the members that need to be declared public in this class:

_____

List the members that need to be declared private in this class:

_____

Planning the Solution for the Employee Class

Write algorithms for the class functions from the information you developed in the problem definition. Remember, if class function members are operating on class data members, the data members are not passed or returned by the functions.

CONSTRUCTOR FUNCTION TO INITIALIZE THE DATA MEMBERS.
  BEGIN

  END.

What will you name this function? _____

What does this function do? _____

Which class data members are operated on by this function? _____

_____

Does this function need to accept or return any data from outside of the class? _____ If so, list the required data items: _____

Write a function header using the scoping operator, ::, to make the connection between the class and function.

_____

FUNCTION TO SET THE INVOICE VALUES FROM USER INFORMATION
BEGIN

END.

What will you name this function? _____

What does this function do? _____

Which class data members are operated on by this function? _____

_____

Does this function need to accept or return any data from outside of the class? _____ If so, list the required data items: _____

Write a function header using the scoping operator, ::, to make the connection between the class and function.

_____

FUNCTION TO CALCULATE THE EXTENDED UNIT PRICE
BEGIN

END.

What will you name this function? _____

What does this function do? _____

Which class data members are operated on by this function? _____

_____

Does this function need to accept or return any data from outside of the class? _____ If so, list the
required data items: _____

Write a function header using the scoping operator, ::, to make the connection between the class and
function.

_____

FUNCTION TO CALCULATE THE SALES-TAX AMOUNT
BEGIN

END.

What will you name this function? _____

What does this function do? _____

Which class data members are operated on by this function? _____

_____

Does this function need to accept or return any data from outside of the class? _____ If so, list the
required data items: _____

Write a function header using the scoping operator, ::, to make the connection between the class and
function.

_____

FUNCTION TO CALCULATE TOTAL INVOICE AMOUNT
BEGIN

END.

What will you name this function? _____

What does this function do? _____

Which class data members are operated on by this function? _____

_____

Does this function need to accept or return any data from outside of the class? _____ If so, list the

241

required data items: _____

Write a function header using the scoping operator, ::, to make the connection between the class and function.

_____

FUNCTION TO DISPLAY THE INVOICE INFORMATION
    BEGIN

    END.

What will you name this function? _____

What does this function do? _____

Which class data members are operated on by this function? _____

_____

Does this function need to accept or return any data from outside of the class? _____ If so, list the required data items: _____

Write a function header using the scoping operator, ::, to make the connection between the class and function.

_____

Construct a UML class diagram for the invoice class, using the member descriptions you developed above.

Planning the Solution for the Application Program

Write the algorithm for function *main()* in the application program to process the invoice by using the functions your developed.. Remember, *main()* must define an invoice object, then use this object to call the public class functions.

main()
BEGIN

END.

 In-the-Lab

Coding the Program

✓ Start Your Editor

Start your C++ editor/IDE.

✓ Create a New Project

Make sure that a new file (and project if required) is open.

✓ Write the Program

Make sure that a new file is open. Using the class UML diagram that you developed, complete the following header file shell.

```
// LAB 10-2 (INVOICE.H)
// AUTHOR : type your name here
// DATE WRITTEN : type the date here

#ifndef INVOICE_H
#define INVOICE_H

// DECLARE INVOICE CLASS
class
{
public:




private:



};

#endif
```

After you have entered the source code for the class declaration, save the header file with the name *invoice.h*.

Invoice Class Implementation File
Open a new file for the function implementation file. Using the function headers and algorithms that you developed, complete the following implementation file shell.

```
// LAB 10-2 (INVOICE.CPP)
// AUTHOR : type your name here
// DATE WRITTEN : type the date here

// PREPROCESSOR DIRECTIVES



#include "invoice.h"        // USE THE " " TO INCLUDE THE EMPLOYEE HEADER FILE
                           // SINCE IT IS LOCATED IN THE WORKING DIRECTORY.

//CONSTRUCTOR IMPLEMENTATION
```

// IMPLEMENTATION OF FUNCTION TO SET INVOICE INFORMATION FROM USER ENTRIES

// IMPLEMENTATION OF FUNCTION TO CALCULATE EXTENDED INVOICE AMOUNT

// IMPLEMENTATION OF FUNCTION TO CALCULATE SALES TAX AMOUNT

// IMPLEMENTATION OF FUNCTION TO CALCULATE INVOICE TOTAL AMOUNT

// IMPLEMENTATION OF FUNCTION TO DISPLAY INVOICE INFORMATION

After you have entered the source code for the function implementation, save the file with the name *invoice.cpp*.

245

Application File

Open a new file for the application program. Using the *main()* algorithm that you developed, complete the following application program shell to define an object for the invoice class and test the implementation functions that you have written.

```
// LAB 10-2 (L10_2.CPP)
// AUTHOR : type your name here
// DATE WRITTEN : type the date here

//PREPROCESSOR DIRECTIVES




#include "invoice.h"          // USE THE " " TO INCLUDE THE INVOICE HEADER FILE
                             // SINCE IT IS LOCATED IN THE WORKING DIRECTORY.

int main ()
{
    // DEFINE Invoice OBJECT



    //CALL FUNCTION TO SET ORDERING INFORMATION FROM USER INFORMATION


    //CALL FUNCTION TO CALCULATE THE EXTENDED INVOICE PRICE


    //CALL FUNCTION TO CALCULATE THE SALES TAX AMOUNT


    //CALL FUNCTION TO CALCULATE THE INVOICE TOTAL


    //CALL FUNCTION TO DISPLAY THE INVOICE


    return 0;

} // END main ()
```

After you have entered the source code for the application program, save the file with the name *L10_2.cpp*.

✓ Compile the Program

Now that you have entered and saved all the files, compile your program. Depending on your environment, the method to do this may vary. Most IDE's have a "Make" or "Build" option that will compile all of the files at one time. If you are working with a command-line compiler, you may have to develop a makefile. Consult your compiler documentation or a knowledgeable programmer for instructions on how to do this for your particular compiler.

✓ Errors?

If there were any errors in the program, you will have to edit the program code to fix the errors, then compile the program again before you can link and run the program. Remember that, when your header file contains a syntax error (such as forgetting a semi-colon after closing a class definition) compilers often register the error in the implementation file rather than in the header file. If you have a tough time getting your entire program to compile at once, try compiling it one file at a time. Be sure to save any files that you change *before* you try to compile again.

✓ Link the Program

If you used a "compile" option rather than a "build" or "make" option, you may have to explicitly tell your compiler to link your program after compiling it.

Testing and Debugging the Program

✓ Run the Program

When the program is successfully compiled and linked, run it to make sure that it does what it is supposed to do.

✓ Check the Program Output

A sample of the input screen from the invoice project is shown in Figure 10-3, and a sample output screen is shown in Figure 10-4. Your input and output should look similar to these.

Documenting the Program

✓ Test and Print Sample Runs of the Program

Get a print-out of a few program runs. See *Printing Console Output From Microsoft Windows* in *Appendix A* if you are running Microsoft Windows and need help with this.

✓ Print the Source Code

Get a print-out of all your program source-code files.

Figure 10-3 Sample input screen for the invoice project

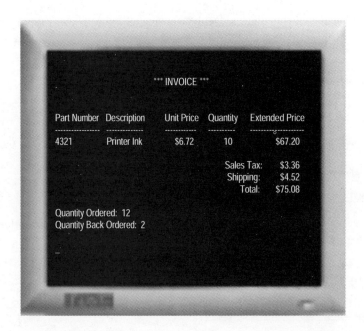

Figure 10-4 Sample output screen for the invoice project

✓ Close the File

When you are finished with the program file, make sure that you have saved any final changes, and then close the file (and project or workspace if required).

Inheritance

OBJECTIVES

In this lab, you will . . .
- ◆ Declare base classes and derived classes.
- ◆ Implement class member functions to manipulate class data members.
- ◆ Define objects for the classes in application programs.
- ◆ Implement your projects using multifile programs.

REQUIRED READING

*Chapter 11: Structured & Object-Oriented Problem Solving Using C++, 3rd edition,
by Andrew C. Staugaard, Jr.*

INTRODUCTION

One of the most important properties of object-oriented programming is ***inheritance***. Inheritance allows newly created classes to inherit members from existing classes. These new ***derived classes*** will include their own members and members inherited from the ***base class***. A collection of classes with common, inherited members are related to each other through inheritance. Such inheritance creates a class hierarchy, or family. The derived class should always be related to its base class via the IS-A relationship.

A base class is declared by using the following format:

> **class** *base class name*
> {
> **public:**
> *Public base class member functions*
>
> **protected:** (OR) **private:**
>   *Protected/private base class member data*
>   *Protected/private base class member functions (utility functions)*
> };

A derived class is declared using the following format:

> **class** *derived class name* : **public** *base class name*
> {
> **public:**
> *Public derived class member functions*
>
> **protected:** (OR) **private:**
>   *Protected/private derived class member data*
>   *Protected/private derived class member functions (utility functions)*
> };

Notice that the base class is declared public in the derived class declaration. This allows the inherited members of the public base class to maintain their access level in the derived class. The members declared as protected have accessibility that is somewhere between that of a private member and a public member. If a member is a private member of a base class, it is not accessible to a derived class. However, a protected member of a base class is accessible to any derived classes. On the other hand, a protected member is "protected" from being accessed outside of the class family, thereby preserving data hiding within the family. You control the amount of data member inheritance by designating the members as private, protected, or public in the base-class declaration.

In Problem 1, you will declare a bank account base class and a credit card derived class. In Problem 2, you will declare a resistor circuit base class. You will then declare series and parallel circuit derived classes. In both problems, you will declare the classes in header files, create implementation files for the member functions, and develop application programs that define objects for the classes and test the function implementations. You will then build a project file, linking the files that you have developed. You will compile, debug, run, test, and print the project files.

In this exercise, you will declare a bank account base class and a credit card account derived class in header files. You will create an implementation file for the member functions. Then you will develop an application program that defines an object for the credit card class and tests the function implementations. Finally, you will build a project linking the files that you have developed. You will compile, debug, run, test, and print the files.

 # Pre-Lab

PROBLEM

Write an application program that defines an object for a credit card class that is derived from a general bank account class. The program should test the required functions to add monthly charges and interest to the card holder's account balance and to subtract monthly credit card payments from the account balance. Produce a credit card statement, reporting the name of the card holder, the account number, the beginning account balance, the monthly credit card charges, the monthly payments, the interest charged at a 15% annual rate of the unpaid account balance, and the ending account balance.

Defining the Problem

Output: What output will be produced, according to the problem statement?

_____

Input: What input will be needed for processing to obtain the required output?

_____

Processing: What processing is required to calculate the new account balance, without interest?

_____

What processing is required to calculate the interest on the new account balance?

_____

What processing is required to calculate the ending account balance, including interest?

_____

According to the problem statement, the program must produce a credit card statement reporting the name of the card holder, the account number, the beginning account balance, the monthly credit card charges, the monthly payments, the interest charged at a 15% annual rate of the unpaid account balance, and the ending account balance. The name of the card holder, the account number, the beginning bank account balance, the monthly payments, and the monthly credit card charges are needed as input from the user. To calculate a new account balance, you will add the monthly credit card charges and subtract the monthly payments from the beginning account balance. To calculate the interest, you will multiply the new balance by 0.15/12. To calculate the ending account balance, you must add the calculated interest to the new account balance.

Before you can develop an application program, you need to declare a bank account base class and a derived credit card class in header files and develop the implementations for the required functions in an implementation file. Finally, you create an application file that defines an object to test your credit card class.

PROBLEM STATEMENT FOR THE BANK ACCOUNT CLASS

Declare a bank account base class as part of a header file. The class is to have data members to store an account number and account balance. The class is to have member functions to perform the following tasks:

- ◆ A function to set the account number from a user entry.
- ◆ A function to set the account balance from a user entry.
- ◆ A function to get the account number.
- ◆ A function to get the account balance.

PROBLEM STATEMENT FOR THE CREDIT CARD CLASS

Declare a derived credit card class to inherit the bank account class members. In addition, it will contain data members to store the card holder's name, monthly credit card charges, monthly payments, interest rate, and interest due. The class is to have member functions to perform the following tasks:

- ◆ A constructor function to initialize the account data members.
- ◆ A function to set the card holder's account information from user entries.
- ◆ A function to add monthly credit card charges to the account balance.
- ◆ A function to subtract the monthly payments from the account balance.
- ◆ A function to calculate and add the monthly interest to the account balance.
- ◆ A function to display the credit card statement.

Defining the Problem for the Bank Account Base Class

What will you name this class? _____

List the members that need to be declared public in this base class:

_____

List the members that need to be declared protected/private in this base class:

_____

Defining the Problem for the Credit Card Derived Class

What will you name this class? _____

Which members will this derived class inherit from its base class? _____

List the additional members that need to be declared public in this derived class:

_____ _____

List the additional members that need to be declared protected/private in this derived class:

_____

Construct a Venn diagram for the class family.

Planning the Solution for the Bank Account Base Class

Write algorithms for the implementation of the functions listed in the bank account base-class problem statement, using the information you developed in the problem definitions.

FUNCTION TO SET THE ACCOUNT NUMBER FROM A USER ENTRY
   BEGIN

   END.

What will you name this function? _____

What does this function do? _____

Which class data members are operated on by this function? _____

_____

Does this function need to accept or return any data from outside of the class? _____ If so, list the required data items: _____

Write a function header using the scoping operator, ::, to make the connection between the class and function.

_____

FUNCTION TO SET THE ACCOUNT BALANCE FROM A USER ENTRY
   BEGIN

   END.

What will you name this function? _____

What does this function do? _____

Which class data members are operated on by this function? _____

_____

Does this function need to accept or return any data from outside of the class? _____ If so, list the required data items: _____

Write a function header using the scoping operator, ::, to make the connection between the class and function.

_____

FUNCTION TO GET THE ACCOUNT NUMBER
   BEGIN

   END.

What will you name this function? _____

What does this function do? _____

Which class data members are operated on by this function? _____

_____

Does this function need to accept or return any data from outside of the class? _____ If so, list the
required data items: _____

Write a function header using the scoping operator, ::, to make the connection between the class and
function.

_____

FUNCTION TO GET THE ACCOUNT BALANCE
   BEGIN

   END.

What will you name this function? _____

What does this function do? _____

Which class data members are operated on by this function? _____

_____

Does this function need to accept or return any data from outside of the class? _____ If so, list the
required data items: _____

Write a function header using the scoping operator, ::, to make the connection between the class and
function.

_____

Construct a UML class diagram for the bank account base class, using the member descriptions you developed above.

Planning the Solution for the Credit Card Derived Class

Write algorithms for the implementation of the functions listed in the credit card class problem statement, using the information you developed in the problem definitions.

CONSTRUCTOR FUNCTION TO INITIALIZE THE CLASS DATA MEMBERS.
   BEGIN

   END.

What will you name this function? _____

What does this function do? _____

Which class data members are operated on by this function? _____

_____

Does this function need to accept or return any data from outside of the class? _____ If so, list the required data items: _____

Write a function header using the scoping operator, ::, to make the connection between the class and function.

_____

256

FUNCTION TO SET THE CARD HOLDER ACCOUNT INFORMATION FROM USER ENTRIES
    BEGIN

    END.

    What will you name this function? _____

    What does this function do? _____

    Which class data members are operated on by this function? _____

    _____

    Does this function need to accept or return any data from outside of the class? _____ If so, list the
    required data items: _____

    Write a function header using the scoping operator, ::, to make the connection between the class and
    function.

    _____

FUNCTION TO ADD CREDIT CARD CHARGES
    BEGIN

    END.

    What will you name this function? _____

    What does this function do? _____

    Which class data members are operated on by this function? _____

    _____

    Does this function need to accept or return any data from outside of the class? _____ If so, list the
    required data items: _____

Write a function header using the scoping operator, ::, to make the connection between the class and function.

_____

FUNCTION TO SUBTRACT MONTHLY PAYMENTS
    BEGIN

    END.

What will you name this function? _____

What does this function do? _____

Which class data members are operated on by this function? _____

_____

Does this function need to accept or return any data from outside of the class? _____ If so, list the required data items: _____

Write a function header using the scoping operator, ::, to make the connection between the class and function.

_____

FUNCTION TO CALCULATE AND ADD THE MONTHLY INTEREST
    BEGIN

    END.

What will you name this function? _____

What does this function do? _____

Which class data members are operated on by this function? _____

_____

Does this function need to accept or return any data from outside of the class? _____ If so, list the required data items: _____

Write a function header using the scoping operator, ::, to make the connection between the class and function.

_____

FUNCTION TO DISPLAY CREDIT CARD STATEMENT
   BEGIN

   END.

What will you name this function? _____

What does this function do? _____

Which class data members are operated on by this function? _____

_____

Does this function need to accept or return any data from outside of the class? _____ If so, list the required data items: _____

Write a function header using the scoping operator, ::, to make the connection between the class and function.

_____

Construct a UML class diagram for the credit card derived class, using the member descriptions you developed above.

Planning the Solution for the Application Program

Write the algorithm for function *main()* in the application program. Remember to define a credit card object and call the functions required to process a credit card account.

main()
BEGIN

END.

In-the-Lab

Coding the Program

✓ Start Your Editor

Start your C++ editor/IDE.

✓ Create a New Project

Make sure that a new file (and project if required) is open.

✓ Write the Program

Bank Account Header File

Make sure that a new file is open. Using the bank account base-class UML diagram that you developed, complete the following header file shell.

```
// LAB 11-1 (ACCOUNT.H)
// AUTHOR : type your name here
// DATE WRITTEN : type the date here

#ifndef ACCOUNT_H
#define ACCOUNT_H

// DECLARE BANK ACCOUNT  BASE CLASS
```

```
#endif
```

After you have entered the source code for the class declaration, save the header file with the name *account.h*.

Credit Card Header File

Make sure that a new file is open. Using the credit card derived-class UML diagram that you developed, complete the following header file shell.

```
// LAB 11-1 (CARD.H)
// AUTHOR : type your name here
// DATE WRITTEN : type the date here

#include "account.h"        // USE THE " " TO INCLUDE THE HEADER FILE
                            // SINCE IT IS LOCATED IN THE WORKING DIRECTORY.


// DECLARE CREDIT CARD DERIVED CLASS
```

After you have entered the source code for the class declaration, save the header file with the name *card.h*.

Bank Account Implementation File

Open a new file for the bank account function implementation file. Using the base-class function headers and algorithms that you developed, complete the following implementation file shell.

```
// LAB 11-1 (ACCOUNT.CPP)
// AUTHOR : type your name here
// DATE WRITTEN : type the date here

#include "account.h"        // USE THE " " TO INCLUDE THE HEADER FILE
                            // SINCE IT IS LOCATED IN THE WORKING DIRECTORY.

// IMPLEMENTATION OF FUNCTION TO SET THE ACCOUNT NUMBER FROM USER



// IMPLEMENTATION OF FUNCTION TO SET THE BEGINNING BALANCE FROM USER
```

// IMPLEMENTATION OF FUNCTION TO GET THE ACCOUNT NUMBER

// IMPLEMENTATION OF FUNCTION TO GET THE ACCOUNT BALANCE

After you have entered the source code for the function implementations, save the file with the name *account.cpp*.

Credit Card Implementation File
Open a new file for the credit card function implementation file. Using the credit card function headers and algorithms that you developed, complete the following implementation file shell.

```
// LAB 11-1 (CARD.CPP)
// AUTHOR : type your name here
// DATE WRITTEN : type the date here

#include "card.h"          // USE THE " " TO INCLUDE THE HEADER FILE
                           // SINCE IT IS LOCATED IN THE WORKING DIRECTORY.
```

// IMPLEMENTATION OF CONSTRUCTOR FUNCTION

// IMPLEMENTATION OF FUNCTION TO SET CARD ACCOUNT INFORMATION FROM USER

// IMPLEMENTATION OF FUNCTION TO ADD THE MONTHLY CREDIT CARD CHARGES

// IMPLEMENTATION OF FUNCTION TO SUBTRACT THE MONTHLY PAYMENTS

// IMPLEMENTATION OF FUNCTION TO CALCULATE AND ADD MONTHLY INTEREST

// IMPLEMENTATION OF FUNCTION TO DISPLAY CREDIT CARD STATEMENT

After you have entered the source code for the function implementations, save the file with the name *card.cpp*.

Application File

Open a new file for the application program. Using the algorithm that you developed for *main()*, complete the following application program shell to define an object for the credit card class, and test the implementation functions that you have written.

```
// LAB 11-1 (CHARGE.CPP)
// AUTHOR : type your name here
// DATE WRITTEN : type the date here

#include <iostream>
#include "account.h"          // USE THE " " TO INCLUDE THE HEADER FILES
#include "card.h"             // SINCE THEY ARE LOCATED IN THE WORKING DIRECTORY.

using namespace std;

int main ()
{

// DEFINE CREDIT CARD OBJECT
```

```
// CALL FUNCTIONS FOR MONTHLY CREDIT CARD TRANSACTIONS
```

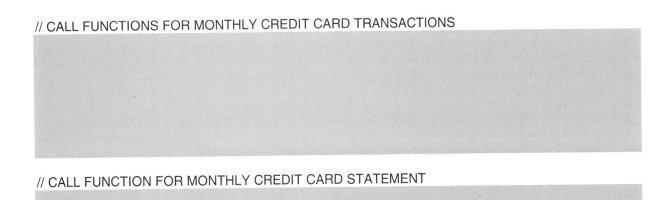

```
// CALL FUNCTION FOR MONTHLY CREDIT CARD STATEMENT
```

```
return 0;
} END main ()
```

After you have entered the source code for the application program, save the file with the name *charge.cpp*.

Testing and Debugging the Program

✓ Compile the Program

Now that you have entered and saved all the files, compile your program. Depending on your environment, the method to do this may vary. Most IDE's have a "Make" or "Build" option that will compile all of the files at one time. If you are working with a command-line compiler, you may have to develop a make file. Consult your compiler documentation or a knowledgeable programmer for instructions on how to do this for your particular compiler. If you are using Visual C++, you can refer to *Appendix B*.

✓ Errors?

If there were any errors in the program, you will have to edit the program code to fix the errors, then compile the program again before you can link and run the program. Remember that when your header file contains a syntax error (such as a forgotten semicolon in closing a class definition), compilers often register the error as in the implementation file rather than in the header file. If you have a tough time getting your entire program to compile at once, try compiling it one file at a time. Be sure to save any files that you change *before* you try to compile again.

✓ Link the Program

If you used a "compile" option rather than a "build" or "make" option, you might have to explicitly tell your compiler to link your program after compiling it.

✓ Run the Program

When the program is successfully compiled and linked, run it to make sure that it does what it is supposed to do.

✓ Check the Program Output

A sample of a program implementation for typical set of transactions is shown in Figure 11-1. Make sure your program produces an output similar to this one.

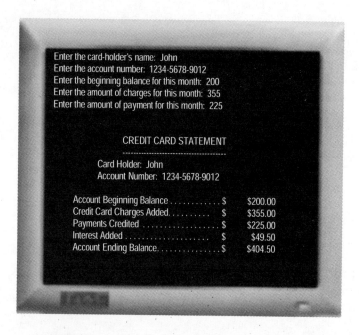

Enter the card-holder's name: John
Enter the account number: 1234-5678-9012
Enter the beginning balance for this month: 200
Enter the amount of charges for this month: 355
Enter the amount of payment for this month: 225

CREDIT CARD STATEMENT

Card Holder: John
Account Number: 1234-5678-9012

Account Beginning Balance . . . . $ $200.00
Credit Card Charges Added . . . . $ $355.00
Payments Credited . . . . $ $225.00
Interest Added . . . . $ $49.50
Account Ending Balance . . . . $ $404.50

Figure 11-1 Sample credit card program screen.

Documenting the Program

✓ Test and Print a Sample Run of the Program

Get print-outs of sample program runs for documentation.

✓ Print the Source Code

Get a print-out of all program source code files.

✓ Close the File

When you are finished with the program file, make sure that you have saved any final changes, and then close the file (and project or workspace if required).

In this exercise, you will declare a resistor circuit base class in a header file and two derived classes for a series circuit and a parallel circuit that inherit the resistor circuit base-class members. You will create implementation files for the member functions, develop an application program that defines an object for the classes, and test the function implementations. Finally, you will build a project file linking the files that you have developed. You will compile, debug, run, test, and print the project file.

Pre-Lab

PROBLEM

Write an application program that defines a series resistance object and a parallel resistance object from a resistor circuit base class. Include statements in the program that test the required functions, allowing the user to enter the number of resistors in the circuit and the resistor values. The program must display the resistor values along with the equivalent resistance of both a series circuit and a parallel circuit.

Defining the Problem

Output: What output will be produced, according to the problem statement?

_____

Input: What input will be needed for processing to obtain the required output?

_____

Processing: What processing is required to calculate the equivalent resistance of a series circuit?

_____

What processing is required to calculate the equivalent resistance of a parallel circuit?

_____

According to the problem statement, the output will be a display reporting the resistor values along with the equivalent resistance of a series circuit and a parallel circuit. The number of resistors and the resistor values are needed as input from the user. The formula to calculate the equivalent resistance of a series circuit is $R_s = R_1 + R_2 + \ldots + R_n$. This is simply the sum of the resistor values. The formula to calculate the equivalent resistance of a parallel circuit is $R_p = 1/(1/R_1 + 1/R_2 + \ldots + 1/R_n)$. This is the inverse of the sum of the inverses of the resistor values.

Before you can develop an application program, you need to declare a resistor circuit base class and derived classes for the series circuit and the parallel circuit in header files, and develop the implementations for the required functions in an implementation file. Finally, you can create a project to combine the separate files into a working application.

PROBLEM STATEMENT FOR THE RESISTOR CIRCUIT BASE CLASS

Declare a resistor circuit base class as part of a header file. The class is to have the following members:

Function Members:

- ♦ A constructor function initializing the resistors to 0.
- ♦ A function that will allow the user to enter the number of resistors in the circuit and the resistor values.
- ♦ A function that will display the resistor values along with the equivalent resistance of the circuit.

Data Members:

- ♦ The resistor values stored in an array.
- ♦ The number of resistors in the circuit.
- ♦ The equivalent resistance of the circuit.

PROBLEM STATEMENT FOR THE SERIES CIRCUIT DERIVED CLASS

Declare a series circuit class inherited from the resistor circuit class, with the following added:

- ♦ A function to calculate the equivalent resistance of a series circuit.

PROBLEM STATEMENT FOR THE PARALLEL CIRCUIT DERIVED CLASS

Declare a parallel circuit class inherited from the resistor circuit class, with the following added:

- ♦ A function to calculate the equivalent resistance of a parallel circuit.

Defining the Problem for the Resistor Circuit Base Class

What will you name this class? _____

List the members that need to be declared public in this base class:

_____

List the members that need to be declared protected/private in this base class:

_____

Defining the Problem for the Series Circuit Derived Class

What will you name this class? _____

Which members will this derived class inherit from its base class? _____

List the additional members that need to be declared public in this derived class:

_____

List the additional members that need to be declared protected/private in this derived class:

_____

Defining the Problem for the Parallel Circuit Derived Class

What will you name this class? _____

Which members will this derived class inherit from its base class? _____

List the additional members that need to be declared public in this derived class:

_____

List the additional members that need to be declared protected/private in this derived class:

_____

Construct a Venn Diagram for the class family.

Planning the Solution for the Resistor Circuit Base Class

Write algorithms for the implementation of the functions listed in the class problem statement, using the information you developed in the problem definition.

CONSTRUCTOR FUNCTION TO INITIALIZE THE CIRCUIT VALUES TO ZERO
   BEGIN

   END.

What will you name this function? _____

What does this function do? _____

Which class data members are operated on by this function? _____

_____

Does this function need to accept or return any data from outside of the class? _____ If so, list the required data items: _____

Write a function header using the scoping operator, ::, to make the connection between the class and function.

_____

FUNCTION TO SET THE NUMBER OF RESISTORS AND THEIR VALUES FROM USER
   BEGIN

   END.

What will you name this function? _____

What does this function do? _____

Which class data members are operated on by this function? _____

_____

Does this function need to accept or return any data from outside of the class? _____ If so, list the

required data items: _____

Write a function header using the scoping operator, ::, to make the connection between the class and function.

_____

FUNCTION TO DISPLAY THE RESISTOR VALUES AND EQUIVALENT RESISTANCE
    BEGIN

    END.

What will you name this function? _____

What does this function do? _____

Which class data members are operated on by this function? _____

_____

Does this function need to accept or return any data from outside of the class? _____ If so, list the required data items: _____

Write a function header using the scoping operator, ::, to make the connection between the class and function.

_____

Construct a UML class diagram for the resistor circuit base class, using the member descriptions you developed above.

Planning the Solution for the Series Circuit Derived Class

Write algorithms for the implementation of the functions listed in the series circuit class problem statement, using the information you developed in the problem definition.

FUNCTION TO CALCULATE THE EQUIVALENT RESISTANCE OF A SERIES CIRCUIT
    BEGIN

    END.

    What will you name this function? _____

    What does this function do? _____

    Which class data members are operated on by this function? _____

    _____

    Does this function need to accept or return any data from outside of the class? _____ If so, list the
    required data items: _____

    Write a function header using the scoping operator, ::, to make the connection between the class and
    function.

    _____

Construct a UML class diagram for the series circuit derived class, using the member descriptions you
developed above.

Planning the Solution for the Parallel Circuit Derived Class

Write algorithms for the implementation of the functions listed in the parallel circuit class problem statement, using the information you developed in the problem definition.

FUNCTION TO CALCULATE EQUIVALENT RESISTANCE OF A PARALLEL CIRCUIT
   BEGIN

   END.

What will you name this function? _____

What does this function do? _____

Which class data members are operated on by this function? _____

_____

Does this function need to accept or return any data from outside of the class? _____ If so, list the required data items: _____

Write a function header using the scoping operator, ::, to make the connection between the class and function.

_____

Construct a UML class diagram for the parallel circuit derived class, using the member descriptions you developed above.

273

Planning the Solution for the Application Program

Write the algorithm for function *main()* in the application program.

main()
BEGIN

END.

In-the-Lab

Coding the Program

✓ Start Your Editor

Start your C++ editor/IDE.

✓ Create a New Project

Make sure that a new file (and project if required) is open.

✓ Write the Program

Resistor Circuit Header File
Make sure that a new file is open. Using the resistor base class UML diagram that you developed, complete the following header file shell.

```
// LAB 11-2 (RESISTOR.H)
// AUTHOR : type your name here
// DATE WRITTEN : type the date here

#ifndef RESISTOR_H
#define RESISTOR_H
// DECLARE RESISTOR  BASE CLASS
```

#endif

After you have entered the source code for the class declaration, save the header file with the name *resistor.h*.

Series Circuit Header File
Make sure that a new file is open. Using the series class UML diagram that you developed, complete the following header file shell.

// LAB 11-2 (SERIES.H)
// AUTHOR : type your name here
// DATE WRITTEN : type the date here

#include "resistor.h"

// DECLARE SERIES CIRCUIT DERIVED CLASS

After you have entered the source code for the class declaration, save the header file with the name *series.h*.

Parallel Circuit Header File
Make sure that a new file is open. Using the parallel class UML diagram that you developed, complete the following header file shell.

// LAB 11-2 (PARALLEL.H)
// AUTHOR : type your name here
// DATE WRITTEN : type the date here

#include "resistor.h"

// DECLARE PARALLEL CIRCUIT DERIVED CLASS

After you have entered the source code for the class declaration, save the header file with the name *parallel.h*.

Resistor Class Implementation File
Open a new file for the resistor circuit function implementation file. Using the resistor class function headers and algorithms that you developed, complete the following implementation file shell.

```
// LAB 11-2 (RESISTOR.CPP)
// AUTHOR : type your name here
// DATE WRITTEN : type the date here

#include "resistor.h"
```

// IMPLEMENTATION OF CONSTRUCTOR FUNCTION

// IMPLEMENTATION OF FUNCTION TO SET NUMBER OF RESISTORS AND VALUES FROM USER

// IMPLEMENTATION OF FUNCTION TO DISPLAY THE RESISTOR VALUES
// AND EQUIVALENT RESISTANCE

After you have entered the source code for the function implementation, save the file with the name *resistor.cpp*.

276

Series Circuit Implementation File

Open a new file for the series circuit function implementation file. Using the header and algorithm that you developed for the series class function, complete the following implementation file shell.

```
// LAB 11-2 (SERIES.CPP)
// AUTHOR : type your name here
// DATE WRITTEN : type the date here

#include "series.h"

// IMPLEMENTATION OF FUNCTION TO CALCULATE THE EQUIVALENT SERIES RESISTANCE
```

After you have entered the source code for the function implementation, save the file with the name *series.cpp*. Compile the file.

Parallel Circuit Implementation File

Open a new file for the parallel circuit function implementation file. Using the header and algorithm that you developed for the parallel class function, complete the following implementation file shell.

```
// LAB 11-2 (PARALLEL.CPP)
// AUTHOR : type your name here
// DATE WRITTEN : type the date here

#include "parallel.h"

// IMPLEMENTATION OF FUNCTION TO CALCULATE THE EQUIVALENT PARALLEL RESISTANCE
```

After you have entered the source code for the function implementation, save the file with the name *parallel.cpp*. Compile the file.

Application File

Open a new file for the application program. Using the algorithm that you developed for *main()*, complete the following application program shell to define objects for the series class and the parallel class. Then, use these objects to test the functions that you have written.

```
// LAB 11-1 (CIRCUIT.CPP)
// AUTHOR : type your name here
// DATE WRITTEN : type the date here

#include <iostream>
#include "series.h"
#include "parallel.h"
using namespace std;
int main ()
{
// DEFINE ANY NEEDED VARIABLES




// DEFINE SERIES RESISTANCE AND PARALLEL RESISTANCE OBJECTS




// CALL FUNCTION TO SET NUMBER OF RESISTORS AND THEIR VALUES FROM USER




// CALL FUNCTION TO CALCULATE EQUIVALENT RESISTANCE OF THE SERIES CIRCUIT




// CALL FUNCTION TO DISPLAY SERIES RESISTOR REPORT




// CALL FUNCTION TO CALCULATE EQUIVALENT RESISTANCE OF THE PARALLEL CIRCUIT




// CALL FUNCTION TO DISPLAY PARALLEL RESISTOR REPORT




return 0;
} END main ()
```

After you have entered the source code, you need to save the program. Name this program *circuit.cpp*.

Testing and Debugging the Program

✓ Compile the Program

Now that you have entered and saved all the files, compile your program. Depending on your environment, the method to do this may vary. Most IDE's have a "Make" or "Build" option that will compile all of the files at one time. If you are working with a command-line compiler, you may have to develop a make file. Consult your compiler documentation or a knowledgeable programmer for instructions on how to do this for your particular compiler. Consult *Appendix B* if you are using Visual C++.

✓ Errors?

If there were any errors in the program, you will have to edit the program code to fix the errors, then compile the program again before you can link and run the program. Remember that when your header file contains a syntax error (such as a forgotten semicolon in closing a class definition), compilers often register the error in the implementation file rather than in the header file. If you have a tough time getting your entire program to compile at once, try compiling it one file at a time. Be sure to save any files that you change *before* you try to compile again.

✓ Link the Program

If you used a "compile" option rather than a "build" or "make" option, you might have to explicitly tell your compiler to link your program after compiling it.

✓ Run the Program

When the program is successfully compiled and linked, run it to make sure that it does what it is supposed to do.

✓ Check the Program Output

A sample input/output screen for the circuit program is shown in Figure 11-2. Your input and output should look similar to this.

Documenting the Program

✓ Test and Print Sample Runs of the Program

Get print-outs of a few program runs. See *Printing Console Output from Microsoft Windows* in *Appendix A* if you are running Microsoft Windows and need help with this.

✓ Print the Source Code

Get a print-out of the program source code.

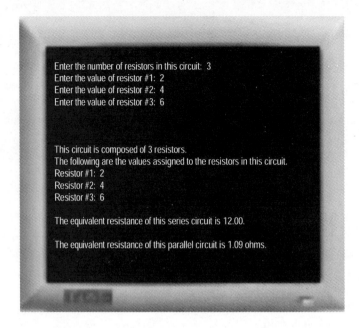

Figure 11-2 Sample input and output for the series and parallel resistor circuits.

✓ Close the File

When you are finished with the program file, make sure that you have saved any final changes, and then close the file (and project or workspace if required).

File I/O

In this lab, you will . . .
- Use classes to define and implement file input and output operations.
- Create menu driven projects to write, read, append, and change file data.

Chapter 12: Structured & Object-Oriented Problem Solving Using C++, 3rd edition,
by Andrew C. Staugaard, Jr.

A file is a sequential data structure that consists of data items that are all of the same data type. Files provide a means for your program to communicate with the outside world. Any I/O operations performed by your program, even keyboard input and display output, are handled via files. Files in C++ can be either ASCII character files or binary files. The default type of file is the character file. If a file is to be a binary file, the binary file mode must be specified when the file stream is opened.

All file I/O in C++ is in the form of file streams that employ predefined classes. The *ifstream* class is used to create input file stream objects, the *ofstream* class is used to create output file stream objects, and the *fstream* class is used to create file stream objects that will be used for both input and output. All three of these file streams are declared in the *fstream* header file (in older compilers, they are declared in *fstream.h*). File streams that you create are called *named* file streams. To create a named file stream, you must define a file stream object for one of the *fstream* file classes and attach the stream object to a particular disk file. This is referred to as ***opening*** a file.

Once a file stream is opened, it is ready for processing. The individual data items within a file are accessed via a file stream window. The window must be positioned over the item to be accessed. When a file is opened, the window, sometimes called a file stream buffer, is automatically created to access the file data items.

Typical tasks that are performed on disk files include writing new files, reading existing files, appending to existing files, and changing the information in existing files. The C++ language has various predefined functions to facilitate the coding of these tasks. Two of these functions are *seekp()* and *seekg()* functions, which allow you to place the file window in a particular position in the file. The *seekp()* function is used in file write operations and the *seekg()* function is used in file read operations.

In Problem 1, you will code a file class declaration, develop the necessary implementation files, and develop an application program that creates a new file to store character data. You will write the data to the file and read the data from the file to the display.

In Problem 2, you will modify the program from Problem 1 so that data can be appended to the end of the file and data already in the file can be modified.

You will declare the file class definition in a header file, create an implementation file for the file manipulation functions, develop an application program that defines file objects for the class, and test the function implementations. You will then build a project, linking the files that you have developed. You will compile, debug, run, test, and print the project files.

In this exercise, you will create a class declaration and function implementations for disk file manipulation. You will develop an application program that defines an object for the file class and tests the function implementations to create and display a parts inventory file. Finally, you will build a project linking the files that you have developed.

Pre-Lab

PROBLEM

Write a file class declaration and implementations for creating/writing a parts inventory file and reading/displaying the file. Write a menu-driven application program that allows the user to make the following choices:

♦ Create and write a parts inventory file that contains the following information:
   Part Name
   Part Number
   Part Price
   Quantity on Hand
♦ Read and display a report of the parts inventory file.
♦ Exit the program.

Defining the Problem

Output: What output will be produced, according to the problem statement?

_____

Input: What input will be needed for processing to obtain the required output?

_____

Processing: What processing is required to create a parts inventory file?

_____

_____

What processing is required to read and display the parts inventory file?

_____

_____

According to the problem statement, the output will be a display reporting the parts inventory. The menu choice, filename and parts data are needed as input from the user. To create a file and write the data to the file, you will create an output file object, accept the data from the user, and write it to the file stream. To read and display the file, you will create an input file object, read the information from the file and display the report.

Before you can develop an application program, you need to declare a file class in a header file, and develop the implementations for the required functions in an implementation file. Finally, you can create a project to combine the separate files into a working application program.

PROBLEM STATEMENT FOR THE FILE CLASS

Declare a file class as part of a header file. The class is to have data members to store the parts inventory information and a data member to store a filename. The class is to have member functions to perform the following tasks:

♦ Initialize the private filename data member with a disk filename entered by the user.
♦ Create and write a new file.
♦ Read and display an existing file.

Defining the Problem for the File Class

What will you name this class? _____

List the members that need to be declared public in this base class:

_____

List the members that need to be declared protected/private in this base class:

_____

Planning the Solution for the File Class

Here are the algorithms for the implementation of the functions listed in the class problem statement. Answer the questions for each function and write the respective function header.

FUNCTION TO SET A FILENAME FROM A USER ENTRY
    BEGIN
        Set the disk file name from a user entry.
    END.

What will you name this function? _____

What does this function do? _____

Which class data members are operated on by this function? _____

_____

Does this function need to accept or return any data from outside of the class? _____ If so, list the required data items: _____

283

Write a function header using the scoping operator, ::, to make the connection between the class and function.

_____

FUNCTION TO WRITE, OR CREATE, A NEW FILE

BEGIN
    Define an output file stream object, and open a disk file.
    Get the new file data items from the user, and write them to the file.
END.

What will you name this function? _____

What does this function do? _____

Which class data members are operated on by this function? _____

_____

Does this function need to accept or return any data from outside of the class? _____ If so, list the required data items: _____

Write a function header using the scoping operator, ::, to make the connection between the class and function.

_____

FUNCTION TO READ AND DISPLAY AN EXISTING FILE

BEGIN
    Define an input file stream object, and open a disk file.
    Read the file data items, and display them to the user.
END.

What will you name this function? _____

What does this function do? _____

Which class data members are operated on by this function? _____

_____

Does this function need to accept or return any data from outside of the class? _____ If so, list the required data items: _____

Write a function header using the scoping operator, ::, to make the connection between the class and function.

_____

Construct a UML class diagram for the file class, using the member descriptions you developed above.

Planning the Solution for the Application Program

Write an algorithm for the steps to be carried out by function *main()* in the application program. Your program should display a menu with the following choices:

♦ Create and write a parts inventory file.
♦ Read and display a report of the parts inventory file.
♦ Exit the program.

(*Hint:* Use a **switch** statement and call the appropriate file manipulation function according to the user's menu choice.)

Of course, your algorithm also needs to begin by setting the file name from a user entry.

main()
BEGIN

END.

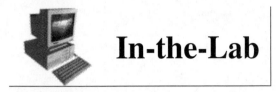

In-the-Lab

Coding the Program

✓ Start Your Editor

Start your C++ editor/IDE.

✓ Create a New Project

Make sure that a new file (and project if required) is open.

✓ Write the Program

File Class Header File

Before you can write the application program, you need to code the class declarations and function implementations for manipulating the file. Make sure that a new file is open. Complete the following file-class declaration shell from your UML diagram to code the file-class header file.

```
// FILE-CLASS DECLARATION HEADER FILE (PARTS.H)

#ifndef PARTS_H
#define PARTS_H

#include <fstream>

using namespace std;

// FILE-CLASS DECLARATION




#endif
```

After you have entered the source code for the file-class declaration, save it with the name *parts.h*.

File-Class Implementation File

Open a new file, and complete the following code for the file-manipulation implementation file, using the function headers and algorithms you developed.

```
// FILE-MANIPULATION IMPLEMENTATION FILE (PARTS.CPP)

#include "parts.h"
#include <string>

// FUNCTION TO SET THE FILENAME FROM A USER ENTRY
```

```
// FUNCTION TO WRITE, OR CREATE, A NEW FILE
```

```
// FUNCTION TO READ AND DISPLAY  AN EXISTING FILE
```

After you have entered the source code for the file-manipulation function implementations, save the file with the name *parts.cpp*.

Application File

Open a new file for the application program, and name it *L12_1.cpp*. Using the algorithm that you developed for *main()*, complete the following application-program shell with a menu interface to create a new disk file, write the file data items, and read and display the parts inventory report.

```
// LAB 12-1 APPLICATION FILE (L12_1.CPP)
// AUTHOR : type your name here
// DATE WRITTEN : type the date here

//PREPROCESSOR DIRECTIVES




int main()
{
// DECLARE FILE OBJECT AND ANY REQUIRED VARIABLES



// CALL FUNCTION TO SET THE FILENAME FROM A USER ENTRY



// DISPLAY MENU AND READ USER CHOICE
// USE THE RESULTS IN A SWITCH STATEMENT TO CALL THE REQUIRED FILE FUNCTIONS







return 0;

} //END main()
```

✓ Compile the Program

Now that you have entered and saved all the files, compile your program. Depending on your environment, the method to do this may vary. Most IDE's have a "Make" or "Build" option that will compile all of the files at one time. If you are working with a command-line compiler, you may have to develop a make file. Consult your compiler documentation or a knowledgeable programmer for instructions on how to do this for your particular compiler. Refer to *Appendix B* if you are using Visual C++.

✓Errors?

If there were any errors in the program, you will have to edit the program code to fix the errors, then compile the program again before you can link and run the program. Remember that when your header file contains a syntax error (such as a forgotten semicolon in closing a class definition), compilers often register the error in the implementation file rather than in the header file. If you have a tough time getting your entire program to compile at once, try compiling it one file at a time. Be sure to save any files that you change *before* you try to compile again.

✓Link the Program

If you used a "compile" option rather than a "build" or "make" option, you might have to explicitly tell your compiler to link your program after compiling it.

Testing and Debugging the Program

✓Run the Program

When the program is successfully compiled and linked, run it to make sure that it does what it is supposed to do.

✓Check the Program Output

A sample program screen with the "Write" choice is shown in Figure 12-1, and a screen with the "Read" choice is shown in Figure 12-2.

Documenting the Program

✓Test and Print a Sample Run of the Program

Get print-outs of sample program runs for documentation. See *Printing Console Output From Microsoft Windows* in *Appendix A* if you are running Microsoft Windows and need help with this.

✓Print the Source Code

Get a print-out of the program source code.

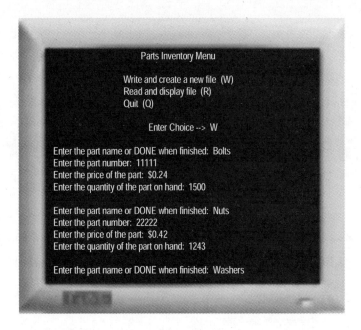

Figure 12-1 Sample output with "Write" choice

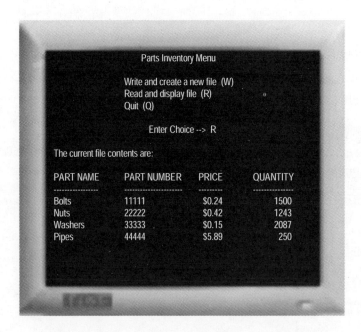

Figure 12-2 Sample output with "Read" choice

✓ Close the File

When you are finished with the program file, make sure that you have saved any final changes, and then close the file (and project or workspace if required).

In this exercise, you will add more functionality to the file-class declaration that you created in Problem 1. You will add function members to append a file and change a file's contents. You will add the implementations for these functions to the *files.cpp* implementation file and add these options to the menu in the application program. You will build a project linking the files that you have modified.

Pre-Lab

PROBLEM

Add options for the user to append additional parts to the parts inventory file created in Problem 1 and to modify, or change, the parts inventory data.

Defining the Problem

Output: What output will be produced, according to the problem statement?

_____

Input: What input will be needed for processing to obtain the required output?

_____

Processing: What processing is required to append additional parts to the parts inventory file?

_____

_____

What processing is required to modify the data already in the parts inventory file?

_____

_____

The input and output will be the same as in Problem 1. The output will be a display reporting the parts inventory. The menu choice, filename, and parts data are needed as input from the user. To append data to a file, you will open the file for output, seek the end of the file, accept the data from the user, and write it to the file stream. To change the data already in the file, you will open the file for input and output, get the component to be changed from the user, search the file for the component, delete the old component, seek the end of the file, and write the new information to the end of the file.

To do this, you must add two new functions to the *parts.h* class header file that will append and change the file, develop and add the implementations for the append and change functions in the *parts.cpp* implementation file, and then modify the menu in the application program to give the user access to the new file operations. Finally, create a project to combine the separate files into a working application.

291

UPDATED PROBLEM STATEMENT FOR THE INVENTORY FILE CLASS

Modify the file-manipulation class header file. The class is to have data members to store the parts inventory information and a data member to store a filename. In addition, the class is to have member functions to perform the following tasks:

♦ Initialize the private filename data member with a disk filename entered by the user.
♦ Create and write a new file.
♦ Read and display an existing file.
♦ Append the file.
♦ Change the file data.

Planning the Solution for the Updated File Class

Here are the algorithms for the implementation of the append and change functions added to the inventory file class. Answer the questions for each function and write the respective function header.

FUNCTION TO APPEND A FILE
    BEGIN
        Define an input/output file stream object, and open an existing disk file.
        Position the file window at the end of the file.
        Get the additional file data items from the user, and write them to the file.
    END.

What will you name this function? _____

What does this function do? _____

Which class data members are operated on by this function? _____

_____

Does this function need to accept or return any data from outside of the class? _____ If so, list the required data items: _____

Write a function header using the scoping operator, ::, to make the connection between the class and function.

_____

FUNCTION TO CHANGE A FILE
    BEGIN
        Define an input/output file stream object, and open a file.
        Get the data item to be changed from the user, and search the file for the data item.
        Seek the position of the data item to be changed.
        Erase the old data item from the file.
        Seek the end-of-file position.
        Write the new data item to the end of the file.
    END.

What will you name this function? _____

What does this function do? _____

Which class data members are operated on by this function? _____

_____

Does this function need to accept or return any data from outside of the class? _____ If so, list the required data items: _____

Write a function header using the scoping operator, ::, to make the connection between the class and function.

_____

Update your a UML class diagram for the inventory file class to show the append and change file function interfaces.

Planning the Solution for the Application Program

Update your *main( )* algorithm to display a menu with the following choices:

- ◆ Create and write a parts inventory file.
- ◆ Read and display a report of the parts inventory file.
- ◆ Append the file.
- ◆ Change the file.
- ◆ Exit the program.

main()
BEGIN

END.

 In-the-Lab

Coding the Program

✓Start Your Editor

Start your C++ editor/IDE.

✓Write the Program

Modify the File-Class Header File
Open the *parts.h* header file. Using your updated UML diagram, add the new function members to the class declaration. After you have modified the source code for the file-class declaration, save it.

Modify the File-Class Implementation File
Open the *parts.cpp* function implementation file. Add the following code to the file-manipulation implementation file.

// HEADER OF FUNCTION TO APPEND A FILE

{
   //DEFINE APPEND FILE OBJECT

   //POSITION FILE WINDOW AT THE END OF THE FILE

   //GET FILE DATA ITEMS AND APPEND TO FILE

} END APPEND IMPLEMENTATION FUNCTION

// HEADER OF FUNCTION TO CHANGE THE FILE

{
   //DEFINE LOCAL VARIABLES AND OBJECTS

   //DEFINE INPUT/OUTPUT FILE OBJECT, AND OPEN FILE

   //GET INVENTORY ITEM TO CHANGE FROM USER, AND SEARCH FILE FOR ITEM

   //IF FOUND, SEEK THE POSITION OF THE FOUND ITEM

   //ERASE THE OLD INVENTORY ITEM FROM THE FILE BY REPLACING IT WITH *'S

   //GET NEW ITEM FROM USER

//SEEK END OF FILE POSITION

//WRITE NEW ITEM TO END OF FILE

//REPORT TO USER IF ITEM NOT FOUND IN FILE

} END CHANGE FILE FUNCTION

After you have added the source code for the new file manipulation function implementations, save the file.

Application File
Open the *L12-1.cpp* application program file. Add the menu options and function calls for appending and changing a file from your updated *main()* algorithm.

✓ Compile the Program

Now that you have entered and saved all the files, compile your program. Depending on your environment, the method to do this may vary. Most IDE's have a "Make" or "Build" option that will compile all of the files at one time. If you are working with a command-line compiler, you may have to develop a make file. Consult your compiler documentation or a knowledgeable programmer for instructions on how to do this for your particular compiler. See *Appendix B* if you are using Visual C++.

✓ Errors?

If there were any errors in the program, you will have to edit the program code to fix the errors, then compile the program again before you can link and run the program. Remember that when your header file contains a syntax error (such as a forgotten semicolon in closing a class definition), compilers often register the error in the implementation file rather than in the header file. If you have a tough time getting your entire program to compile at once, try compiling it one file at a time. Be sure to save any files that you change *before* you try to compile again.

✓ Link the Program

If you used a "compile" option rather than a "build" or "make" option, you might have to explicitly tell your compiler to link your program after compiling it.

Testing and Debugging the Program

✓ Run the Program

When the program is successfully compiled and linked, run it to make sure that it does what it is supposed to do.

✓ Check the Program Output

A sample program screen with the "Append" choice is shown in Figure 12-3, and a screen with the "Change" choice is shown in Figure 12-4. The modified file contents are displayed in Figure 12-5.

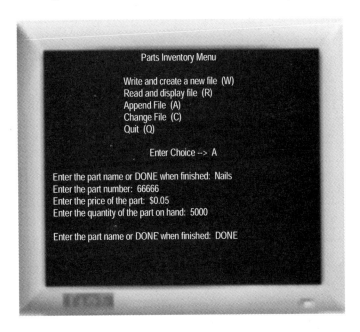

Figure 12-3 Sample output with "Append" choice

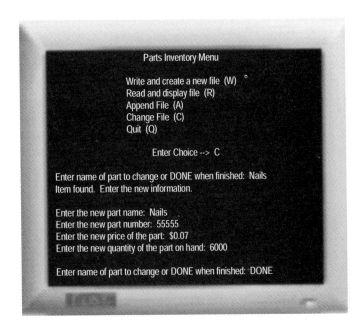

Figure 12-4 Sample output with "Change" choice

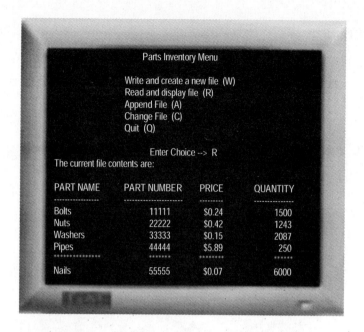

Figure 12-5 Final inventory file contents displayed with "Read" choice

Documenting the Program

✓ Test and Print Sample Runs of the Program

Get print-outs of sample program runs for documentation. See *Printing Console Output From Microsoft Windows* in *Appendix A* if you are running Microsoft Windows and need help with this.

✓ Print the Source Code

Get a print-out of the program source code.

✓ Close the File

When you are finished with the program file, make sure that you have saved any final changes, and then close the file (and project or workspace if required).

Pointers

In this lab, you will . . .

♦ Define pointers and use them to access and manipulate data.

♦ Determine whether a word is a palindrome, using pointers.

♦ Implement an invoice class, using pointers.

Chapter 13: Structured & Object-Oriented Problem Solving Using C++, 3rd edition,
by Andrew C. Staugaard, Jr.

What is a pointer? A pointer represents an actual memory address. Pointers provide a powerful and efficient means of accessing data, especially when that data is part of a data structure, such as an array. The reference parameters and array names that you have been working with are *constant pointers*, because the address they point to can never be changed by the program. A *variable pointer*, on the other hand, is a pointer that can be altered to point to any data of the same type by the program.

To define a pointer, you must tell the compiler what type of data the pointer is pointing to. For example *int *intPointer;* would be used to point to integer data. The asterisk, *, in front of a pointer variable denotes "the contents of." In other words, *intPointer* is read as "the contents of the memory location where *intPointer* is pointing."

When you assign a value to pointer, you must be careful not to "mix apples and oranges." Remember, a pointer points to an address in memory. You can assign a pointer to an address, such as an array name or the address reference of a variable–&value, for example. You can *not* assign a pointer to an element of the array or the variable itself. For example, *p1 = names*, if *names* has been defined as an array, and *p2 = &value*, if *value* has been defined as a variable, are legal pointer assignments. However, *p1 = &value* is not a legal assignment, because *p1* refers to data and *&value* refers to an address. If you get the data and address assignments mixed up in your program, it will produce a data-type mismatch error.

You can add or subtract integer values to or from a pointer. The result will be a pointer that is displaced from the original pointer value by the number added or subtracted. If you subtract two pointers pointing to the same array, you get the number of elements between the two pointer locations. You should not add, multiply, or divide pointers, because the results can often be unpredictable.

In Problem 1, you will develop a problem definition, an algorithm, and a program that uses pointers to determine whether a word is a palindrome.

In Problem 2, you will modify your invoice program from Project 10 to employ pointers to implement the solution.

In both problems, you will write the source code for the program that accepts the required input and produces an output report. You will compile, link, run, test, and print your programs.

In this exercise, you will write a program that will determine whether a word is a palindrome. You will accept a word from the keyboard and place it into an array. Once the word has been read, you will use pointers to compare the character elements to determine whether the word is a palindrome. (*Note:* A palindrome is a word that is spelled the same way both forward and backward. For example, "MOM" is a palindrome.)

Pre-Lab

PROBLEM

Write a program that will determine whether a word is a palindrome. Place a word entered by the program user into an array, and use pointers to compare the character elements for the palindrome determination. Notify the program user as to whether the word is a palindrome.

Defining the Problem

Output: What output is needed, according to the problem statement?

_____

Input: What input will be needed for processing to obtain the required output?

_____

Processing: What processing is required to determine whether the word is a palindrome?

_____

_____

    According to the problem statement, the output will be a message to the user as to whether the word entered is a palindrome. The word is needed as input from the program user. To determine whether the word is a palindrome, you will compare the first and last characters of the word, then continue comparing the other characters in the word, moving toward the center of the word for each comparison, until you reach the center of the word. If each set of characters matches, the word is a palindrome and can be spelled the same both forward and backward. If any of the comparisons does not match, the word is not a palindrome.

Planning the Solution

Here is an initial algorithm for function *main()*. Write a more detailed algorithm for the input, output, and processing.

main()
BEGIN
    Get a word from the program user.
    Test to determine whether the word is a palindrome, and notify user of results.
END.

    GET A WORD FROM THE PROGRAM USER AND PLACE IN AN ARRAY.
BEGIN

END

    TEST TO DETERMINE WHETHER THE WORD IS A PALINDROME, AND NOTIFY USER OF RESULTS. (*Hint:* Make one pointer point to the first character in the array and a second pointer point to the last array character. Then, using a loop, compare the elements located by the pointers, move the pointers toward the center of the array, and continue comparing the other array elements, moving toward the center of the word for each comparison until you reach the center of the word. Set a Boolean flag to false if two characters do not match, then test the Boolean flag later to determine whether the word was a palindrome.)
BEGIN

END

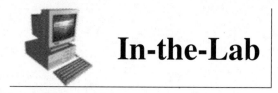

In-the-Lab

Coding the Program

✓ Start Your Editor

Start your C++ editor/IDE.

✓ Create a New Project

Make sure that a new file (and project if required) is open.

✓ Enter the Source Code

Using the algorithm that you developed, complete the following program shell. (*Hint:* You can use the *strlen()* function to find the last character of the array.)

```
// LAB 13-1 (L13_1.CPP)
// AUTHOR : type your name here
// DATE WRITTEN : type the date here

#include <iostream>
#include <string>

using namespace std;

int main()
{
// DECLARE ARRAY SIZE CONSTANT


//DEFINE A BOOLEAN FLAG TO TEST RESULTS


// DEFINE CHARACTER ARRAY AND TWO CHARACTER POINTERS


// FILL ARRAY FROM USER ENTRIES
```

// MAKE p1 POINT TO FIRST ARRAY CHARACTER

// MAKE p2 POINT TO LAST ARRAY CHARACTER

// ASSUME WORD IS A PALINDROME BY SETTING BOOLEAN FLAG TO TRUE

// TEST ARRAY FOR PALINDROME BY COMPARING CHARACTERS USING POINTERS
// SET BOOLEAN FLAG TO FALSE IF CHARACTERS DON'T MATCH

// DISPLAY PALINDROME RESULTS ACCORDING TO BOOLEAN FLAG

```
    return 0;

} // END main()
```

✓ Save the Program

After you have entered the source code, save the program. Name this program *L13_1.cpp*.

Testing and Debugging the Program

✓ Compile the Program

Now that you have entered and saved the program, compile it.

✓ Errors?

If there were any errors in the program, you will have to edit the program code to fix the errors, then compile the program again before you can link and run the program. Be sure to save the program again after you correct any errors.

✓ Link the Program

If you used a "compile" option rather than a "build" or "make" option, you might have to explicitly tell your compiler to link your program after compiling it.

✓ Run the Program

When the program is successfully compiled and linked, run it to make sure that it does what it is supposed to do.

✓ Check the Program Output

Check the results of the program run. Sample results from the program are shown in Figure 13-1 and Figure 13-2. Your results should look similar to these.

Figure 13-1 Sample program results where the word entered is not a palindrome

Figure 13-2 Sample results where the word entered is a palindrome

Documenting the Program

✓ Test and Print a Sample Run of the Program

Get print-outs of sample program runs of the palindrome program. See *Printing Console Output From Microsoft Windows* in *Appendix A* if you are running Microsoft Windows and need help with this.

✓ Print the Source Code

Get a print-out of the program source code.

✓ Close the File

When you are finished with the program file, make sure that you have saved any final changes, and then close the file (and project or workspace if required).

In this exercise, you will declare an invoice class in a header file, create an implementation file for the member functions, develop an application program that defines an object for the invoice class, and test the functions implementations. This problem is similar to Problem 2 in Project 10. However, in this problem we will employ pointers to implement the solution. You will build a project file linking the files that you have developed. You will compile, debug, run, test, and print the project file.

 # Pre-Lab

PROBLEM

Create a dynamic invoice object that contains all the information necessary to process one line of an invoice. Assume that the invoice must include the following data and functions:

> *Data:*
> > Quantity Ordered
> > Quantity Shipped
> > Part Number
> > Part Description
> > Unit Price
> > Extended Price
> > Sales-Tax Rate
> > Sales-Tax Amount
> > Shipping
> > Total

Use dynamic pointers to implement the object data.

> *Functions:*
> - A constructor function to initialize all the data items to 0 except the sales-tax rate, which should be initialized to 5%.
> - A function to allow the user to initialize the data items from the keyboard.
> - A function to calculate the extended price of the item.
> - A function to calculate the sales-tax amount of the item.
> - A function calculate the total amount of the invoice.
> - A function to display the invoice data with header information in a business-like format.
> - Because the object data will be implemented by using dynamic pointers, we will add a destructor function to dispose of the pointer data at the end of the program.

Defining the Problem

Output: What output will be produced, according to the problem statement?

_____

Input: What input will be needed for processing to obtain the required output?

_____

Processing: What processing is required to calculate the extended price of the item?

_____

_____

What processing is required to calculate the sales-tax amount?

_____

_____

What processing is required to calculate the total amount on the invoice?

_____

_____

According to the problem statement, the output will be a display of the invoice data in a business-like format. Because the quantity ordered might be different from the quantity shipped, you should display any quantity backordered. The part number, part description, unit price, quantity ordered, quantity shipped, and amount of shipping are needed as input. To process the extended price, the quantity shipped must be multiplied by the unit price. To process the amount of sales tax on the order, multiply the extended price by the sales-tax rate. The invoice total is simply the sum of the extended price, the sales-tax amount, and the amount of shipping.

Before you can develop an application program, you need to declare an invoice class in a header file and develop implementations for the required functions in an implementation file. Finally, you can create a project to combine the separate files into a working application.

PROBLEM STATEMENT FOR THE INVOICE CLASS

Declare an invoice class as part of a header file. The class is to have *pointer* data members to store the following:

> Quantity Ordered
> Quantity Shipped
> Part Number
> Part Description
> Unit Price
> Extended Price
> Sales-Tax Rate
> Sales-Tax Amount
> Shipping
> Total

The class is to have member functions to perform the following tasks:

- A constructor function to initialize all the data items to 0 except the sales-tax rate, which should be initialized to 5%.
- A function to allow the user to initialize the data items from the keyboard.
- A function to calculate the extended price of the item.
- A function to calculate the sales-tax amount of the item.
- A function calculate the total amount of the invoice.
- A function to display the invoice data with header information in a business-like format.
- A destructor function to dispose of the pointer data at the end of the program.

Defining the Problem for the Updated File Class

What will you name this class? _____

List the members that need to be declared public in this base class:

_____

List the members that need to be declared protected/private in this base class:

_____

Planning the Solution for the Updated File Class

Here is a list of functions required for the invoice class. Write algorithms and answer the questions for these functions from the information you developed in the problem definition. Remember, if class function members are operating on class data members, the data members are not passed or returned by the functions.

- Constructor function to initialize all the data members.
- Function to allow the user to initialize the data items from the keyboard.
- Function to calculate the extended price of the item.
- Function to calculate the sales-tax amount of the item.
- Function calculate the total amount of the invoice.
- Function to display the complete invoice.
- Destructor function to dispose of the invoice data.

CONSTRUCTOR FUNCTION
BEGIN

END.

What will you name this function? _____

What does this function do? _____

Which class data members are operated on by this function? _____

_____

Does this function need to accept or return any data from outside of the class? _____ If so, list the required data items: _____

Write a function header using the scoping operator, ::, to make the connection between the class and function.

_____

FUNCTION TO SET ORDER INFORMATION FROM USER ENTRIES
BEGIN

END.

What will you name this function? _____

What does this function do? _____

Which class data members are operated on by this function? _____

_____

Does this function need to accept or return any data from outside of the class? _____ If so, list the required data items: _____

Write a function header using the scoping operator, ::, to make the connection between the class and function.

_____

FUNCTION THAT CALCULATES EXTENDED PRICE
BEGIN

END.

What will you name this function? _____

What does this function do? _____

Which class data members are operated on by this function? _____

_____

Does this function need to accept or return any data from outside of the class? _____ If so, list the
required data items: _____

Write a function header using the scoping operator, ::, to make the connection between the class and
function.

_____

FUNCTION THAT CALCULATES SALES TAX
BEGIN

END.

What will you name this function? _____

What does this function do? _____

Which class data members are operated on by this function? _____

_____

Does this function need to accept or return any data from outside of the class? _____ If so, list the
required data items: _____

Write a function header using the scoping operator, ::, to make the connection between the class and
function.

_____

FUNCTION THAT CALCULATES INVOICE TOTAL
BEGIN

END.

What will you name this function? _____

What does this function do? _____

Which class data members are operated on by this function? _____

_____

Does this function need to accept or return any data from outside of the class? _____ If so, list the required data items: _____

Write a function header using the scoping operator, ::, to make the connection between the class and function.

_____

FUNCTION THAT DISLAYS INVOICE DATA
BEGIN

END.

What will you name this function? _____

What does this function do? _____

Which class data members are operated on by this function? _____

_____

Does this function need to accept or return any data from outside of the class? _____ If so, list the required data items: _____

Write a function header using the scoping operator, ::, to make the connection between the class and function.

_____

DESTRUCTOR TO DISPOSE OF POINTER DATA
BEGIN

END.

What will you name this function? _____

What does this function do? _____

Which class data members are operated on by this function? _____

_____

Does this function need to accept or return any data from outside of the class? _____ If so, list the required data items: _____

Write a function header using the scoping operator, ::, to make the connection between the class and function.

_____

Construct a UML class diagram for the invoice class, using the member descriptions you developed above.

Planning the Solution for the Application Program

Write the algorithm for the steps to be carried out by function *main( )* in the application program.

main( )
BEGIN

END.

 # In-the-Lab

Coding the Program

✓ Start Your Editor

Start your C++ editor/IDE.

✓ Write the Program

Invoice Class Header File
Make sure that a new file is open. Using the class description from your UML diagram, complete the following header file shell. Make sure to declare the class data as *pointer* data.

```
// LAB 13-2 (L13_2.H)
// AUTHOR: type your name here
// DATE WRITTEN: type the date here
// INVOICE CLASS DECLARATION HEADER FILE

#ifndef INVOICE_H
#define INVOICE_H
```

// INVOICE CLASS DECLARATION

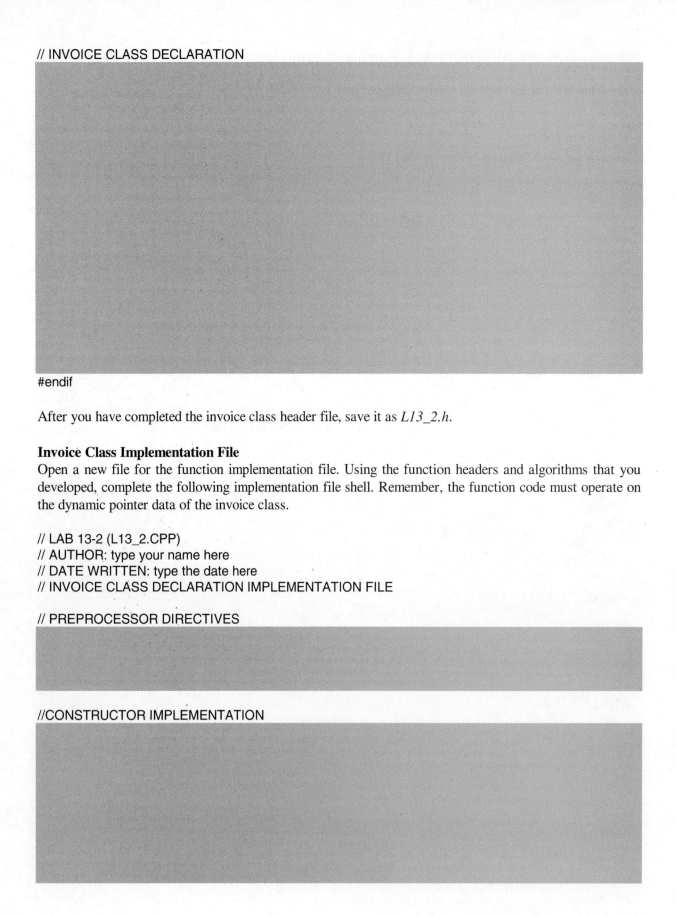

#endif

After you have completed the invoice class header file, save it as *L13_2.h*.

Invoice Class Implementation File
Open a new file for the function implementation file. Using the function headers and algorithms that you developed, complete the following implementation file shell. Remember, the function code must operate on the dynamic pointer data of the invoice class.

// LAB 13-2 (L13_2.CPP)
// AUTHOR: type your name here
// DATE WRITTEN: type the date here
// INVOICE CLASS DECLARATION IMPLEMENTATION FILE

// PREPROCESSOR DIRECTIVES

//CONSTRUCTOR IMPLEMENTATION

// IMPLEMENTATION OF FUNCTION TO SET INVOICE INFORMATION FROM USER ENTRIES

// IMPLEMENTATION OF FUNCTION TO CALCULATE EXTENDED INVOICE AMOUNT

// IMPLEMENTATION OF FUNCTION TO CALCULATE SALES TAX AMOUNT

// IMPLEMENTATION OF FUNCTION TO CALCULATE INVOICE TOTAL AMOUNT

// IMPLEMENTATION OF FUNCTION TO DISPLAY INVOICE INFORMATION

315

// DESTRUCTOR IMPLEMENTATION

After you have entered the source code for the function implementation, save the file with the name *L13_2.cpp*.

Application File
Open a new file for the application program. Using the *main()* algorithm that you developed, complete the following application-program shell to define an object for the invoice class and test the functions that you have written. Make sure to define a pointer object for your invoice class and to delete the pointer object at the end of *main()*.

```
// LAB 13-2 (L13_2APP.CPP)
// AUTHOR: type your name here
// DATE WRITTEN: type the date here


// PREPROCESSOR DIRECTIVES




int main()
{







return 0;
} //END main()
```

After you have entered the source code for the application program, save the file with the name *L13_2APP.cpp*.

✓ Compile the Program

Now that you have entered and saved all the files, compile your program. Depending on your environment, the method to do this may vary. Most IDE's have a "Make" or "Build" option that will compile all of the files at one time. If you are working with a command-line compiler, you may have to develop a make file. Consult your compiler documentation or a knowledgeable programmer for instructions on how to do this for your particular compiler. Refer to Appendix B if you are using Visual C++.

✓ Errors?

If there were any errors in the program, you will have to edit the program code to fix the errors, then compile the program again before you can link and run the program. Remember that when your header file contains a syntax error (such as a forgotten semicolon in closing a class definition), compilers often register the error in the implementation file rather than in the header file. If you have a tough time getting your entire program to compile at once, try compiling it one file at a time. Be sure to save any files that you change *before* you try to compile again.

✓ Link the Program

If you used a "compile" option rather than a "build" or "make" option, you might have to explicitly tell your compiler to link your program after compiling it.

Testing and Debugging the Program

✓ Run the Program

When the program is successfully compiled and linked, run it to make sure that it does what it is supposed to do.

✓ Check the Program Output

A sample of the input screen from the invoice project is shown in Figure 13-3, and a sample output screen is shown in Figure 13-4. Your input and output should look similar to these.

Documenting the Program

✓ Test and Print Sample Runs of the Program

Get print-outs of sample program runs for documentation. See *Printing Console Output From Microsoft Windows* in *Appendix A* if you are running Microsoft Windows and need help with this.

✓ Print the Source Code

Get a print-out of the program source code.

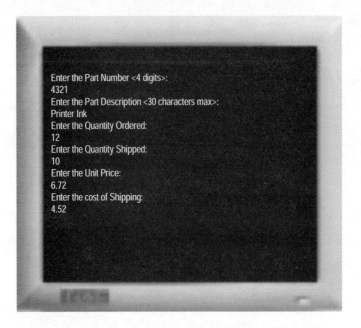

Figure 13-3 Sample input screen for the invoice project

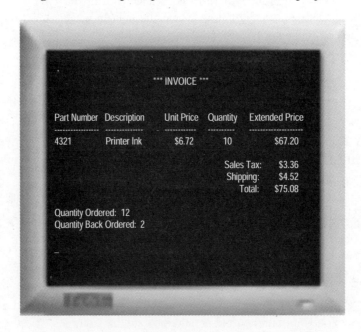

Figure 13-4 Sample output screen for the invoice project

✓ Close the File

When you are finished with the program file, make sure that you have saved any final changes, and then close the file (and project or workspace if required).

Abstract Data Types

In this lab, you will . . .

♦ Declare classes to implement ADTs.

♦ Define objects for the ADT classes in application programs.

♦ Use stacks and queues to determine whether a word is a palindrome.

♦ Use an ordered linked list to manipulate character data.

♦ Use the STL's stack and queue classes.

REQUIRED READING

Chapter 14: Structured & Object-Oriented Problem Solving Using C++, 3rd edition, by Andrew C. Staugaard, Jr.

INTRODUCTION

Abstract data types, or ADTs, provide for data abstraction. The idea behind data abstraction is to combine data with a set of operations that are defined for that data in an encapsulated package called an ADT. You know what the ADT does, and you can use the ADT interface without worrying about details of how the computer implements the data or its operations.

An ADT is not the same thing as a data structure. A data structure provides a way of structuring, or organizing, data within a programming language. You will be concerned about data structures when you implement an ADT, because you will have to decide how to organize and store the ADT data.

The data in an ADT must be private, which means that it is hidden from any operations that are not defined for the ADT. The ADT includes operations, or functions, that manipulate the ADT data. These operations are public, which means that they are used by outside applications to access and manipulate the private ADT data. Because the data must be private and the functions are public, the class in C++ provides an ideal implementation for an ADT.

You will be using three ADTs in this lab project. They are the stack, the queue, and the linked list. The differences between these ADTs lie in the way that you have access to the data elements.

The *stack* is a collection of data elements and related operations where all the insertions and deletions of elements to and from the stack are made at one end of the stack called the *top*. A stack operates on the last-in, first-out (LIFO) principle. In general, a stack is used to reverse the order of data placed in it.

The *queue* is a collection of data elements where all insertions of elements into the queue are made at one end of the queue, called the *rear* of the queue, and all deletions of elements from the queue are made at the other end of the queue, called the *front* of the queue. A queue operates on the first-in, first-out (FIFO) principle. The queue preserves the order of the elements from input to output.

A *list* is a sequence of data elements whose basic operations are insertion and deletion of elements to and from the list. A *linked list* is a sequential collection of data elements such that, given any element in the list, the location of its successor element is specified by an explicit link, rather than by its natural position in the collection. An *ordered linked list* is a linked list where all the data elements are in some natural order from the first node to the last node in the list. An alphabetized list of elements is an example of an ordered linked list. To create an ordered linked list, the algorithm to insert a node must search the list for the correct insertion point prior to adding the node to the list.

A linked list consists of a sequence of nodes. A node contains two things: an *element* and a *locator*, or *link*. The element is the information that is stored in the node, and the locator is the link that locates the next node in the list. A **struct** is used to declare a node in C++. For more information on **struct**s, see Chapter 14 in Staugaard's text.

In Problem 1, you will code the class declarations for a stack and queue, enter the code for the implementation files, and develop an application program that uses a stack and a queue to determine whether a word is a palindrome. You will then modify the program to use only stacks to solve the problem.

In Problem 2, you will code the class declaration for a linked list, enter the code for the implementation file, and develop an application program to use an ordered linked list to store character data in ascending order.

You will use your experience from Problems 1 and 2 in Problem 3, where you will modify the stack and queue ADT's that you will develop in Problem 1 to hold information in a linked list (rather than an array). You will create dynamically resizable stacks and queues.

Problem 4 will again tackle the palindrome problem, but this time you will modify your program to use the STL's built-in stack and queue classes.

In all problems, you will declare the classes in header files, create implementation files for the member functions, and develop application programs that define objects for the classes and test the function implementations. You will then build a project, linking the files that you have developed. You will compile, debug, run, test, and print the project files.

In this exercise, you will use class declarations and implementations for a stack and queue. You will develop an application program that defines an object for the stack and queue classes and tests the function implementations to determine whether a word entered by the user is a palindrome. Finally, you will build a project linking the files that you have developed. You will compile, debug, run, test, and print the files.

Pre-Lab

PROBLEM

Enter the code for the class declarations and necessary implementations for a stack and queue. Write an application program that allows the user to enter a word and uses a stack and a queue to test the word to determine whether it is a palindrome. Produce a report to the user as to whether the word is a palindrome. (Recall that a word is a palindrome if it is spelled the same both forward and backward.)

Defining the Problem

Output: What output is needed, according to the problem statement?

_____

Can functions be used to produce the output? _____

Input: What input will be needed for processing to obtain the required output?

_____

Can functions be used to accept the input? _____

Processing: What processing is required to obtain the output?

_____

Can functions be used to do the processing? _____

According to the problem statement, the output will be a display reporting whether the word entered is a palindrome. The word to test is needed as input from the user. To determine whether the word is a palindrome, you will compare the characters of the word to determine if they are the same both forward and backward.

PROBLEM DEFINITION FOR THE STACK CLASS

The stack class will need data members for the top element and an array to store the stack elements. Use the following summary of legal stack operations when defining the function members of the stack class.

createStack( ) - Creates an empty stack.
push( ) - Places an element on the top of a stack.
pop( ) - Removes an element from the top of a stack.
topElement( ) - Inspects the top element of the stack, leaving the stack unchanged.
emptyStack( ) - Determines whether the stack is empty.
fullStack( ) - Determines whether the array that is being used to hold the stack is full.

Defining the Problem for the Stack Class

What will you name this class? _____

List the members that need to be declared public in this class:

_____

List the members that need to be declared private in this class:

_____

Planning the Solution for the Stack Class

Develop algorithms for the functions to implement the legal stack operations listed in the stack class problem definition.

createStack( ) - CREATES AN EMPTY STACK.
BEGIN

END

Which class data members are operated on by this function? _____

_____

Does this function need to accept or return any data from outside of the class? _____ If so, list the required data items: _____

Write a function header using the scoping operator, ::, to make the connection between the class and function.

_____

push( ) - PLACES AN ELEMENT ON THE TOP OF A STACK.
BEGIN

END

    Which class data members are operated on by this function? _____

_____

    Does this function need to accept or return any data from outside of the class? _____ If so, list the
required data items: _____

    Write a function header using the scoping operator, ::, to make the connection between the class and
function.

_____

pop( ) - REMOVES AN ELEMENT FROM THE TOP OF A STACK.
BEGIN

END

    Which class data members are operated on by this function? _____

_____

    Does this function need to accept or return any data from outside of the class? _____ If so, list the
required data items: _____

    Write a function header using the scoping operator, ::, to make the connection between the class and
function.

_____

topElement( ) - INSPECTS THE TOP ELEMENT OF THE STACK, LEAVING THE STACK UNCHANGED.
BEGIN

END

    Which class data members are operated on by this function? _____

_____

    Does this function need to accept or return any data from outside of the class? _____ If so, list the required data items: _____

    Write a function header using the scoping operator, ::, to make the connection between the class and function.

_____

emptyStack( ) - DETERMINES WHETHER THE STACK IS EMPTY.

    Which class data members are operated on by this function? _____

_____

    Does this function need to accept or return any data from outside of the class? _____ If so, list the required data items: _____

    Write a function header using the scoping operator, ::, to make the connection between the class and function.

_____

fullStack( ) - DETERMINES WHETHER THE ARRAY BEING USED TO HOLD THE STACK IS FULL.

    Which class data members are operated on by this function? _____

_____

    Does this function need to accept or return any data from outside of the class? _____ If so, list the required data items: _____

Write a function header using the scoping operator, ::, to make the connection between the class and function.

Construct a UML class diagram for the stack class, using the member descriptions you developed above.

PROBLEM STATEMENT FOR THE QUEUE CLASS

The queue class will need data members for the front element, rear element, and element count and an array to store the queue elements. Use the following summary of legal queue operations when defining the members of the queue class.

createQueue( ) - Creates an empty queue.
insert( ) - Adds an element on the rear of a queue.
remove( ) - Removes an element from the front of a queue.
frontElement( ) - Copies the front element of a queue, leaving the queue unchanged.
emptyQueue( ) - Determines whether the queue is empty.
fullQueue( ) - Determines whether the array is full that is used to hold the queue.

Defining the Problem for the Queue Class

What will you name this class? _____

List the members that need to be declared public in this class:

_____

List the members that need to be declared private in this class:

_____

325

Planning the Solution for the Queue Class

Develop algorithms for the functions to implement the legal queue operations listed in the queue class problem definition.

createQueue( ) - CREATES AN EMPTY QUEUE.
BEGIN

END

    Which class data members are operated on by this function? _____

_____

    Does this function need to accept or return any data from outside of the class? _____ If so, list the required data items: _____

    Write a function header using the scoping operator, ::, to make the connection between the class and function.

_____

insert( ) - ADDS AN ELEMENT TO THE REAR OF A QUEUE.
BEGIN

END

    Which class data members are operated on by this function? _____

_____

    Does this function need to accept or return any data from outside of the class? _____ If so, list the required data items: _____

    Write a function header using the scoping operator, ::, to make the connection between the class and function.

_____

remove( ) - REMOVES AN ELEMENT FROM THE FRONT OF A QUEUE.
BEGIN

END

    Which class data members are operated on by this function? _____

_____

    Does this function need to accept or return any data from outside of the class? _____ If so, list the required data items: _____

    Write a function header using the scoping operator, ::, to make the connection between the class and function.

_____

frontElement( ) - COPIES THE FRONT ELEMENT OF A QUEUE, LEAVING THE QUEUE UNCHANGED.
BEGIN

END

    Which class data members are operated on by this function? _____

_____

    Does this function need to accept or return any data from outside of the class? _____ If so, list the required data items: _____

    Write a function header using the scoping operator, ::, to make the connection between the class and function.

_____

emptyQueue( ) - DETERMINES WHETHER THE QUEUE IS EMPTY.
BEGIN

END

Which class data members are operated on by this function? _____

_____

Does this function need to accept or return any data from outside of the class? _____ If so, list the required data items: _____

Write a function header using the scoping operator, ::, to make the connection between the class and function.

_____

fullQueue( ) - DETERMINES WHETHER THE ARRAY BEING USED TO HOLD THE QUEUE IS FULL.

BEGIN

END

Which class data members are operated on by this function? _____

_____

Does this function need to accept or return any data from outside of the class? _____ If so, list the required data items: _____

Write a function header using the scoping operator, ::, to make the connection between the class and function.

_____

Construct a UML class diagram for the queue class, using the member descriptions you developed above.

Planning the Solution for the Application Program

Write an algorithm for the steps to be carried out by function *main()* in the application program using a stack and a queue to determine whether a word is a palindrome. Employ the legal stack and queue operations developed above. (*Hint:* be sure to include a loop to fill the stack and queue and a loop to empty and compare the stack and queue for testing whether the word is a palindrome.)

main()
BEGIN

END.

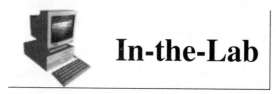 **In-the-Lab**

Coding the Program

✓Start Your Editor

Start your C++ editor/IDE.

✓Create a New Project

Make sure that a new file (and project if required) is open.

✓Write the Program

Stack-Class Header File

Before you can write the application program, you need to code the class declarations and function implementations for the stack and queue. Make sure that a new file is open. Use the class description from the stack-class UML diagram that you developed to complete the following header file shell.

```
//STACK CLASS DECLARATION HEADER FILE (STACK.H)

#ifndef STACK_H
#define STACK_H

// DECLARE CONSTANTS AND VARIABLES




// STACK CLASS DECLARATION
class
{
 public:




 private:



};
#endif
```

After you have entered the source code for the stack-class declaration, save it with the name *stack.h*.
Queue Class Header File

Make sure that a new file is open. Use the class description from the queue-class UML diagram that you developed to complete the following header file shell.

//QUEUE CLASS DECLARATION HEADER FILE (QUEUE.H)

#ifndef QUEUE_H
#define QUEUE_H

//DEFINE CONSTANTS AND VARIABLES

// DECLARE QUEUE CLASS
class
{
public:

private:

};
#endif

After you have entered the source code for the queue-class declaration, save it with the name *queue.h*.

Stack-Class Implementation File
Open a new file for the stack function implementation file. Use the function headers and algorithms that you developed for the stack class to complete the following implementation file shell.

// STACK IMPLEMENTATION FILE (STACK.CPP)

//PREPROCESSOR DIRECTIVES

#include "stack.h"

// CONSTRUCTOR TO IMPLEMENT createStack( )

//IMPLEMENTATION OF emptyStack()

//IMPLEMENTATION OF fullStack()

//IMPLEMENTATION OF push()

//IMPLEMENTATION OF pop()

//IMPLEMENTATION OF topElement()

After you have entered the source code for the stack function implementations, save the file with the name *stack.cpp*.

Queue-Class Implementation File

Open a new file for the queue function implementation file. Use the function headers and algorithms that you developed for the queue class to complete the following implementation file shell.

//QUEUE IMPLEMENTATION FILE (QUEUE.CPP)

//PREPROCESSOR DIRECTIVES

#include "queue.h"

// CONSTRUCTOR TO IMPLEMENT createQueue()

//IMPLEMENTATION OF emptyQueue()

//IMPLEMENTATION OF fullQueue()

//IMPLEMENTATION OF insert()

//IMPLEMENTATION OF remove()

//IMPLEMENTATION OF frontElement()

After you have entered the source code for the queue function implementations, save the file with the name *queue.cpp*.

Application File
Open a new file for the application program. Use the problem definition and *main()* algorithm that you developed to complete the following application program shell. Make sure to use a stack and a queue for determining whether a word entered by the user is a palindrome.

```
// LAB 14-1 APPLICATION FILE (L14_1.CPP)
// AUTHOR : type your name here
// DATE WRITTEN : type the date here
```

```
//PREPROCESSOR DIRECTIVES
```

```
#include "stack.h"
#include "queue.h"

int main()
{
// DEFINE STACK AND QUEUE OBJECTS
```

// DEFINE ANY REQUIRED VARIABLES

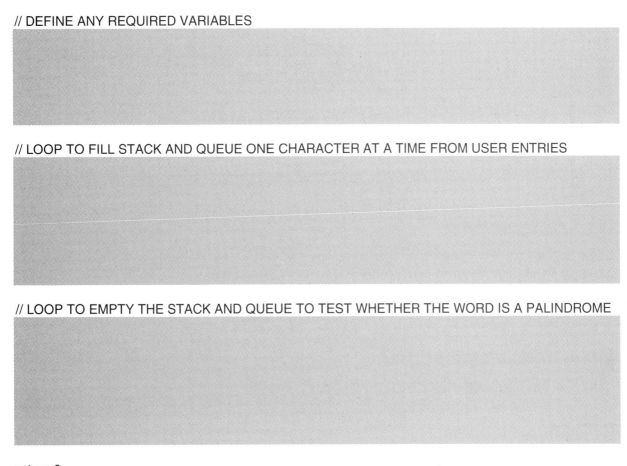

// LOOP TO FILL STACK AND QUEUE ONE CHARACTER AT A TIME FROM USER ENTRIES

// LOOP TO EMPTY THE STACK AND QUEUE TO TEST WHETHER THE WORD IS A PALINDROME

return 0;

} //END main()

After you have entered the source code for the application program, save the file with the name *L14-1.cpp*.

✓ Compile the Program

Now that you have entered and saved all the files, compile your program. Depending on your environment, the method to do this may vary. Most IDE's have a "Make" or "Build" option that will compile all of the files at one time. If you are working with a command-line compiler, you may have to develop a make file. Consult your compiler documentation or a knowledgeable programmer for instructions on how to do this for your particular compiler. See *Appendix B* if you are using Visual C++.

✓ Errors?

If there were any errors in the program, you will have to edit the program code to fix the errors, then compile the program again before you can link and run the program. Remember that when your header file contains a syntax error (such as a forgotten semicolon in closing a class definition), compilers often register the error in the implementation file rather than in the header file. If you have a tough time getting your entire program to compile at once, try compiling it one file at a time. Be sure to save any files that you change *before* you try to compile again.

✓ Link the Program

If you used a "compile" option rather than a "build" or "make" option, you might have to explicitly tell your compiler to link your program after compiling it.

Testing and Debugging the Program

✓ Run the Program

When the program is successfully compiled and linked, run it to make sure that it does what it is supposed to do.

✓ Check the Program Output

Sample output screens from the palindrome project are shown in Figure 14-1 and Figure 14-2. Your input and output should look similar to these.

Documenting the Program

✓ Test and Print a Sample Run of the Program

Get print-outs of a few sample program runs. See *Printing Console Output From Microsoft Windows* in *Appendix A* if you are running Microsoft Windows and need help with this.

✓ Print the Source Code

Get a print-out of the program source code.

✓ Challenge Yourself

When you are finished with the program file, make sure that you have saved any final changes, and then close the file (and project or workspace if required).
Modify your program to the following specifications:
- Move your current code to test a word using stacks and queues into a separate function.
- Add another function to test whether a word is a palindrome using only stacks. (*Hint:* You will need 3 stacks to do this. Why?)
- Modify *main()* to display a menu to give the user a choice between using stacks and queues to test whether a word is a palindrome (as in the current implementation) and using only stacks to determine whether a word is a palindrome.

✓ Close the File

When you are finished with the program file, make sure that you have saved any final changes, and then close the file (and project or workspace if required).

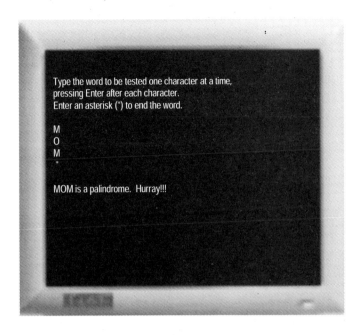

Figure 14-1 Sample output screen for a word that is a palindrome

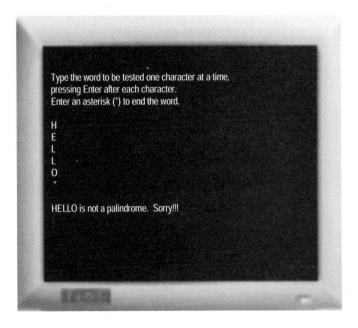

Figure 14-2 Sample output screen for a word that is not a palindrome

In this exercise, you will develop a linked-list class declaration, related function implementations, and an application program that defines an object for the linked-list class. The program will test the function implementations to manipulate an ordered linked list ADT storing character data in ascending order. You will add characters to the list, delete characters from the list, and display the list. You will build a project to exercise the ordered linked list.

Pre-Lab

PROBLEM

An ordered linked list is one in which the information in the list is ascending or descending from the first node to the last node in the list. To develop an ordered linked-list ADT, the *insertNode()* operation needs to search for the proper insertion point of the information being added to the list prior to inserting the node into the list.

Write an application program to develop an ordered linked-list ADT that will store character data in ascending order, from the beginning to the end of the list. Your program should allow the user to add characters to the list, display the list contents, add additional characters to the ordered linked list, display the list with the new elements, delete characters from the ordered linked list, and display the list after you have deleted the characters.

Defining the Problem

Output: What output is needed, according to the problem statement?

_____

Can functions be used to produce the output? _____

Input: What input will be needed for processing to obtain the required output?

_____

Can functions be used to accept the input? _____

Processing: What processing is required to obtain the output?

_____

Can functions be used to do the processing? _____

According to the problem statement, the output will be the contents of the original ordered linked list, the list contents after adding more characters, and the list contents after you have deleted characters. The characters are needed as input from the user. To add a character to the list, you must search for the correct

338

insertion point and insert the character. To delete a character from the list, you must search for the character and remove its node.

PROBLEM DEFINITION FOR THE LINKED-LIST CLASS

The linked-list class will need a data member for locating the first element in the linked list. Use the following summary of linked-list operations when defining the function members of the linked-list class.

> *createList( )* - Creates an empty list.
> *insertNode( )* - Adds a node to the list.
> *deleteNode( )* - Removes a specified node from the list.
> *traverseList( )* - Traverses the list, processing the list information as required.
> *emptyList( )* - Determines whether the list is empty.

Defining the Problem for the Linked-List Class

What will you name this class? _____

List the members that need to be declared public in this class:

_____

List the members that need to be declared private in this class:

_____

Planning the Solution for the Linked-List Class

Develop algorithms for the functions to implement the linked-list operations listed in the linked-list class problem definition.

createList( ) - CREATES AN EMPTY LIST.
BEGIN

END

Which class data members are operated on by this function? _____

_____

Does this function need to accept or return any data from outside of the class? _____ If so, list the required data items: _____

Write a function header using the scoping operator, ::, to make the connection between the class and function.

_____

insertNode( ) - ADDS A NODE TO AN ORDERED LINKED LIST.
BEGIN

END

    Which class data members are operated on by this function? _____

_____

    Does this function need to accept or return any data from outside of the class? _____ If so, list the required data items: _____

    Write a function header using the scoping operator, ::, to make the connection between the class and function.

_____

deleteNode( ) - REMOVES A SPECIFIED NODE FROM THE LIST.
BEGIN

END

    Which class data members are operated on by this function? _____

_____

    Does this function need to accept or return any data from outside of the class? _____ If so, list the required data items: _____

Write a function header using the scoping operator, ::, to make the connection between the class and function.

_____

traverseList( ) - TRAVERSES THE LIST, PROCESSING (DISPLAYING) THE LIST INFORMATION.
BEGIN

END

Which class data members are operated on by this function? _____

_____

Does this function need to accept or return any data from outside of the class? _____ If so, list the required data items: _____

Write a function header using the scoping operator, ::, to make the connection between the class and function.

_____

emptyList( ) - DETERMINES WHETHER THE LIST IS EMPTY.
BEGIN

END

Which class data members are operated on by this function? _____

_____

Does this function need to accept or return any data from outside of the class? _____ If so, list the required data items: _____

Write a function header using the scoping operator, ::, to make the connection between the class and function.

_____

Construct a UML class diagram for the linked-list class, using the member descriptions you developed above.

Planning the Solution for the Application Program

Here is an initial algorithm for the steps to be carried out by function *main()* in the application program by using an ordered linked to manipulate character elements. Write algorithms for the functions to allow the user to enter characters into the linked list, to allow the user to remove a character from the linked list, and to display the contents of the linked list. Be sure to employ the legal linked-list operations developed above. (*Note:* These functions must call upon the linked list functions to perform their designated task.)

main()
BEGIN
    Call function to add characters to the list.
    Call function to display the list.
    Call function to add more characters to the list.
    Call function to display the list.
    Call function to remove characters from the list.
    Call function to display the list.
END.

ADD CHARACTERS FUNCTION
BEGIN

END.

What will you name this function? _____

What does this function do? _____

Which class data members are operated on by this function? _____

_____

Does this function need to accept or return any data from outside of the class? _____ If so, list the
required data items: _____

Write a function header using the scoping operator, ::, to make the connection between the class and
function.

_____

REMOVE CHARACTERS FUNCTION
BEGIN

END.

What will you name this function? _____

What does this function do? _____

Which class data members are operated on by this function? _____

_____

Does this function need to accept or return any data from outside of the class? _____ If so, list the required data items: _____

Write a function header using the scoping operator, ::, to make the connection between the class and function.

_____

DISPLAY FUNCTION
BEGIN

END.

What will you name this function? _____

What does this function do? _____

Which class data members are operated on by this function? _____

_____

Does this function need to accept or return any data from outside of the class? _____ If so, list the required data items: _____

Write a function header using the scoping operator, ::, to make the connection between the class and function.

_____

In-the-Lab

Coding the Program

✓ Start Your Editor

Start your C++ editor/IDE.

✓ Create a New Project

Make sure that a new file (and project if required) is open.

✓ Write the Program

Linked-List Class Header File

Before you can write the application program, you need to code the class declaration and function implementations for the linked list. Make sure that a new file is open. Use the description that you developed in the UML diagram to complete the following header file shell.

```cpp
//LAB 14-2 (LIST.H)      // HEADER FILE FOR LINKED LIST STORING
                         // CHARACTERS IN ASCENDING ORDER

#ifndef LIST_H
#define LIST_H

// DEFINE VARIABLES



struct Node
{
  char character;        //CHARACTER IN THE LIST
  Node *next;            //POINTS TO NEXT NODE IN MEMORY
};

// DEFINE LINKED LIST CLASS
class
{
public:


```

```
private:
```

```
};
#endif  // LIST.H
```

After you have entered the source code for the class declaration, save it with the name *list.h*.

Linked-List Class Implementation File

Open a new file for the linked-list function implementation file. Use the list-class function headers and algorithms that you developed; complete the following implementation file shell.

```
// LAB 14-2 (LIST.CPP)   //LINKED-LIST IMPLEMENTATION FILE
```

```
//PREPROCESSOR DIRECTIVES
```

```
#include "list.h"
```

```
// CONSTRUCTOR TO IMPLEMENT createList()
```

```
// IMPLEMENTATION OF insertNode()
```

//IMPLEMENTATION OF deleteNode()

//IMPLEMENTATION OF traverseList()

//IMPLEMENTATION OF emptyList()

After you have entered the source code for the linked-list function implementations, save it with the name *list.cpp*.

Application File

Open a new file for the application program. Use the *main()* and function algorithms that you developed to complete the following application-program shell.

347

```
// LAB 14-2 (L14_2.CPP)
// AUTHOR : type your name here
// DATE WRITTEN : type the date here

//PREPROCESSOR DIRECTIVES




#include "list.h"

//FUNCTION PROTOTYPES




int main()
{

//DEFINE LIST OBJECT


//CALL FUNCTION TO ADD CHARACTERS TO THE LIST


//CALL FUNCTION TO DISPLAY THE LIST CONTENTS


//CALL FUNCTION TO ADD MORE CHARACTERS TO THE LIST


//CALL FUNCTION TO DISPLAY THE LIST CONTENTS


// CALL FUNCTION TO REMOVE CHARACTERS FROM THE LIST


//CALL FUNCTION TO SHOW THE LIST CONTENTS


return 0;
} //END main()
```

// FUNCTION TO DISPLAY THE CURRENT CONTENTS OF THE LIST

// FUNCTION TO ADD NEW CHARACTERS TO THE LIST

// FUNCTION TO REMOVE CHARACTERS FROM THE LIST

After you have entered the source code for the application program, save the file with the name *L14_2.cpp* and compile it.

✓ Compile the Program

Now that you have entered and saved all the files, compile your program. Depending on your environment, the method to do this may vary. Most IDE's have a "Make" or "Build" option that will compile all of the files at one time. If you are working with a command-line compiler, you may have to develop a make file. Consult your compiler documentation or a knowledgeable programmer for instructions on how to do this for your particular compiler. See *Appendix B* if you are using Visual C++.

✓Errors?

If there were any errors in the program, you will have to edit the program code to fix the errors, then compile the program again before you can link and run the program. Remember that when your header file contains a syntax error (such as a forgotten semicolon inclosing a class definition) compilers often register the error in the implementation file rather than in the header file. If you have a tough time getting your entire program to compile at once, try compiling it one file at a time. Be sure to save any files that you change *before* you try to compile again.

✓Link the Program

If you used a "compile" option rather than a "build" or "make" option, you might have to explicitly tell your compiler to link your program after compiling it.

Testing and Debugging the Program

✓Run the Program

When the program is successfully compiled and linked, run it to make sure that it does what it is supposed to do.

✓Check the Program Output

Sample screens from the ordered linked list project (spread over two screens) are shown in Figures 14-3 and 14-4. Your input and output should look similar to these.

Documenting the Program

✓Test and Print Sample Runs of the Program

Get print-outs of a few program runs for documentation. See *Printing Console Output From Microsoft Windows* in *Appendix A* if you are running Microsoft Windows and need help with this.

✓Print the Source Code

Get a print-out of the program source code.

✓Close the File

When you are finished with the program file, make sure that you have saved any final changes, and then close the file (and project or workspace if required).

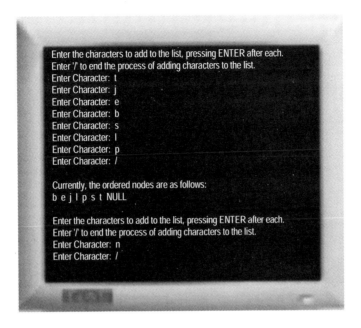

Figure 14-3 The first screen in a sample run of the ordered linked-list program

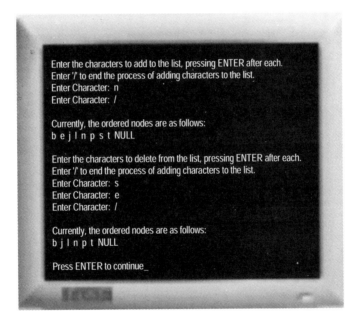

Figure 14-4 The second screen in a sample run of the ordered linked-list program

Using the knowledge gained in Problems 1 and 2, implement the stack and queue ADT's by using linked lists. Then, repeat Problem 1 to test for word palindromes. For the stack implementation, make *top* point to the first node in the list. Then, always insert and delete at this first node when you push and pop data. For the queue implementation, make *front* point to the first node in the list and *rear* point to the last node in the list. See Chapter 14 in Staugaard's text for more details.

Remember that a linked list grows dynamically, so you will not need the *fullStack()* and *fullQueue()* function. Good luck!

So far in this project, you have developed your own implementation of the stack and queue ADT's. Now it is time to learn a little about the stack and queue implementations available in the STL. In this problem, you will once again be testing words to check whether they are palindromes, but this time you will be using the STL stack and queue classes. (*Note*: Your compiler must support the C++ Standard Template Library to complete this project. If you are using a compiler that does not comply with the latest C++ ANSI/ISO standard, you may not be able to work through this problem.)

You can modify your application file from Problem 1 or Problem 3 to create STL stacks and queues rather than your own. All you have to do is include *stack* and *queue* rather than your own *"stack.h"* and *"queue.h"*. Then, define your stack object as *stack <**char**>* and your queue object as *queue <**char**>*. Remember to include **char** in angle brackets after the class name and before the object name. Because these classes are C++ template classes, they must be told what class of data they will contain. Once objects are defined for the STL stack and queue classes, you must change the function calls to match the STL class equivalents of your stack and queue functions.

Tables 14-1 and 14-2 below summarize the differences between your stack and queue functions and the STL stack and queue functions. The main difference has to do with retrieving information. The STL stack's *pop()* function does not return the data that is removed from the stack. *You must read the data by using the STL stack's top() function, then call the pop() function to remove the element from the stack.*

For example, in your earlier code you might have a line similar to this:

```
cout << stackObject.pop() << endl;
```

You would have to replace this line with *two* lines in your new program:

```
cout << stackObject.top() << endl;
stackObject.pop();
```

Similarly, the STL equivalent of your queue's *remove()* function is called, incidentally and somewhat confusingly, *pop()*, which does not return the element that it removes. For example, your current program may have a line similar to this:

```
cout << queueObject.remove() << endl;
```

This line must be replaced with the following two lines:

```
cout << queueObject.front() << endl;
queueObject.pop();
```

Other than these important differences, the STL functions will take the same arguments and return the same data as your function implementations.

TABLE 14-1 STL EQUIVALENTS OF YOUR STACK FUNCTIONS

STL Stack Function	Your Stack Function
push()	*push()*
top() then *pop()*	*pop()*
top()	*topElement()*
empty()	*emptyStack()*

TABLE 14-2 STL EQUIVALENTS OF YOUR QUEUE FUNCTIONS

STL Queue Function	Your Queue Function
push()	*insert()*
front() then *pop()*	*remove()*
front()	*frontElement()*
empty()	*emptyQueue()*

You will not have to call *createStack()* or *createQueue()* functions, because the STL class constructors take care of all initialization for you, and, as in Problem 3, you do not need the *fullStack()* or *fullQueue()* functions, because the STL implements stacks and queues dynamically. Also, remember to remove your stack and queue implementation files (*stack.cpp* and *queue.cpp*) from the project if you are modifying your project from Problem1 or Problem 3.

Multidimensional Arrays

In this lab, you will . . .
♦ Define, fill, manipulate, and display multidimensional arrays.
♦ Pass multidimensional arrays to user-defined functions for manipulation.
♦ Develop both structured and object-oriented programs to manipulate multidimensional arrays.

Chapter 15: Structured & Object-Oriented Problem Solving Using C++, 3rd edition, by Andrew C. Staugaard, Jr.

A multidimensional array is an extension of a one-dimensional array that stores multiple lists of elements. For example, a two-dimensional array stores lists in a two-dimensional table format of rows and columns, where each row is a list. The rows provide the vertical dimension of the array and the columns provide the horizontal array dimension. A three-dimensional array stores lists in a three-dimensional format of rows, columns, and planes, where each plane is a two-dimensional array. The rows provide the vertical dimension, the columns provide the horizontal dimension, and the planes provide the depth dimension of the array.

You will be using the most common multidimensional array, the *two-dimensional* array shown in Figure 15-1, in this lab project. You can see that a two-dimensional array contains multiple rows combined to form a single rectangular structure of data. You can think of this rectangular data structure as a *table* of elements.

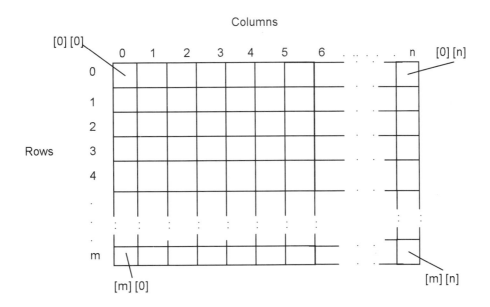

Figure 15-1 The structure of a two-dimensional array.

The elements in a two-dimensional array are located by their row and column indices. The rows are labeled on the vertical axis and range from 0 to m. The columns are labeled on the horizontal axis and range from 0 to n. The size of a two-dimensional array is determined by how many rows and columns it contains. Each dimension starts with 0, the last row position is m, and the last column position is n.

In general, if the last row index is m, how many rows does a two-dimensional array contain? _____

In general, if the last column index in n, how many columns does a two-dimensional array contain? _____

Since a two-dimensional array has $m + 1$ rows and $n + 1$ columns, its dimension, or size, is $m + 1$ rows by $n + 1$ columns. The dimension can be written as $(m + 1) \times (n + 1)$.

The elements stored in the array are located by their row and column index values. For example, the element in the upper left corner is located at index [0][0], as shown in Figure 15-1. The element in the lower right corner is located at index [m][n]. The row index is listed before the column index in accessing a two-dimensional array.

Remember that all arrays in C++ must be defined. Just as with one-dimensional arrays, you must specify the data type of the data elements, the name of the array, and the size of the array in the definition. The only difference when defining a two-dimensional array is in the size specification. You must specify both the row and column sizes. Refer to your text for more information on defining arrays.

Recall that there is a major restriction on the array elements: *The elements in a given array must all be of the same data type.*

Accessing the array elements in a two-dimensional array is done in much the same way as for a one-dimensional array. You can use direct assignment statements, read/write statements, or loops. The difference is that, to locate the elements in a two-dimensional array, you must specify a row index and a column index. The **for** loop structure is the most common way of accessing multiple array elements. When you use a loop to access a multidimensional array, you *must* use a separate loop for each dimension of the array, and the loops must be nested.

In Problem 1, you will develop a problem definition, an algorithm, and a program that defines a 3 x 5 two-dimensional array to accept 15 integer elements and display the elements in a 5 x 3 table format. You will use functions to fill and display the array.

In Problem 2, you will develop a problem definition, an algorithm, and a program that uses a two-dimensional array to store the monthly rental price for resort cabins over a five-year period. You will develop functions to fill the array, compute and store the total rental income for each cabin by year, compute and store the percentage of increase/decrease in price between adjacent years for each cabin, and produce a displayed report for each data array. You will use a structured-programming approach to solve this problem. Then, in Problem 3, you will convert your Problem 2 structured program to an object-oriented program that solves the resort cabin problem.

In all problems, you will write the source-code program that accepts the required input and produces an output report. You will compile, link, run, test, and print your programs.

In this exercise, you will accept elements from the keyboard and will use a two-dimensional array to store them. Once the elements have been read, you will display the array with the rows and columns reversed, or flipped. You will develop functions to fill and display the array.

 # Pre-Lab

PROBLEM

Write a program that will accept 15 integers from the keyboard and use a two-dimensional array to store them. Once the elements have been read, display them as a 3×5 array and then as a 5×3 array. (*Hint:* reverse the rows and columns to display the flipped array.) Develop functions to fill and display the array.

Defining the Problem

Output: What output is needed, according to the problem statement?

_____

Can a function be used to produce the output? _____

Input: What input will be needed for processing to obtain the required output?

_____

Processing: What processing is required to compute the total rental income for each cabin by year?

_____

According to the problem statement, the output will be the array displayed in both 3×5 and 5×3 format. The 5×3 "flipped" array results from reversing the rows and columns of the original array. The array elements are needed as input from the program user. No processing is required for this problem, because the array elements do not need to be manipulated in any way. The input and output can be programmed by using functions that are called by *main()*.

Planning the Solution

Here is an initial algorithm for function *main()*. Write an algorithm for the input and output functions that you developed in the problem definition.

BEGIN
    Call a function to fill a 3 x 5 array of integers from user entries.
    Call a function to display a 3 x 5 array of integers.
    Call a function to display a 3 x 5 array of integers in a 5 x 3 format.
END.

357

FUNCTION TO FILL A 3x5 ARRAY FROM USER ENTRIES
BEGIN

END.

What will you name this function?

_____

What does this function do?

_____

Accepts: What data items must this function accept from *main( )* to perform its designated task?

_____

Returns: What data items must this function return to *main( )*?

_____

Will this function be a void function or a non-void function? _____

List any required parameters and designate each parameter as value or reference.

_____

Write a prototype/header for this function.

_____

FUNCTION TO DISPLAY A 3x5 ARRAY OF INTEGERS
BEGIN

END.

What will you name this function?

_____

What does this function do?

_____

Accepts: What data items must this function accept from *main()* to perform its designated task?

_____

Returns: What data items must this function return to *main()*?

_____

Will this function be a void function or a non-void function?   _____

List any required parameters and designate each parameter as value or reference.

_____

Write a prototype/header for this function.

_____

FUNCTION TO DISPLAY THE 3x5 ARRAY OF INTEGERS IN 5x3 FORMAT
    BEGIN

    END.

What will you name this function?

_____

What does this function do?

_____

Accepts: What data items must this function accept from *main()* to perform its designated task?

_____

Returns: What data items must this function return to *main()*?

_____

Will this function be a void function or a non-void function? _____

List any required parameters and designate each parameter as value or reference.

_____

Write a prototype/header for this function.

_____

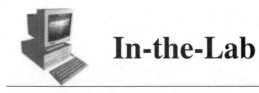 **In-the-Lab**

Coding the Program

✓ Start Your Editor

Start your C++ editor/IDE.

✓ Create a New Project

Make sure that a new file (and project if required) is open.

✓ Write the Program

Using the algorithms and prototypes that you developed, complete the following program shell.

```
// LAB 15-1 (L15_1.CPP)
// AUTHOR : type your name here
// DATE WRITTEN : type the date here

//PREPROCESSOR DIRECTIVES



// FUNCTION PROTOTYPES

```

```
// DECLARE GLOBAL CONSTANTS FOR ARRAY SIZE




int main()
{
// DEFINE INTEGER ARRAY




//CALL FUNCTION TO FILL ARRAY FROM USER ENTRIES




// CALL FUNCTION TO DISPLAY 3x5 ARRAY




// CALL FUNCTION TO DISPLAY 3x5 ARRAY IN 5x3 FORMAT




return 0;
END main()


// THIS FUNCTION WILL FILL THE ARRAY FROM USER ENTRIES.

{










} // END INPUT FUNCTION

// THIS FUNCTION WILL DISPLAY THE 3x5 ARRAY.

{





} // END DISPLAY 3x5 ARRAY FUNCTION
```

// THIS FUNCTION WILL DISPLAY THE 3x5 ARRAY IN 5x3 FORMAT.

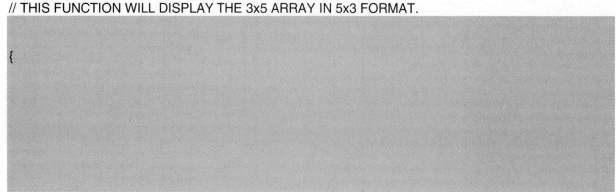

{

} // END DISPLAY 3x5 ARRAY IN 5x3 FORMAT FUNCTION

✓ Save the Program

After you have entered the source code, you need to save the program. Give this program the name *L15_1.cpp*.

Testing and Debugging the Program

✓ Compile the Program

Now that you have entered and saved the program, compile it.

✓ Errors?

If there were any errors in the program, you will have to edit the program code to fix the errors, then compile the program again before you can link and run the program. Be sure to save the program again after you correct any errors.

✓ Link the Program

If you used a "compile" option rather than a "build" or "make" option, you might have to explicitly tell your compiler to link your program after compiling it.

✓ Run the Program

When the program is successfully compiled and linked, run it to make sure that it does what it is supposed to do.

✓ Check the Program Output

A sample run of the program (spread over two screens) is shown in Figure 15-2 and Figure 15-3. Your input and output should look similar to these.

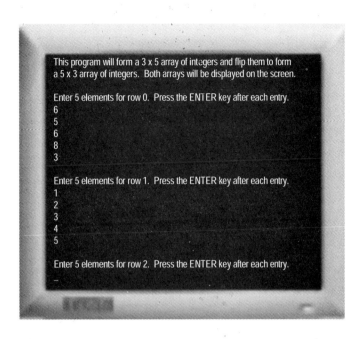

Figure 15-2 Input screen from a sample run of the array-flip program.

Figure 15-3 Output screen from a sample run of the array-flip program.

Documenting the Program

✓ Test and Print a Sample Run of the Program

Get print-outs of sample program runs for documentation. See *Printing Console Output From Microsoft Windows* in *Appendix A* if you are running Microsoft Windows and need help with this.

✓ Print the Source Code

Get a print-out of the program source code.

✓ Close the File

When you are finished with the program file, make sure that you have saved any final changes, and then close the file (and project or workspace if required).

In this exercise, you will develop a problem definition, an algorithm, and a C++ program that will employ functions and two-dimensional arrays to do the following: fill and store the monthly rental price of six resort cabins over a five-year period, compute the total rental income for each cabin by year, compute the percentage increase/decrease in price between adjacent years for each cabin, and display a formatted report.

 # Pre-Lab

PROBLEM

Assume the following table represents the monthly rental price of six resort cabins over a five-year period.

		YEAR				
		FIRST	SECOND	THIRD	FOURTH	FIFTH
	1	200	210	225	300	235
	2	250	275	300	350	400
CABIN	3	300	325	375	400	450
	4	215	225	250	250	275
	5	355	380	400	404	415
	6	375	400	425	440	500

Write a program that uses functions to perform the following tasks:

♦ Fill a two-dimensional array with the above table.
♦ Compute the total rental income for each cabin by year, and store the yearly totals in a second array.
♦ Compute the percentage increase/decrease in price between adjacent years for each cabin, and store the percentages in a third array.
♦ Display a report showing each of the three arrays in table form, with appropriate row/column headings.

Defining the Problem

Output: What output is needed, according to the problem statement?

_____

Can a function be used to produce the output? _____

Input: What input will be needed for processing to obtain the required output?

_____

Processing: What processing is required to compute the total rental income for each cabin by year?

                      What processing is required to compute the percentage increase/decrease in price between adjacent years for each cabin?

According to the problem statement, the output will be a display of reports showing the monthly cabin rental price, total yearly income per cabin, and price increase/decrease in tabular form, with appropriate row/column headings. The rental price array must be filled, but the problem does not specify how it must be filled. Therefore, you have three options: 1) fill the array from user entries, 2) fill the array by using direct assignment with hard-coded values, or 3) fill the array by reading the values from a text file. We will leave this decision up to you and/or your instructor. To compute the total yearly income per cabin, simply multiply the monthly price values by 12 and store the results in a second array. To compute the percentage increase/decrease in price between adjacent years, subtract year *a* from year *b* and divide by year *a*, then multiply this quotient by 100 to place the answer in percent form. Place the computed percentages in a third array.

Planning the Solution

Here is an initial algorithm for function *main()*. Using the input, output, and processing developed in the problem definition, write algorithms for the functions required by the program.

BEGIN
    Call a function to fill the *cabins* array with rental prices.
    Call a function to calculate yearly rental totals and place them in a second array.
    Call a function to calculate % increase/decrease between adjacent years and place it in a third array.
    Call a function to display the rental-cabin reports.
END.

FUNCTION TO FILL CABINS ARRAY
    BEGIN

    END.

What will you name this function?

What does this function do?

_____

Accepts: What data items must this function accept from *main( )* to perform its designated task?

_____

Returns: What data items must this function return to *main( )*?

_____

Will this function be a void function or a non-void function?   _____

List any required parameters and designate each parameter as value or reference.

_____

Write a prototype/header for this function.

_____

FUNCTION TO COMPUTE YEARLY TOTALS
   BEGIN

   END.

What will you name this function?

_____

What does this function do?

_____

Accepts: What data items must this function accept from *main( )* to perform its designated task?

_____

Returns: What data items must this function return to *main()*?

_____

Will this function be a void function or a non-void function? _____

List any required parameters and designate each parameter as value or reference.

_____

Write a prototype/header for this function.

_____

FUNCTION TO CALCULATE % INCREASE/DECREASE
    BEGIN

    END.

What will you name this function?

_____

What does this function do?

_____

Accepts: What data items must this function accept from *main()* to perform its designated task?

_____

Returns: What data items must this function return to *main()*?

_____

Will this function be a void function or a non-void function? _____

List any required parameters and designate each parameter as value or reference.

_____

Write a prototype/header for this function.

_____

FUNCTION TO DISPLAY REPORTS
    BEGIN

    END.

What will you name this function?

_____

What does this function do?

_____

Accepts: What data items must this function accept from *main( )* to perform its designated task?

_____

Returns: What data items must this function return to *main( )*?

_____

Will this function be a void function or a non-void function? _____

List any required parameters and designate each parameter as value or reference.

_____

Write a prototype/header for this function.

_____

 **In-the-Lab**

Coding the Program

✓ Start Your Editor

Start your C++ editor/IDE.

✓ Create a New Project

Make sure that a new file (and project if required) is open.

✓ Enter the Source Code

Make sure that a new file is open. Using the above algorithms, complete the following program shell for the rental-cabin input, calculations, and report.

```
// LAB 15-2 (L15_2.CPP)
// AUTHOR : type your name here
// DATE WRITTEN : type the date here

//PREPROCESSOR DIRECTIVES




// GLOBAL CONSTANT FOR ARRAY SIZE


// FUNCTION PROTOTYPES



int main()
{
// DEFINE ARRAYS




```

```
// CALL FUNCTION TO FILL CABINS ARRAY WITH RENTAL PRICES



// CALL FUNCTION TO CALCULATE YEARLY TOTALS AND PLACE IN TOTALS ARRAY



// CALL FUNCTION TO CALCULATE % INCREASE/DECREASE AND PLACE IN PERCENTS ARRAY



// CALL FUNCTION TO DISPLAY CABIN-RENTAL REPORTS



return 0;

}  // END MAIN

// THIS FUNCTION WILL FILL THE CABINS ARRAY WITH THE MONTHLY RENTAL INCOME

{










}  // END FILL FUNCTION

// THIS FUNCTION WILL CALCULATE THE YEARLY TOTALS
// AND PLACE THEM IN THE TOTALS ARRAY

{








}  // END YEARLY TOTALS FUNCTION
```

// THIS FUNCTION WILL CALCULATE % INCREASE/DECREASE
// AND PLACE IN PERCENTS ARRAY

```
{


}  // END % FUNCTION
```

// THIS FUNCTION WILL DISPLAY THE CABIN-RENTAL REPORTS

```
{


}  // END REPORT FUNCTION
```

✓ Save the Program

After you have entered the source code, you need to save the program. Name this program *L15_2.cpp*.

Testing and Debugging the Program

✓ Compile the Program

Now that you have entered and saved the program, compile it.

372

✓Errors?

If there were any errors in the program, you will have to edit the program code to fix the errors, then compile the program again before you can link and run the program. Be sure to save the program again after you correct any errors.

✓Link the Program

If you used a "compile" option rather than a "build" or "make" option, you might have to explicitly tell your compiler to link your program after compiling it.

✓Run the Program

When the program is successfully compiled and linked, run it to make sure that it does what it is supposed to do.

✓Check the Program Output

Figures 15-4, 15-5, and 15-6 show the cabin reports. If your output is not similar, edit the program code so that it produces correct results.

Documenting the Program

✓Test and Print Sample Runs of the Program

Get print-outs of program runs for documentation. See *Printing Console Output From Microsoft Windows* in *Appendix A* if you are running Microsoft Windows and need help with this.

✓Print the Source Code

Get a print-out of the program source code.

✓Close the File

When you are finished with the program file, make sure that you have saved any final changes, and then close the file (and project or workspace if required).

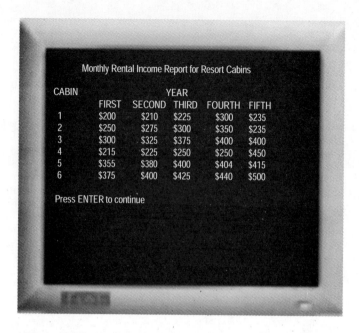

Figure 15-4 The monthly rental report of the resort cabins.

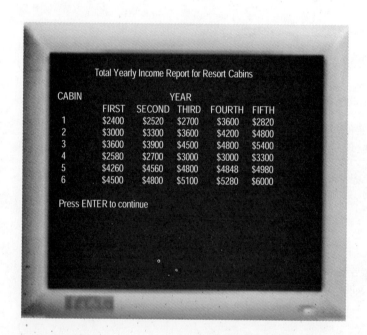

Figure 15-5 The yearly income report of the resort cabins.

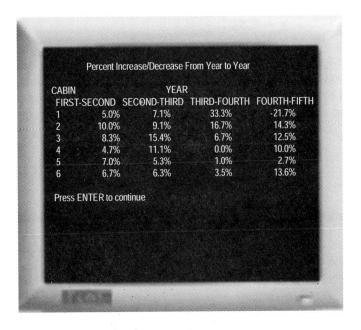

Figure 15-7 The increase/decrease profit report of the resort cabins.

Convert the structured program that you developed in Problem 2 to an object-oriented program. Compile, run, and test your object-oriented program. To perform the conversion, you must declare a *Cabins* class that includes the functions that you developed in Problem 2 as public members of the class and the three cabin arrays as private members of the class. Remember, the function prototypes will be different, because when a public function operates directly on a private member of the same class, the private member is not passed to or from the function. The *Cabins* class should be a separate header file. The function code that you developed earlier should be in a separate implementation file, and *main()* should be in a separate application file. You now have all the tools and know-how to do this conversion. Good luck!

Working With Consoles
In Microsoft Windows

INTRODUCTION

As a PC user, you are probably accustomed to a point-and-click window interface using the basic desktop metaphor for accessing files and programs and for navigating through your computer. As a beginning programmer, you will not create programs for this graphical environment. You will, instead, create programs that utilize console windows. If you stick with programming, you will graduate to creating graphical environments later, but that topic is separate from the basic programming concepts covered in this lab manual and the accompanying text.

The drawbacks to consoles are that they are neither pretty nor intuitive. A black screen and a blinking cursor are a little daunting to the novice user. However, it is a good environment for learning to program, because input and output (the task of writing information to the screen and the task of getting information from the user) are relatively straightforward. Programmers normally begin in a console environment, such as DOS or Unix, to learn the basic concepts of programming, then graduate to a graphical environment, such as Windows, after mastering these concepts.

Microsoft Windows supports DOS-style programs via a console (or MS-DOS) window. You will use this tool for learning to program.

CONSOLE INPUT & OUTPUT

The programs that you write will send standard output to the command-prompt window and will receive standard input through keyboard entry into the command-prompt window. All there is to console input and output is text. Your program writes text (including carriage-return line-feeds and other whitespace) to the console window, which directly outputs the text. The program user will type any required input directly into the console window, which sends the data to the program in a text form that can be easily read.

There are two basic console display modes within Microsoft Windows: window and full screen. When running in window mode, the console looks just like any other window, except that it contains a command prompt. The window can be moved, resized, minimized, or maximized. Depending on your version of Windows, the console window could also have a vertical scroll bar, allowing you to scroll up and view previous content. When running in full-screen display mode, the console window mimics the view of DOS. The mouse and all other windows are hidden. The contents of the console window expand to fill the entire screen. You can switch between window mode and full screen mode by pressing *Alt + Enter*.

Original DOS screens could display 25 rows of 80 characters on the default screen. With this rigid structure, it was not difficult to use a chart to lay out a text-based program nicely. While older versions of Windows mimic this 80x25 screen quite nicely, you cannot always predict the size and layout of a console screen in newer versions of Windows. For this reason, sample programs in the book do not get any more fancy than tabular columns when displaying information.

PRINTING CONSOLE OUTPUT FROM MICROSOFT WINDOWS

Because printing sample runs of your programs is important for program documentation, you should know how to go about printing console screens from within Microsoft Windows. It seems like a simple task, but it really isn't as straightforward as it should be.

Back in the DOS days, printing the content of your screen was as easy as pressing the *PrintScreen* key (often marked *PrtScn* or something similar) on your keyboard. This key's functionality has changed in Windows. We will look at three ways to print the contents of a console window: *Shift + PrintScreen*, copy and paste a screenshot, and copy and paste console text. The *Shift + PrintScreen* method will work *only* with Microsoft Windows 95/98/ME systems. The other two methods will work on all versions of Microsoft Windows.

Shift + PrintScreen

If you are running a derivative of Microsoft Windows 95 (e.g., Windows 95/98/ME), this is the easiest way for you to print the contents of a console window. Here are the steps:

(1) Make sure the console either is in full-screen mode or is the active window.
(2) Press *Shift + PrtScn*.
(3) If required, force your printer to print its buffer.

Steps 1 and 2 are very straightforward. Step 3 is printer specific. Depending on the model and software setup of your printer, it may not immediately print your console text. The information will be sent to the printer, but the printer may store the information in its memory buffer. Generally, you must send a form feed to the printer. Most printers have a button that you can push to do this. If your computer has sent the information to your printer, and you cannot get the console information to print, consult your printer documentation.

Copy and Paste a Screenshot

The second way to print the contents of a console window is to copy a screenshot of the console window to the Windows clipboard, then print it, using an image-editing program.

(1) Make sure the console either is in full-screen mode or is the active window.
(2) Press *Alt + PrtScn*.
(3) Launch an image-editing program.
(4) Paste the clipboard contents as a new image.
(5) Print the image.

Steps 1 and 2 are, once again, straightforward. If you do not have an image-editing program that you normally use, you can use Microsoft Paint (under the *Start* menu → *Programs* → *Accessories* → *Paint*) to print the program. Within the image editor, you should find the command to paste the clipboard contents into a new image; in some image editors, the general paste command (under the Edit menu) will create a new image; in other editors, there will be a separate command for pasting the clipboard contents as a new image. After you have successfully pasted the console window screenshot, use the editor's print command to print it. Figure 1 shows a console screenshot that has been pasted into Microsoft Paint.
The graphical paste method works, but it is not the best method, because the contents of the console are printed exactly as they appear on the screen—with a black background and white (or light gray) writing. This uses an excessive amount of ink (or toner).

Copy and Paste Console Text

If you are running a derivative of Microsoft Windows NT (e.g., Windows NT 4 or Windows 2000), this is the best method to print console output:

(1) Make sure the console is the active window.
(2) If you are running a Windows 95 derivative, click the *Mark* button on the toolbar of the console window. This button has an image of a dashed square and is shown in Figure 2.
(3) Move your mouse to point above and to the left of the contents that you wish to copy.

378

(4) Press and hold your mouse button, then drag the mouse below and to the right of the contents that you wish to copy and let up on the mouse button.

(5) You will see the colors of the selected area turn inverted (i.e. white background with black letters as shown in Figure 3). Make sure all of the text that you wish to print is within the inverted color area; if it isn't, repeat steps 3 and 4 to highlight everything that you want to print.

(6) Press the *Enter* key on your keyboard. The highlight will disappear.

(7) Launch a text editor.

(8) Paste the copied text into a blank document.

Step 2 is should be skipped if you are running a Windows NT derivative, because the *Mark* button is not available for the console windows in these operating systems, and, by default, the console windows are set to "quick edit" mode, which means that the window will automatically go into *Mark* mode as soon as you try to highlight a section of it.

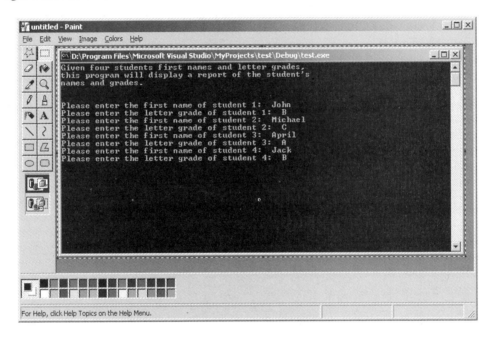

Figure 1 A console screenshot that has been pasted into Microsoft Paint

Figure 2 Windows 98 console window showing *Mark* button

379

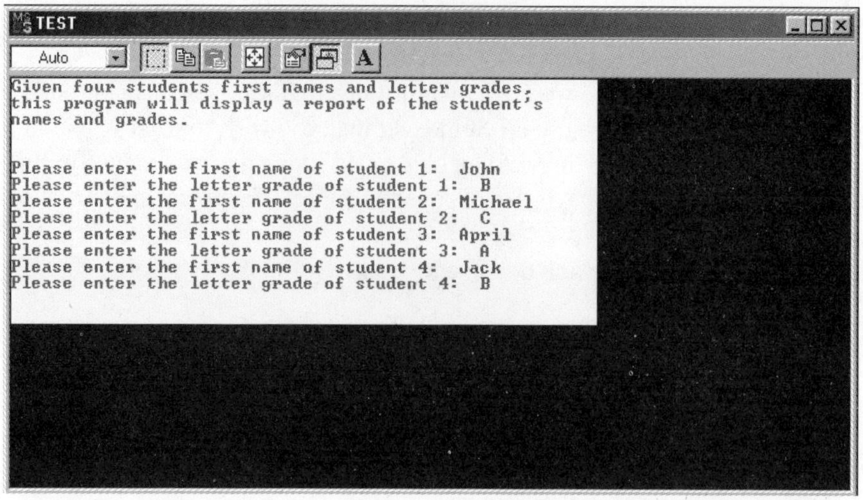

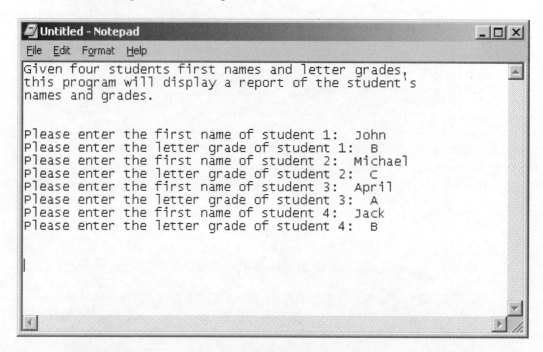

Figure 3 Windows 98 console window in *Mark* mode with highlighted text

Once you have copied the text to the clipboard, you can copy it into any image program that supports pasting text from the clipboard. If you do not have a word-processor, you can use Notepad (*Start* menu → *Programs* → *Accessories* → *Notepad*) to print the text. Figure 4 shows some text that has been copied from a console window and pasted into Notepad.

Figure 4 Console text that has been pasted into Notepad

Microsoft Visual C++ Tutorial

Who should use this tutorial?

You should, first of all, have a working knowledge of Windows before you attempt to program in a Windows environment. Knowing how to launch programs from the start menu and use standard Windows menus, buttons, etc., is a minimum. Having a general knowledge of the Windows file structure (i.e., how and where files are stored) will also help you out. You can often pick up these basics simply by surfing the internet for awhile or even by playing a few simple games of solitaire. Once you have the basics down, you will be well equipped to begin to learn how to program in C++.

It helps to know C++ before trying to master the Visual Studio environment. Likewise, it is easier to learn C++ if you are familiar already with Visual Studio. This puts the beginner in a distinct catch-22. This tutorial is written with the beginner in mind. It attempts to give the new user some insight into the Visual Studio environment without addressing C++ concepts. The drawback is that a new user will probably not have the knowledge of C++ to proceed through the entire tutorial.

Instead, future programmers should attempt to read through enough of this tutorial to become familiar enough with Visual Studio to learn how to program in C++. As a novice programmer learns new concepts (such as multifile projects and classes), he or she can refer to the later sections of the tutorial to learn how to apply these concepts in Visual Studio.

If you do not have any knowledge of C++, you should go through sections 2, 3, and 4 to get accustomed to the Visual Studio environment so that you can continue learning C++. Once you have a little experience with C++, go through the rest of the sections. If you are already familiar with the Visual Studio environment (i.e., you have used Visual Basic, Visual J++, or another Visual Studio product) this tutorial will probably not help much.

What is this tutorial?

We will cover how to use the Visual Studio environment. We will use Visual C++ 6.0 Service Pack 5. C++ concepts are not presented. You should use this tutorial in conjunction with a book (or a class) that teaches standard C++ programming. It is possible to read through the all the sections and go through all the examples without knowing anything about C++, but you will probably not gain anything from it.

Why Microsoft Visual Studio?

Some might argue that Visual Studio is too advanced for beginning programmers. This is a valid argument. After all, Visual Studio is an advanced *IDE* (Integrated Development Environment). It is the IDE that is used by Visual C++, Visual Basic, Visual J++, Visual Foxpro, Visual Interdev, and others. As a result, if you can program in Visual C++, then learning to program with Visual Basic, Visual J++, et al., is a matter of learning a new language without learning a new environment.

Others might argue that Visual Studio does too much for beginners. They might say that the debugger catches mistakes too easily, so that new programmers will not learn from them, or that the automation of compile options puts new programmers at a disadvantage if they ever have to deal with a command-line-based compiler. This is another valid point; however, a new programmer would not know what all the command-line options were for anyway, and entering these options would simply be the student's algorithm for compiling a program. Sure, new programmers do eventually learn what all the command-line options mean, but the same new programmer could instead learn C++ in Visual Studio and learn how to compile with a command line if and when that need arises.

Microsoft Visual Studio is an excellent IDE, and Visual C++ is an excellent implementation of the C++ language. Once a new programmer gets a good handle on the Visual Studio environment, he or she will be able to concentrate on learning C++ with minimal complications.

Getting Started

We will assume that you have already installed Microsoft Visual C++. If you do not have Visual C++ installed, please refer to the documentation that comes with the program.

Launch Visual C++ from the Windows *Start* Menu (probably in *Programs→Microsoft→Visual Studio 6.0→Microsoft Visual C++ 6.0*). You will be sitting in front of a screen that looks similar to that in figure 1. If your screen has a dialog box showing the "Tip of the Day," click on the *Close* button and you will be left with the screen shown in Figure 2.1.

First Visual C++ Program

This section will take you through building a simple console program. We will begin by creating a new C++ file, then we will type in a very simple program. Finally, we will compile and run the program.

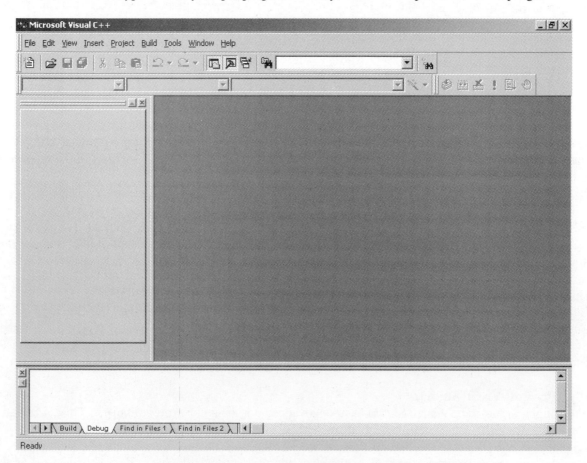

Figure 1 – Empty Visual C++ Window

In Visual C++, we must have a *project* in order to compile a program. Similarly, we must have an active *workspace* in which to create a project. If no project exists, Visual C++ helpfully creates a default project within a default workspace. We will allow VC++ to do this for us when we compile our program.

Creating a New C++ Source File

The first step is to create a new C++ file. Click on the *File* menu, then click on *New...* in the dropdown menu. A window that is shown in Figure 2 will appear.

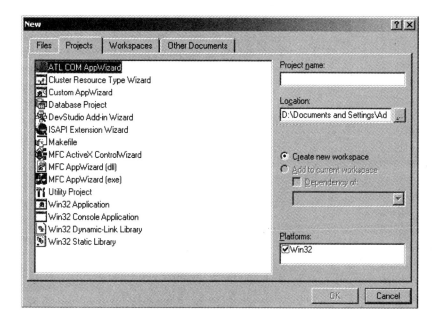

Figure 2 – *New* Window (*Projects* tab)

Click on the *Files* tab along the top of the screen, and you will be presented with the window shown in Figure 3. Click once on the icon labeled *C++ Source* File. Next, type *hello* into the text box labeled *File name:*. (Because *C++ Source File* is highlighted, Visual C++ will automatically add a *.cpp* extension to the end of the file name to identify it as a C++ source file.)

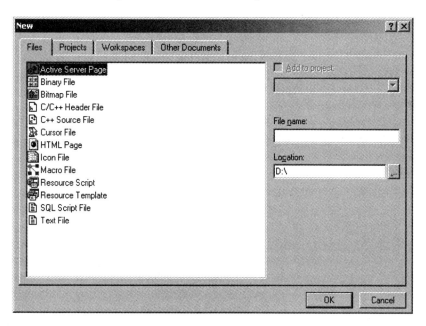

Figure 3 – *New* Window (*Files* tab)

Below the *File name:* text box, there is another box labeled *Location:*. If you know the path of the directory where you would like to create the file, type it in the text box; otherwise, click the button to the right of the box to show a dialog window similar to the one shown in Figure 4. Use this dialog window to browse to the folder where you would like to save your new C++ file, then click on the button labeled *OK*. You should see the path of the folder that you chose in the text box labeled *Location*.

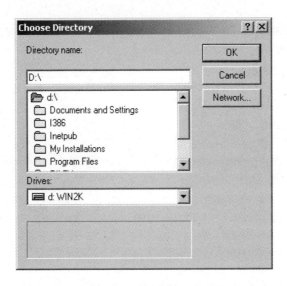

Figure 4 – *Choose Directory* **Dialog Window**

The Project Directory

It is a good idea to save your C++ file in its own directory. When Visual C++ creates a default project, it will designate the folder where your file is saved as the project folder. In other words, it creates several files and even subfolders within the folder where you save your file. In the big scheme of things, all those other files don't matter, because the compiler can rebuild them. If you aren't careful, though, they will clutter up your hard drive.

The typical practice is to create a folder with the name of your project (in this example, the project is called *hello*), then create the file within that folder. If you need to create a folder, then click cancel on the open dialog windows, minimize Visual C++, create the folder, then go back to Visual C++.

Also, keep in mind that because Visual C++ creates several files (including the executable) within the project folder and its subfolders, a 1.44-MB floppy disk is not a good place to create your file. If you need to save your project on a floppy disk, create your file in a temporary folder on the hard drive or on a network drive somewhere; then, when you are through working, copy *only* the C++ source file to the floppy disk.

Once you have decided where to save your file, click on the *OK* button in the *New* window. You should be presented with a screen similar to Figure 5. Where the gray background was in Figure 1, there is now an empty file showing. The cursor should be blinking in the top left of the empty file portion of the window. This is the part of the window that shows the contents of the current file being edited.

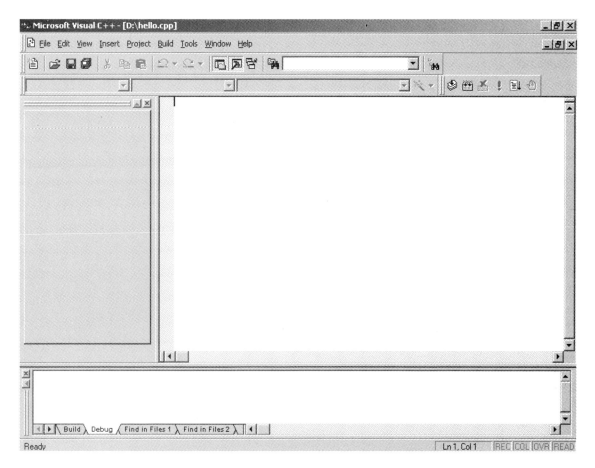

Figure 5 – Visual C++ Window with empty C++ file opened

Type in the Code

Now we are ready to type in our first Visual C++ program. Type in the following code exactly as it is shown:

```cpp
#include <iostream.h>

int main()
{
    cout << "Hello World!" << endl;

    return 0;
} //END main()
```

Notice that Visual C++ highlights the C++ keywords *#include*, *int*, and *return*. Syntax highlighting is one of the many features that Visual C++ provides to make writing programs simpler.

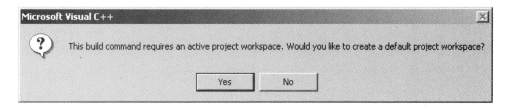

Figure 6 – Prompt to create a default project and workspace

Build the Program

Now we need to compile, link, and run the program. First, save your file. Either click on the *File* menu, then select *Save* from the dropdown menu, or simply type *ctrl+s* (hold down the *Ctrl* key and type *s*). Now Click on the *Build* menu, then select *Build* from the dropdown menu (or type the *F7* key, which is the hot key for the *Build* command). A dialog box like the one in Figure 6 should appear. Click the *Yes* button to allow Visual C++ to create a default project and workspace.

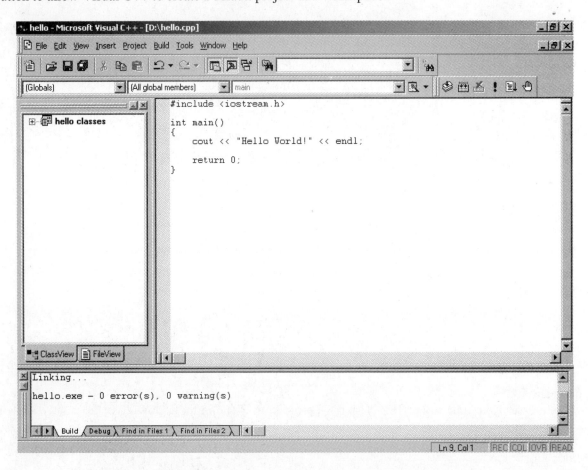

Figure 7 – Visual C++ window with active workspace and project

Your screen should now look similar to Figure 7. If any errors show in the bottom portion of the window, make sure that your code is typed correctly. If you are sure your code is correct, first ask someone to double-check it for you. It is very easy to miss something when copying code, particularly if you are not familiar with C++.

In the event that your code is right and you are still getting an error, you should look for other problems. Your first step should be to quit Visual C++, then reopen it and try to build your program again. If that doesn't help, try rebooting your computer. If you still have trouble, it is possible that Visual C++ is not installed properly. It is also possible that you do not have the file permissions within the operating system to write in the directory where your project is located. If you have built your project on a floppy disk, you may not have enough disk space to build the project. You may need to consult your computer and software manuals and/or technical support.

Explore the Environment

In general, your program will compile, and you will be ready to run your program. Before running the program, take a moment to explore the Visual C++ environment now that you have an active workspace and project.

At the left side of the screen is a window containing "hello classes." This is the *Workspace* window. Click on the plus sign (+) next to "hello classes." A folder with the word "Globals" will appear with

386

another plus sign next to it. Click on this plus sign and "main()" will appear underneath it. If you double-click on "main()" or the icon next to it, the editor window will become active, and the cursor will appear at the beginning of the line "int main()" within your code.

At the bottom of the *Workspace* window, there are two tabs labeled *Class View* and *File View*. By default, *Class View* is the active tab. Click on the tab labeled *File View*. Now the *Workspace* window should show "Workspace 'hello': 1 project(s)" on the first line and "hello files" on the next line. Click the plus sign next to "hello files" and "hello.cpp" will appear. You should recognize this as the name of the file that you typed into the *New* window in the *File Name* text box.

If you look at the very top right corner of the screen, you should see two rows of the standard window buttons (from left to right: Minimize, Restore/Maximize, and Close). Click the close button on the lower row. The editor where you typed the code will disappear, leaving nothing but a gray background. (If you are prompted to save at this time, double-check that you haven't accidentally made any unwanted changes to the code, then click *Yes*.) Now double-click on "hello.cpp" in the *Workspace* window. The editor window will reappear, code and all.

Now look at the window at the bottom of the screen. The window that says "hello.exe – 0 Error(s), 0 Warning(s)" is called the *Output* window. Notice that there are several tabs at the bottom of the *Output* window labeled *Build*, *Debug*, etc. The active tab is the *Build* tab, and, interestingly enough, it contains output created when you built your program.

Notice that on the right side of the *Output* window there is a vertical scroll bar. Right now it is at the bottom of the window. Try scrolling up. You should see that there was more output from the build that had just automatically scrolled past. There is also a horizontal scrollbar along the right part of the bottom of the window. You can scroll right if you want, but there is nothing over there now. Sometimes the output lines are too wide to fit on the screen. Rather than wrap around to the next line, the output will extend off the screen.

Run the Program

Click on the *Build* menu, then select *Execute hello.exe* (or type *ctrl+F5*). A console screen will appear showing the output of your program and prompting you to press any key as in Figure 8. When you press a key, the window will disappear.

Congratulations! You have created your first program with Visual C++. Let's look at a synopsis of the steps you took:

1. Created a new C++ file (*File→New...*, *Files*, *C++ Source File*, enter file name and location)
2. Typed in the code
3. Compiled, linked, and ran the program (*Build→Build*, *Build→Execute*)

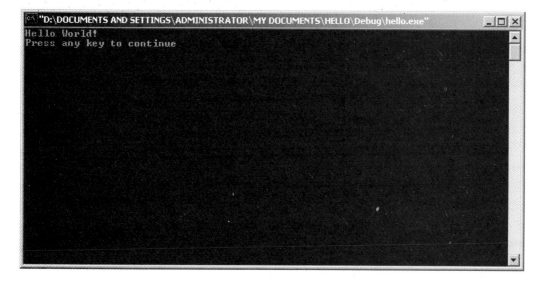

Figure 8 – Console output from hello.exe

387

Syntax Errors

Syntax errors occur when you do not correctly follow the rules for writing a program–for instance, if you forget a semicolon at the end of a line or if you mistype a keyword or a variable name. A program will not compile if it has syntax errors. It follows that these are the first errors you will have to fix. They are relatively easy to find and fix. Visual C++ does an excellent job of finding and helping you fix syntax errors. With most errors, it stops just short of fixing them for you.

Let's create a syntax error in the program from Section 2 to see how C++ handles it. Delete the semicolon from the end of the line that begins with "cout." Your code should now look like this:

```
#include <iostream.h>

int main()
{
    cout << "Hello World!" << endl

    return 0;
} //END main()
```

Now push *Ctrl+s* to save the file, then push *F7* to build the program. The last line of the *Output* window should now show "hello.exe - 1 error(s), 0 warning(s)." If you scroll up, you will see a description of the error. The line will begin with the full path and filename of the *hello.cpp* file followed by the line number where the error was found in parentheses, then a colon and the description of the error. The error should read: "error C2143: syntax error : missing ';' before 'return'." (A missing semicolon always shows up as a syntax error on the line after the line missing the semicolon.)

Now that we know where the error is, it's time to fix it. Double-click anywhere on the line that shows the error description. You will be pleasantly surprised to see what happens. Your screen should look similar to Figure 9. The error line in the *Output* window will be highlighted, the error description will appear at the very bottom of the main Visual C++ window, the cursor jumps to the beginning of the line indicated in the error, and a small marker appears just to the left of the line indicated in the error.

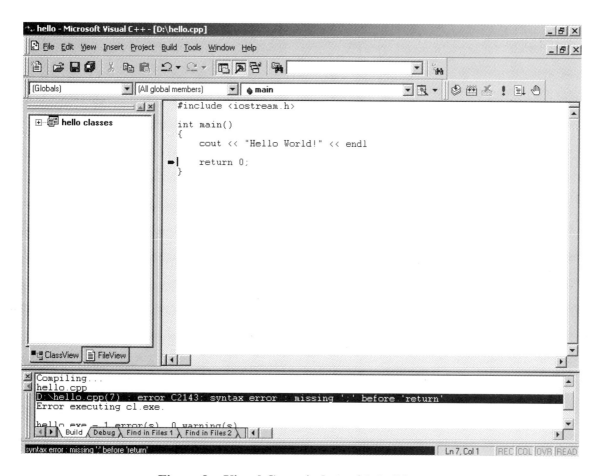

Figure 9 – Visual C++ window with build error

In a large program, this error finding will speed things up tremendously. From here, you can fix the error and rebuild your program. Take some time to play around. Delete things, add things—get a feel for the syntax-error reporting in Visual C++.

Using the Debugger

Syntax errors in code are the least of your worries. *Logic* errors are much harder to find. A logic error occurs when your code does not do what you want or expect it to do. These errors do not keep your program from compiling or running (although sometimes they cause your program to crash), and the compiler will not find them for you. The debugger, however, is a great tool for finding these errors.

To get a feel for the debugger, retype the *Hello World* program. Here is the code:

```
#include <iostream.h>

int main()
{
    cout << "Hello World!" << endl;

    return 0;
} //END main()
```

After typing in the code, hit *Ctrl+s* to save then *F7* to build the program. Now you are ready to *step through* the program (run it by executing one line of code at a time, using the debugger). To begin, simply type the *F10* key. You will see a console window briefly appear, then disappear, and your Visual C++ window will change to look similar to Figure 10.

389

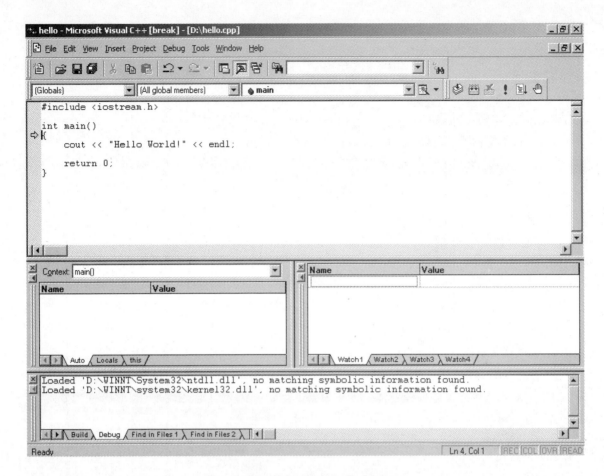

Figure 10 – Visual C++ Debugger

Notice that the *Workspace* window has disappeared from the left side of the screen, and, although the *Output* window is still at the bottom of the screen, it is now set to the *Debug* tab. There are also two new windows just above the *Output* window. The one on the left is called the *Variables* window, and the one on the right is called the *Watch* window.

Look at the menu bar. The *Build* menu has been replaced with a *Debug* menu. If you click on this menu heading, you will see the dropdown menu shown in Figure 11. The only two commands we will use right now are *Step Over* and *Go*. As you can see in the Figure 11, the hot key for *Step Over* is *F10*—the key you used to start the debugger, and the key you will use to step through the program. The hot key for *Go* is *F5*. You will use this command to run the rest of the way through the program when you are finished stepping through it.

If you look back at the main Visual C++ screen, you may notice a small yellow arrow next to the opening brace of main() (the '{' on the line following "int main()"). This arrow marks the current line of code. The line that is marked with the yellow arrow is the line that will be executed when you hit *F10*.

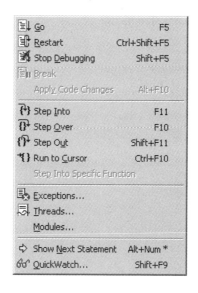

Figure 11 – Debug menu

Hit *F10*, and you should see the yellow arrow drop down one line. Because that line didn't contain any code, nothing else happened, but the arrow should now be pointing at the line with the *cout* statement.

Hit *F10* again, and your program will write "Hello World!" to the console screen, which is running as a separate program in Windows. Use either the task bar or *Alt+Tab* to look at the console screen. After verifying that the output is displayed correctly, click anywhere on the Visual C++ window to make it the active window once again. Another *F10* will execute the *return* statement, bringing the arrow to the closing brace. From here you can keep pushing *F10*, but Visual C++ will pop open unfamiliar files where the code to end the program is located. It's easier to simply push *F5* and allow the debugger to run through the rest of the code on its own.

Go ahead and push *F5* to allow the program to finish. You may see the console window appear briefly again. If you recall, when you used *Ctrl+F5* to execute the program without the debugger, the console window stayed open until you pressed a key to close it. The debugger does not do this. It simply runs through the program and closes the console window.

Finding Logic Errors with the Debugger
Delete everything in your *hello.cpp* file. Then type in the following code containing logic errors. This program is supposed to prompt the user for the number of people to greet, then prompt for each person's name. As you type in the program, see whether you can catch some of the logic errors. (*Hint: There are three logic errors in the code.*) Even if you find the errors, type the code exactly as it is shown, so that the errors will be there when we use the debugger.

```
#include <iostream.h>

int main()
{
        //DEFINE LOCAL VARIABLES
        int count=0;              //A LOOP COUNTER
        int numberOfPeople=0; //HOLDS THE NUMBER OF PEOPLE TO SAY HELLO TO
        char name[25]=" ";       //HOLDS THE NAME OF A PERSON TO SAY HELLO TO

        //PROMPT USER FOR THE NUMBER OF PEOPLE TO SAY HELLO TO
        cout << "How many people do you want to say hello to?  " << flush;
        cin >> numberOfPeople;
        cout << endl;
```

```
        for ( count = 1 ; count < numberOfPeople ; count++);
        {
                //GET THE NAME OF THE FIRST PERSON
                cout << "Please type the name of person #" << count << ":  " << flush;
                cin.getline(name,25);

                //SAY HELLO TO THE PERSON
                cout << "Hello, " << name << '.' << endl << endl;
        } //END FOR

        return 0;
} //END main()
```

After you type in the code, hit *Ctrl+s* to save, then hit *F7* to build the program. (If you end up with any syntax errors, fix them, then try to build the program again.) Now, hit *Ctrl+F5* to run the program. What happens? Figure 12 shows a sample output of the program.

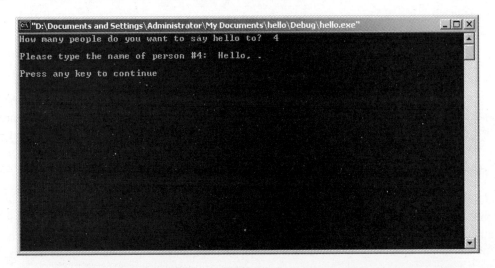

Figure 12 – Sample output of program with logic errors

When the program runs, it first prompts you for the number of people to greet. In the sample run, we entered 4. After that, the program doesn't act right. Rather looping through and prompting for four names, it writes the name prompt once, then immediately outputs "Hello, ."

Before using the debugger, you should look at the output and decide where to look for the error. Right away, you should suspect the *for* loop, since the program only runs through the code within the loop one time. Press a key to make the run window disappear, then press *F10* to start debugging.

Press *F10* one more time to get to the first line of actual code. Now take a second to explore the *Variables* window. Right now, the *Auto* tab is active, and the window is showing the variable *count* with a random value, since the line where count is initialized to 0 has not been executed yet.

Click on the *Locals* tab. You will see all three local variables that exist in the program (*numberOfPeople*, *name*, and *count*) along with their values, which are currently random garbage. Press *F10* once and watch what happens. The values of *name* and *count* have turned red. Click back on the *Auto* tab. Notice that *numberOfPeople* has appeared on the list of variables. Press *F10* again and watch what happens. This time, *count* disappears from the list, and the value of *numberOfPeople* has turned red.

The Auto tab shows only the variables that are in the current line of code (which will be executed on the next *Step Over*) and the previous line of code. When the value of a variable has just been changed, it turns red. The *Local* tab shows a list of all variables that are local to the current function–in this case, main(). When a variable's value is changed, that value turns red.

Because there are only three variables in this program, the *Local* tab will make it easy to see everything that is going on, so click on the *Local* tab. Then turn your attention to the variable *name*. You may have noticed that the *name* has a small plus sign next to it. Click on the plus sign, and the variable (which is a string) will expand so that each of the 25 characters set aside to represent the variable appears on a separate line. Because the value is still random garbage, this isn't easy to see, so press *F10* again to execute the line that initializes *name* to a string containing a single space.

Now the line after the name line (labeled with "[0]") shows the value "32 ' '." This is the ASCII value of the character (for a space it is 32), then the character itself enclosed in single quotes. The rest of the characters (lines labeled "[1]" through "[24]") all show an ASCII value of 0, the null terminator, which ends a string. If you don't understand this, don't worry—just make a mental note that it is possible to look at individual characters in a string should you ever need to.

Click on the minus sign next to *name* (where the plus sign was) to hide the individual characters. It's time to continue searching for the logic errors. Press *F10* to execute the *cout* statement. Then press it again to execute the *cin* statement. You'll notice that the arrow doesn't move to the next line after you execute the *cin* statement. The program is expecting input here.

You need to enter a number into the console screen where the program is running. Use the task bar or *Alt+Tab* to switch to the console window, then type in the number 4 and press *Enter*. Click anywhere in the Visual C++ window to make it active again. The arrow will have moved on to the next line now, and in the *Variables* window the value of *numberOfPeople* should be 4. Press *F10* again, and the program will go to the *for* loop.

Before executing the next line, look at the value of *count* in the *Variables* window. Its value is 0. Now press *F10* and watch what happens to the value. The arrow goes to the next line, and the value of *count* changes to 4. This isn't supposed to happen. The value should become 1, because that is what the *for* statement sets it to for the first time through the loop. There is something wrong with the statement.

If you look at the *for* statement, you'll see that it ends with a semicolon; however, *for* statements should not normally end with a semicolon (even though C++ syntax allows it). This is the first error. The semicolon causes the program to execute that single line four times rather than executing the loop four times.

Now that you've found the first error, press *F5* to allow the program to finish executing, then delete the semicolon from the end of the *for* statement. Press *Ctrl+s* to save the change, then press *F7* to build the program. Now, run the program again by pressing *Ctrl+F5*. What happens this time?

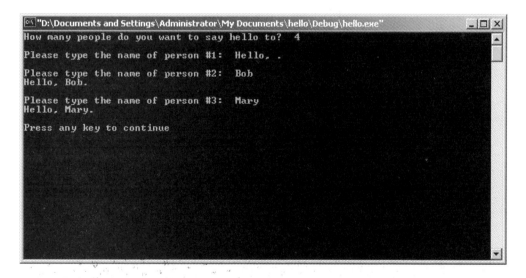

Figure 13 - Sample output of program with 1 logic error fixed

As you can see from Figure 13, there are still errors with the program. First, the program doesn't read in the name of person #1. It just skips by without waiting for input. Also, the program should prompt for a person #4, but it stops after #3.

You'll have to step through the program again to find these errors. You should know from the output that there is a problem with the *cin.getline()* statement the first time it runs in the *for* loop. You should also see that the loop is running one time less than it should. Armed with that knowledge, it's time to debug again.

Press *F10* to begin debugging. Click on the *Locals* tab in the *Variables* window to show all the local variables. Step through until you get to the *for* statement, and when you are prompted for the number of people, enter 4. Press *F10* one more time and look at the variables. The value of *count* is now 1, which is what it should be. Execute the next line of code and the arrow will be at the *cin.getline()* statement. Because this is the first time through the loop, this is one of the problem areas that you need to look at.

Before you execute the *cin.getline* statement, look at the value of *name*. It is set to a space (" "). Now press *F10*. You know from executing *cin* statements in the debugger that the program should stop here until you enter a value into the console window; however, the arrow continues to the next line without waiting for input. If you look at the value of *count*, you will see that it is red, indicating a change. If you look a little closer, you will see that the new value is the empty string ("") rather than a string consisting of a single space.

Now you know what happened, if not why it happened. Let's find the next error. Continue stepping through the program. You will see the arrow jump back up to the for statement after the last line of code within the loop. Keep stepping through the program. Notice that count increments each time through the *for* loop. Also notice that each time you execute the *cin.getline()* statement, you have to switch to the console where the program is running and enter a name.

After the third time through the loop, the arrow jumps back up to the *for* statement, but then jumps to the *return* line next. Stop right there and check your variables. You'll see that *count* is four. You know that the program should be going through the loop, four times; therefore, the loop should be executed when *count* is equal to four. If you look at the *for* loop though, you'll see that in order for the loop to execute, *count* must be less than *numberOfPeople*. If you look at the value of *numberOfPeople*, you'll see that it is also four. Because four is not less than four, the loop does not execute the last time. This is the error.

Press *F5* to finish debugging. The last error is an easy one to fix: simply change the test in the *for* loop from *count < numberOfPeople* to *count <= numberOfPeople*. The other problem is a little tougher to figure out, though. It turns out to be a quirk of the C++ language having to do with input buffers and carriage-return-line-feeds. It suffices to say that you should put the following line before a *cin.getline()* statement:

```
cin >> ws;
```

When a *cin* statement is used to read in data, it leaves the carriage-return-line-feed in the input buffer, and *cin.getline()* does not take that into account. It follows that whenever a *cin.getline()* statement appears after a *cin* statement, it reads what is left in the buffer rather than prompting for more input. If you didn't catch that, don't worry about it. Just remember that a *cin* before a *cin.getline()* requires a *cin >> ws*. Here is the complete, corrected code:

```
#include <iostream.h>

int main()
{
        //DEFINE LOCAL VARIABLES
        int count=0;              //A LOOP COUNTER
        int numberOfPeople=0;  //HOLDS THE NUMBER OF PEOPLE TO SAY HELLO TO
        char name[25]=" ";       //HOLDS THE NAME OF A PERSON TO SAY HELLO TO
```

```
//PROMPT USER FOR THE NUMBER OF PEOPLE TO SAY HELLO TO
cout << "How many people do you want to say hello to?  " << flush;
cin >> numberOfPeople;
cout << endl;

for ( count = 1 ; count <= numberOfPeople ; count++)
{
        //GET THE NAME OF THE FIRST PERSON
        cout << "Please type the name of person #" << count << ":  " << flush;
        cin >> ws;
        cin.getline(name,25);

        //SAY HELLO TO THE PERSON
        cout << "Hello, " << name << '.' << endl << endl;
} //END FOR

        return 0;
} //END main()
```

Using the *Watch* window

The *Variables* window can get very crowded in a program with more than three or four variables. There are also times that you may want to keep an eye on an expression rather than on just variables.

To learn how to use the *Watch* window, use the program from the last section. With the program open, hit *F10* to begin debugging. Once the debugger is started, you can use the *Watch* window. The premise behind the *Watch* window is simple: you simply type the variable name or expression whose value you want to watch.

If you look down at the *Watch* window, you will see a dotted rectangle in the *Name* column and another in the *Value* column. Click on the rectangle in the *Name* column. The cursor will appear in the rectangle. Now type *count* in the box and hit *Enter*. The *Value* column will show an error because the program execution is not yet running your code. Hit *F10* again and the uninitialized value of *count* will appear.

Find the variable name *numberOfPeople* within the code and double-click it with your mouse to highlight it. Once it is highlighted, use your mouse to drag it to the dotted rectangle on the second row of the *Watch* window in the *Name* column. The row should now contain *numberOfPeople* in the *Name* column and its uninitialized value in the *Value* column. This is an alternative way to add a variable to the *Watch* window.

Now add a watch for *name*, using whichever method you prefer. Notice that the *name* has a plus sign next to it, just as it did in the *Variables* window. This can be used to look at individual characters that make up the string exactly the same way as it worked in the *Variables* window.

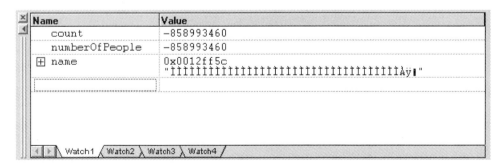

Figure 14 – Watch window showing uninitialized variables

In this program, it may also be useful to know when the *for* loop will break. You can enter the conditional statement (*count <= numberOfPeople*) contained in the *for* statement into the *Watch* window, either by typing it in the next row or by highlighting the expression and dragging it to the next row. You can now step through the program.

Notice that the value of *count <= numberOfPeople* is represented by a "1" when it is true and a "0" when it is false. In general, this is how Boolean values are represented in both the *Watch* and *Variables* windows.

Take some time to play around with the *Watch* window to get a feel for how it works. Try entering different expressions (e.g. *1+2* and *count - numberOf People*). When you feel comfortable with the us of the *Watch* window, click on the *File* menu and select *Close Workspace* from the dropdown menu.

Section 4   VISUAL C++ PROJECTS

Introduction to Projects
Until now, you have probably pictured the C++ source file as the basis for C++ programming. You started with an empty file, filled it with code, and allowed the compiler to create a default project around it. It is time to look at it from a different perspective. Visual C++ provides several different types of projects—each type can be thought of as a template or framework for which you, the programmer, provide functionality.

The default project which Visual C++ built around the *hello.cpp* file was a *Win32 Console Application*. You didn't write the code that caused a console window to appear, and you didn't write the code that prompted the user to "Press any key to continue" when the program was finished running. The *Win32 Console Application* project (in conjunction with Windows) took care of that. What you did was fill in the gap between the opening of the console widow and the "Press any key to continue" prompt.

To create a program in Visual C++, you begin with a project, and you plug in your own C++ source code to provide functionality. When you think about it that way, you should not have any trouble imagining how one project can contain several files.

Creating a New Project
Click on the *File* menu, then select *New...*from the dropdown list, or simply type *Ctrl+n*. You will be presented with the *New* window with the *Projects* tab active. Figure 2 shows this window. You will see a list of the projects available in Visual C++ 6. *Win32 Console Application* is listed third from the bottom. Click it once to highlight it.

Now you need to choose a location and a project name. Keep in mind that you are creating a project rather than a file. Visual C++ will create a folder in the location that you choose, and it will call the folder by the project name.

Type "rps" in the *Project Name* text box, then choose a location for your project and click *OK*. In case you're wondering, "rps" stands for Rock-Paper-Scissors. Another window similar to Figure 15 will appear to prompt you for more information on your project. Make sure "An empty project" is selected, then click *Finish*. One more window will appear, asking you to finalize your choices. Click *OK*, and your project will be created.

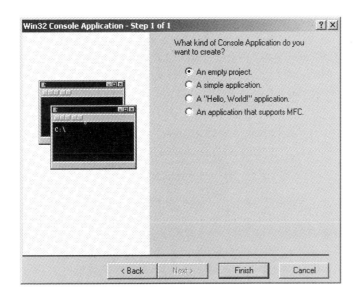

igure 15 – Win32 Console Application Wizard

Adding Multiple Files to a Project

Now you need to add a file to the project. Press *Ctrl+n* to bring up the *New* window (see Figure 16). Since you have a project open, the window defaults to the *Files* tab. Click once on *C++ Source File* to select it, then enter "rps" in the *File Name* box. The *Location* box defaults to the project folder, so there is no need to change it.

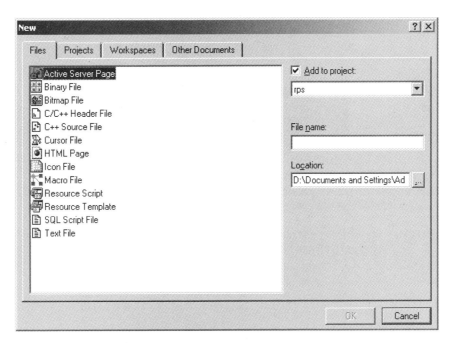

Figure 16 – *New* window on *Files* tab with rps project open

Notice the checkbox labeled *Add to project*. Because this is checked, this file will be added to the project. It is possible for a file to exist within the project folder, yet not be part of the project, so you want to make sure this box is checked. If the file is not added to the project, it will not be compiled with the project, and it might as well not exist.

Click *OK*, and you will be presented with an empty source file. Enter the following code. (If you are connected to the Internet, you can download the *rps.cpp* file from Staugaard's text Web site at and insert it into the edit window.)

```
//ROCK-PAPER-SCISSORS PROGRAM FILE (rps.cpp)

//INCLUDE HEADER FILES
#include <iostream>
#include <string>
using namespace std;

#include <stdlib.h>             //FOR srand() AND rand()
#include <time.h>               //FOR time() (USED FOR RANDOM SEED)

#include "rpsGlobals.h"         //FOR RPS PROTOTYPES AND CONSTANTS

//MAIN FUNCTION
int main()
{
        //DEFINE LOCAL VARIABLES
        int wins=0;        //NUMBER OF ROUNDS THE PLAYER HAS WON
        int losses=0;      //NUMBER OF ROUNDS THE PLAYER HAS LOST
        int pAttack=0;     //PLAYER'S CURRENT ATTACK
        int cAttack=0;     //COMPUTER'S CURRENT ATTACK
        char again=' ';    //TO PROMPT WHETHER TO PLAY AGAIN

        //INITIALIZE RANDOMIZATION
        srand(time( NULL ));

        //DISPLAY PROGRAM DESCRIPTION
        writeProgramDescription();

        //BEGIN do / while LOOP FOR PROMPTING TO PLAY AGAIN
        do
        {
                //CLEAR VARIABLES
                wins=0;
                losses=0;

                //PLAY GAME
                //THE for LOOP WILL BREAK AFTER THE LAST ROUND
                //OR WHEN wins OR losses IS OVER HALF OF ROUNDS
                for( int i=0 ;
                    i<ROUNDS && wins<(ROUNDS / 2)+1 && losses<(ROUNDS /2)+1 ;
                    i++)
                {
                        //SHOW CURRENT ROUND AND SCORE
                        cout << "Round " << i+1 << ':' << endl;
                        writeScore(i,wins,losses);

                        //GET PLAYER'S ATTACK
                        pAttack=getPlayerAttack();

                        //ECHO ATTACK
                        cout << "You attack with " << writeAttack(pAttack) << '.' << endl;

                        //GENERATE COMPUTER'S ATTACK
                        cAttack = rand() % 3;

                        //WRITE COMPUTERS ATTACK
                        cout << "Computer attacks with " << writeAttack(cAttack) << endl;
```

398

```
                    //DECIDE WHO WINS
                    writeRoundResult(wins, losses, pAttack, cAttack);
            }//END FOR

                    //SHOW FINAL SCORE
                    cout << "FINAL SCORE:" << endl;
                    writeScore(i,wins,losses);

                    //DECLARE WHO THE WINNER IS
                    writeFinalResults(wins, losses);

                    //PROMPT USER TO PLAY AGAIN
                    cout << "Press 'Y' the <ENTER> to play again." << endl;
                    cin >> again;
            } while (again=='Y' || again=='y');

            return 0;
}//END main()
```

There are several constants and function calls that are not defined within this code. In the interest of simplifying things, they have been separated out into different files. The constants and the function prototypes exist in a file called *rpsGlobals.h*, which is included in this file with a *#include* statement.

To create this file, press *Ctrl+n* to open the *New* window. Click on *C/C++ Header File* to select it, then type "rpsGlobals" in the *File Name* box. The location will automatically be set to the project folder, so make sure *Add to project* is checked, and click *OK*.

You will be presented with another blank file. Type in the following code. (If you are connected to the Internet, you can download the *rpsGlobals.h* file from Staugaard's text Web site at and insert it into the edit window.)

```
//GLOBAL VALUES FOR ROCK-PAPER-SCISSORS (rpsGlobals.h)

//DECLARE CONSTANTS
const int ROCK = 0;
const int PAPER = 1;
const int SCISSORS = 2;
const int ROUNDS = 5;

//FUNCTION PROTOTYPES
void writeProgramDescription();
void writeScore(int round, int wins, int losses);
int getPlayerAttack();
string writeAttack(int attack);
void writeRoundResult(int &wins, int&losses, int pAttack, int cAttack);
void writeFinalResults(int wins, int losses);
```

Now, all that is left is the actual code for the functions. Press *Ctrl+n* again to bring up the *New* window. Select *C++ Source File*, and type "rpsFunctions" in the *File Name* box. Once again, the location should be correct, so make sure *Add to project* is checked and click *OK*. Type this code into the new file. (If you are connected to the Internet, you can download the *rpsFunctions.cpp* file from Staugaard's text Web site at   and insert it into the edit window.)

```
//FUNCTIONS FOR ROCK-PAPER-SCISSORS (rpsFunctions.cpp)

//INCLUDE HEADER FILES
#include <iostream>
#include <iomanip>
#include <string>
```

```cpp
using namespace std;

#include "rpsGlobals.h"  //FOR RPS PROTOTYPES AND CONSTANTS
//THIS FUNCTION WRITES A PROGRAM DESCRIPTION MESSAGE
void writeProgramDescription()
{
        //HEAR IS THE PROGRAM DESCRIPTION
        cout << "                    ROCK - PAPER - SCISSORS" << endl << endl;
        cout << "It's time to play Rock-Paper-Scissors against the computer.  Decide" << endl;
        cout << "what your attack is, then see what the computer chose.  Play best" << endl;
        cout << "of " << ROUNDS << ", then decide whether to play again.  "
             << "Remember that" << endl;
        cout << "Rock smashes Scissors, Scissors cuts Paper, and Paper covers Rock."
             << endl << endl;
}//END writeProgramDescription()

//THIS FUNCTION DISPLAYS THE SCORE
void writeScore(int round=0, int wins=0, int losses=0)
{
        cout << "   Player: " << setw(4) << wins << flush;
        cout << "   Computer: " << setw(4) << losses << flush;
        cout << "   Draw: " << setw(4) << round-(wins+losses) << endl;
}// END writeScore()

//THIS FUNCTION PROMPTS FOR THE PLAYER TO ENTER ATTACK
//       THEN READS IT IN AND RETURNS IT
int getPlayerAttack()
{
        //DEFINE LOCAL VARIABLE
        int attack=0;

        //DISPLAY PROMPT
        cout << "0  ROCK" << endl;
        cout << "1  PAPER" << endl;
        cout << "2  SCISSORS" << endl;

        //READ IN ATTACK UNTIL A VALID VALUE IS ENTERED
        do
        {
                cout << "What is your attack?  " << flush;
                cin >> attack;
        } while (attack!=0 && attack!=1 && attack!=2);

        return attack;
} //END getPlayerAttack()

//THIS FUNCTION WILL RETURN A STRING TO REPRESENT AN ATTACK GIVEN THE
//ATTACK NUMBER
string writeAttack(int attack=0)
{
        //DECIDE WHICH STRING TO SEND BACK
        switch (attack)
        {
        case ROCK:
                return "ROCK";
                break;
        case PAPER:
                return "PAPER";
                break;
```

400

```cpp
        case SCISSORS:
                return "PAPER";
                break;

        default:
                return "ROCK";
                break;
        } // END SWITCH
} //END writeAttack()

//THIS FUNCTION DISPLAYS THE RESULTS OF A ROUND GIVEN PLAYER AND COMPUTER
//ATTACKS
//IT ALSO ACCEPTS wins AND losses BY REFERENCE AND INCREMENTS WHEN NEEDED
void writeRoundResult(int &wins, int&losses, int pAttack=0, int cAttack=0)
{
        //WRITE THE RESULTS
        switch ((pAttack - cAttack + 3) % 3)
        {
        case 0:
                //IT WAS A TIE
                cout << "Its a tie." << endl << endl;
                break;

        case 1:
                //PLAYER WON
                cout << "You Win!" << endl << endl;
                ++wins;
                break;

        case 2:
                //PLAYER LOST
                cout << "Computer Wins." << endl << endl;
                ++losses;
                break;
        } //END SWITCH
} //END writeRoundResult()

//THIS FUNCTION DISPLAYS THE FINAL RESULTS OF THE PROGRAM
void writeFinalResults(int wins=0, int losses=0)
{
        if (wins>losses)
        {
                cout << "YOU WIN THE GAME!!!" << endl;
        }//END IF
        else
        {
                if (wins<losses)
                {
                        cout << "The computer won." << endl;
                }//END IF
                else
                {
                        cout << "It's a draw...but you didn't lose." << endl;
                } // END ELSE
        } //END ELSE
} // END writeFinalResults()
```

You should now make sure that all three files are saved. If you click on the *FileView* tab of the workspace window (at the left side of the screen), the click on the plus next to "rps files," you will see the three files listed. If you double-click on one of them, that file will open (if it is not open) and move to the front of the code-editing portion of the screen. You can then push *Ctrl+s* to save that file.

When all the files are saved, push *F7* to build the program. If you have mistyped anything, the compiler will let you know it now. Use messages in the *Output* window to fix any syntax errors if the program doesn't compile. After it compiles correctly, run it.

It is sometimes helpful to split a large program into several files. For instance, if a program has several functions that do calculations and several others that display messages on the screen, it may be helpful to separate those categories of functions so they are easier to find later. When you do this, it is a good idea to create a header file to contain all global information (such as constants and function prototypes) and include it in each C++ file. In general, programs that you will write while learning to program will not be large enough to warrant this kind of separation, but you should know how to do it.

Adding Classes to a Project

To create a class, you can add source files and header files one at a time as described in the previous section, but Visual C++ offers an easier way. In this section, you'll create a simple class using the *New Class...* command.

If you have a project open, click the *File* menu, and select *Close Workspace* from the dropdown menu. Create a new project by pressing *Ctrl+n* and selecting *Win32 Console Application*. Name the project "geometry," and click *OK*. In the next window, make sure *An Empty Project* is selected and then click *Finish*. Click *OK* in the next window, and you'll be ready to start.

Let's create the class right away. If the *ClassView* tab is not active in the *Workspace* window, click on it. The window should have a line that says "geometry classes" with a plus sign to the left of it. Right-click on the text, then select *New Class...* from the dropdown menu. A window similar to Figure 17 will appear. Type "Rectangle" into the *Name* text box and then click *OK*.

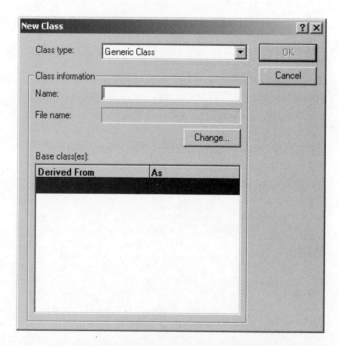

Figure 17 – *New Class* **window**

Visual C++ will now create files called *Rectangle.cpp* and *Rectangle.h*. You can open these files by clicking on the *FileView* tab of the *Workspace* window, clicking the plus sign next to "geometry files," clicking the plus sign next to either "source files" (for *Rectangle.cpp)* or "header files" (for *Rectangle.h),* then double-clicking on the file name. However, Visual C++ provides an easier way to create member functions and variables.

In the *Workspace* window, with the *ClassView* tab active, click the plus sign next to "geometry classes," then click the plus sign next to *rectangle* when it appears. Under "Rectangle" is a list of the class's member functions. Visual C++ has already added a constructor (*Rectangle()*) and a destructor (*~Rectangle()*) by default.

You will need to add variables to contain the length and width of the rectangle as integers and functions to calculate the perimeter and area of the rectangle. Begin by adding the variables. Right-click on "rectangle" in the *Workspace* window and select *Add Member Variable* from the dropdown menu. You will be presented with a window similar to Figure 18.

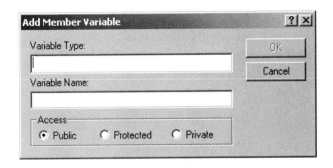

Figure 18 - *Add Member Variable* window

Type "double" in the *Variable Type* box, and type "length" in the *Variable Name* box. Click on the radio button next to *Private* to make the variable private, then click *OK*. Repeat the process to create a private double named *width*.

To add the member functions, right-click on "Rectangle" within the *Workspace* window, and select *Add Member Function....* A window similar to Figure 19 will appear. Type "double" into the *Function Type* box and "perimeter" into the *Function Declaration* box. Click *OK*. (The *Rectangle.cpp* file will open, but ignore that for now.) Repeat the process to create a public member function of type double called *area*.

Figure 19 - *Add Member Variable* window

Now add a new member function of type void. This will be the *setLength()* function, so it will have to accept a parameter. Type "void" in the *Function Type* box and then type "setLength(double l=0.0)" in the *Function Declaration* box. Notice that if you want a default parameter, this is where you set it. Repeat this to create a function of type void called *setWidth()* that accepts a double called *w* with a default value of 0.0.

You should now have a screen similar to Figure 20. Type the following code into the constructor (Rectangle::Rectangle()):

```
length=0;
width=0;
```

Now put this code into the perimeter function (Rectangle::perimeter()):

return (2 * length) + (2 * width);

Finally, put this code into the area function (Rectangle::area()):

return length * width;

Here is the code for the function that sets the length (Rectangle::setLength()):

length=l;

Here is the code for the function to set the width (Rectangle""setWidth()):

width=w;

When you have entered the code, press *Ctrl+s* to save the file. The rectangle class is now complete. It may help you to see exactly what the compiler has done, so right-click "Rectangle" in the *Workspace* window and select *Go to Definition* from the dropdown list. The file *Rectangle.h* will open in the editor. Aside from a very small amount of Visual C++ specific information, this file should look exactly as if you created it yourself (except for commenting).

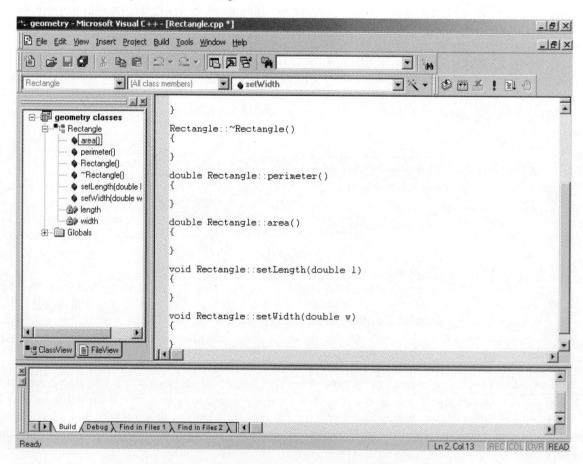

Figure 20 - Rectangle class with empty member functions

You may now create a new C++ source file to test the class functions. Press *Ctrl+n* again to bring up the *New* window. Select *C++ Source File*, and type "geometry" in the *File Name* box. Once again, the location should be correct, so make sure *Add to project* is checked, and click *OK*. Type the following code into the edit window. (If you are connected to the Internet, you can download the *geometry.cpp* file from Staugaard's text Web site at   and insert it into the edit window.)

```cpp
//GEOMETRY PROJECT MAIN FILE (geometry.cpp)

#include <iostream.h>          //FOR cin AND cout
#include "Rectangle.h"         //FOR Rectangle CLASS

void main()
{
          //DEFINE LOCAL VARIABLES
          Rectangle rect;               //RECTANGLE OBJECT
          double l=0.0;                 //LENGTH OF RECT
          double w=0.0;                 //WIDTH OF RECT

          //SET LENGTH AND WIDTH
          cout << "Enter the length of the rectangle:  " << flush;
          cin >> l;
          rect.setLength(l);

          cout << "Enter the width of the rectangle:  " << flush;
          cin >> w;
          rect.setWidth(w);

          //DISPLAY THE PERIMETER AND AREA
          cout << "The perimeter is " << rect.perimeter() << endl;
          cout << "The area is " << rect.area() << endl;
}//END main()
```

Using the Debugger with Functions and Classes

There are two crucial areas of the debugger that have not been covered yet in this tutorial: the differences between stepping over, stepping in, and stepping out of statements, and the setting of breakpoints.

If you consult Figure 11, you will see that in addition to the *Step Over* command that you used to step through the program, there are also *Step Into* and *Step Out* commands. To see the differences between these commands, make sure you have the geometry project from the previous section open, and then press *F10* to begin debugging.

Use *F10* (the *Step Over* command) to step through the program until you reach the line that contains "rect.setLength(l)." (When you are prompted for a length, type any number in.) Now press *F10* one more time to run this line. You might expect the debugger to go to the code within the *setLength()* function, but this does not happen. The debugger executes the function as if it was just another program statement. The debugger steps over the function.

Keep pressing *F10* until you are at the line that contains "rect.setWidth(w)." This time, instead of pressing *F10* to step over the function, press *F11* to step into the function. The debugger will now open the *Rectangle.cpp* file and it will be ready to step through the *setWidth()* function.

Use *F10* to step through the function. When you reach the end of the function, keep stepping through, and the debugger will jump back to the *geometry.cpp* file. You should be ready to execute the first *cout* statement.

Press *F11* to step into the statement. The debugger will jump into the *perimeter()* function in *Rectangle.cpp*. Instead of stepping through this function, press *Shift+F11* to step out of the function. The debugger will jump back to *geometry.cpp*. The debugger executed the rest of the function, then handed control back to you.

You should notice that the program flow did not move to the next line. There are actually two functions in this line: the *perimeter()* function, which you entered, and the output function used by *cout*. If

405

you want to see some confusing code, step into the output function by pressing *F11*. If you do this, you should step back out with *Shift+F11*, being careful not to accidentally change any of the code here.

In general, you should not step into any of Visual C++'s built-in functions. If you aren't careful, the debugger allows you to step all the way down to assembly level code, and then you'll be really lost. If you find yourself hopelessly buried within unknown source files within the debugger, it's a good idea to simply press *F5* to allow the program to finish running or *Shift+F5* to stop the debugger.

Breakpoints are another feature of the debugger that you should be familiar with. If you are still in the debugger, press *F5* to let the program finish. Open the *geometry.cpp* file if it is not already open. (To do this, click on the *FileView* tab in the *Workspace* window, click on the plus next to "geometry files," click on the plus next to "Source Files," then double-click "geometry.cpp."

Right-click anywhere on the line that contains "rect.setLength(l)." Select *Insert/Remove Breakpoint* from the dropdown list. A solid circle will appear to the left of the line. Now open the *Rectangle.cpp* file. Within the *setWidth()* function, create a breakpoint on the line that contains "width=w" by right-clicking on the line and selecting *Insert/Remove Breakpoint* from the dropdown list.

Now you should begin debugging. Instead of pressing *F10* to step through the program, press *F5* to run the program in the debugger. (This is called the *Go* command.) The program will begin to run. The console window will appear and prompt you for a length. Enter any number in, then press enter. After this, the program appears to freeze. If you click on the Visual C++ window, you will see that the program execution has halted at the line where you set the breakpoint.

At this time, it is important to point out that if you run the program with *Ctrl+F5*, it will ignore all breakpoints. However, since the *Go* command runs the program within the debugger, it will halt when it reaches a breakpoint in the code.

Now use *F10* to step through the code until you come to the line containing "rect.setWidth(w)." (Remember, you set a breakpoint within this function.) When you reach this line, press *F10* one more time to step over it. What happens?

Because the program encountered a breakpoint within the function, it halted the program flow when it reached the breakpoint, even though you stepped over the function. The debugger opened the *Rectangle.cpp* file and it is ready to execute the line where you inserted the breakpoint. Right-click on this line and select *Remove Breakpoint* to get rid of the breakpoint on this statement.

Take some time to play around with stepping into/over/out of statements and with inserting and removing breakpoints. These are very important features of the debugger, and you should be familiar with using them. When you are done, click on the *File* menu and select *Close Workspace* from the dropdown menu.

Windows Project

In a console application, every program runs within a console window. Even if a program has no input or output, the console window will appear when the program runs. A Windows application, however, has no such dependency on a console window. Input and output are handled by the Windows *APIs* (Application Programming Interface), which is a set of classes and functions that programs can call to create an interface that is standard within Windows and is, therefore, easy for people to use.

Windows projects contain a lot of code and have a particular structure, and this tutorial will not go through all that is required. However, if you are learning Windows programming, it will be help to know how to build a Windows project.

Press *Ctrl+F7* to bring up the *New* window. The *Projects* tab should be active. Figure 2 shows this window. If you are creating a Windows program by typing in all of the code, you should select "Win32 Application" (listed fourth from the bottom), then select "An Empty Project" when you are prompted. If you want to quickly build an application using visual tools, select "MFC AppWizard (exe)"; then answer the following prompts as fits your program. If you are learning to program, you will generally want to create an empty "Win32 Application" so that nothing will be hidden or automated.

Visual C++ 6 Specific Comments

Visual C++ 6 is a very good compiler and is generally compliant with the ANSI standard, with one notable exception: *string*. This is forgivable, because the standard did not contain the *string* type until after Visual C++ 6 was released, and Microsoft has created a fix so that you can use the string type.

To use the *string* type, you normally have to include *string.h* along with *iostream.h* to use *cin* and *cout* with strings and *iomanip.h* to use *cout* formatting. In Visual C++ 6, you should include *iostream*, *iomanip*, and *string* instead (notice that the *.h* is dropped). You should also type *using namespace std* on a line with your includes. A program that uses the *string* type with *cin* or *cout* would contain the following:

```
#include <iostream>
#include <string>
using namespace std;
```

If you need to use formatting functions such as *setw()*, your program must contain

```
#include <iostream>
#include <iomanip>
#include <string>
using namespace std;
```

You cannot also include *iostream.h* or *iomanip.h*; otherwise your program will not compile.

Visual C++ 6 is a very good and easy-to-use program, but, like any large program, it's not perfect. You are bound to run into some strange behaviors if you use it long enough. If it does not seem to be working properly, sometimes simply closing the program then reopening it is enough to fix it. If that doesn't work, try rebooting your computer.

Section 5   CONCLUSION

It is beyond the scope of this tutorial to cover every aspect of Visual C++ 6, but after going through the tutorial, you should have a good working knowledge of its basic functions. There are several features of the program that have not even been mentioned here; however, everything you need to get started using Visual C++ 6 to create programs is here. Good luck.

Microsoft Visual Studio
Hot Key Summary

Here is a list of keyboard shortcuts for common tasks.

Action	Hot Key
Create New File or Project	Ctrl + N
Open File, Workspace, etc.	Ctrl + O
Save Current File	Ctrl + S
Print Current File	Ctrl + P
Compile Current File	Ctrl + F7
Make Project	F7
Execute Program	Ctrl + F5
Go (Run Program in Debugger)	F5
Restart Debugging	Ctrl + Shift + F5
Stop Debugging	Shift + F5
Step Into	F11
Step Out	Shift + F11
Step Over	F10

ASCII Character Table

Dec	Char	Dec	Char	Dec	Char	Dec	Char
0	^@ NUL	32	SPC	64	@	96	`
1	^A SOH	33	!	65	A	97	a
2	^B STX	34	"	66	B	98	b
3	^C ETX	35	#	67	C	99	c
4	^D EOT	36	$	68	D	100	d
5	^E ENQ	37	%	69	E	101	e
6	^F ACC	38	&	70	F	102	f
7	^G BEL	39	'	71	G	103	g
8	^H BS	40	(	72	H	104	h
9	^I HT	41	)	73	I	105	i
10	^J LF	42	*	74	J	106	j
11	^K VT	43	+	75	K	107	k
12	^L FF	44	,	76	L	108	l
13	^M CR	45	-	77	M	109	m
14	^N SO	46	.	78	N	110	n
15	^O SI	47	/	79	O	111	o
16	^P DLE	48	0	80	P	112	p
17	^Q DC1	49	1	81	Q	113	q
18	^R DC2	50	2	82	R	114	r
19	^S DC3	51	3	83	S	115	s
20	^T DC4	52	4	84	T	116	t
21	^U NAK	53	5	85	U	117	u
22	^V SYN	54	6	86	V	118	v
23	^W ETB	55	7	87	W	119	w
24	^X CAN	56	8	88	X	120	x
25	^Y EM	57	9	89	Y	121	y
26	^Z SUB	58	:	90	Z	122	z
27	^[ESC	59	;	91	[	123	{
28	^\ FS	60	<	92	\	124		
29	^] GS	61	=	93	]	125	}
30	^^RS	62	>	94	^	126	~
31	^_ US	63	?	95	_	127	DEL

Optional Program Grading Sheet

On the following two pages are a lab submission cover and grading sheet. Feel free to make copies of these sheets as needed.

PROJECT ___, PROBLEM ___

Name: _____   **Date:** _____   **Section:** _____

Item	Required By Instructor to Hand-in	Completed
	☑	☑
Problem Definition	☐	☐
Initial Algorithm	☐	☐
Refined Algorithm(s)	☐	☐
Source Code Listing	☐	☐
Program Run Samples	☐	☐
Executable Program on Disk	☐	☐

PROGRAM GRADING
(To Be Filled Out By The Instructor)

Rating: 0 to 5 points each (See back of page for rating criteria.)

		Rating	Weight	Percent
A.	Program Design	_____	5% =	_____
B.	Program Execution	_____	4% =	_____
C.	Specification Satisfaction	_____	4% =	_____
D.	Coding Style	_____	3% =	_____
E.	Comments	_____	2% =	_____
F.	Creativity	_____	2% =	_____

Late Submission Penalty   (_____)

Total % =   _____

Program Point Value =   _____

Your Score =   _____

Grading Notes:

PROGRAM GRADING CRITERIA

A. Program Design (25%)

Rating	Criteria
5	Solution well thought out
3	Solution partially planned
1	Ad hoc solution; program "designed at the keyboard"

B. Program Execution (20%)

Rating	Criteria
5	Program runs correctly
3	Program produces correct output half of the time
1	Program runs, but is mostly incorrect
0	Program does not compile or run at all

C. Specification Satisfaction (20%)

Rating	Criteria
5	Program satisfies specifications completely and correctly
3	Many parts of the specification not implemented
1	Program does not satisfy specification

D. Coding Style (15%)

Rating	Criteria
5	Well-formatted, understandable code; appropriate use of language capabilities
3	Code hard to follow in one reading; poor use of language capabilities
1	Incomprehensible code; appropriate language capabilities unused

E. Comments (10%)

Rating	Criteria
5	Concise, meaningful, well-formatted comments
3	Partial, poorly written or poorly formatted comments
1	Wordy, unnecessary, incorrect, or badly formatted comments
0	No comments at all

F. Creativity (10%)

0 to 5 points to programs that usefully extend the requirements, that use the capabilities of the language particularly well, that use a particularly good algorithm, or that are particularly well written.